Foreword

When I was at School, I had no aspirations to join my Dad in his coach firm, in fact he discouraged me, advising me to get a 'proper job'.

Nearing the end of my fifth year at school my half-brother arranged an interview with his manager at a local company Rediffusion. I was offered an indoor workshop job on the proviso I stayed at school for my exams! Sadly, I had only been at work for a few months when Dad passed away.

My attitude changed and somehow, I managed to talk my Mum into keeping the company running and reluctantly she agreed. When I think back, our local bank, Barclays, must have been very understanding to support a sixteen year old, with not much idea of business, supported by his Mother.

Only now in retirement, can I look back at the legacy of this decision and share with you my own personal story.

Colin Rowland
former proprietor of Rambler Coaches

RAMBLER COACHES
The Rowland Years

Best wishes

RAMBLER COACHES
The Rowland Years

STEPHEN DINE

Rambler Coaches – The Rowland Years
is an Empress Publishing book

Published in Great Britain by
Empress Publishing
St Margaret's Road
St Leonards-on-sea
East Sussex
TN37 6EH

This edition published 2023

All illustration credits listed in brackets after each picture caption. Every effort has been made to trace picture authors but if they are unknown the publisher invites the copyright holder to get in touch and a credit will be added for future reprints.

978-0-9564119-3-8

1 3 5 7 9 10 8 6 4 2

Typeset in 13/18 pt Goudy by Falcon Oast Graphic Art Ltd, www.falcon.uk.com
Printed and Bound by Printed Word Publishing part of the Scantech Group Ltd, www.printedwordpublishing.com

To find out more on other titles available from the author please visit
www.stephendinebooks.com

Contents

References

Memoirs of John Goodwin
Memoirs of Gordon Rowlands
Memoirs of Clive Richardson 'Blue Badge Guide'
Brighton Coach Rallies
Personalised number plates
Bus services
Service vans and breakdown trucks
Interesting Bedford's
Bedford re-power – the Cummins project
Coaches for export
Fleet list
The Gallery
The Skinners AEC

Introduction

It has been my pleasure and privilege to be able to write this long awaited book for my friends and fellow coach operators Colin Rowland and to the late and much-missed John Goodwin, who was Colin's business partner from 1974 until his death in 2016. In my formative years their company visibly set the benchmark in the South of England on how immaculately presented coaches should be operated.

Although the high quality of the business operation has spoken very much for itself, the men behind it however were modest enough not to actually put themselves forward to 'blow their own trumpet' so to speak, on the long and endless hours of hard work and determination that gained them this enviable reputation. It is not uncommon in business that the dynamics required to maintain running at a high level of operation can almost seem easy to achieve for one looking in from outside, but the struggle behind the success from these modest men disguised the fact that much of their own personal lives took a regretful second place in order for them to reach the top of their industry. It has been important to record the Rambler Coaches story and I am pleased that it can now finally be told.

Whether you have been connected to the company in some way over the years, are a customer and would like to know more about Rambler

Coaches, or just like to read on how a business succeeded through many decades of changing social and economic times, by reading this book you have booked your seat to enjoy an excursion which will be a long, but enjoyable one. The story has many highlights, humour and a little sadness, but we hope you will enjoy your journey with us.

Stephen Dine
Westfield
East Sussex.

Acknowledgements

The time I shared with the late John Goodwin, business partner in Rambler Coaches was entertaining in order to record his stories and memoirs with me, also those of Clive Richardson, Pauline Rowland, Gordon Rowlands, Tony Patten and Jacqueline Rowland.

A huge thank you must go to Derek Jones for the wealth of information on the pre-war activities of the company and for the large task in assistance, corrections, and verifications to both the Rambler manuscript and fleet list of vehicles operated. Thank you to Paul Green for verifications and advice and to The Bus Archive for supplying copies of a selection of bus timetables from their excellent research facility of routes operated over the years.

To Bob Cook for sharing his many years of research alongside the late and well respected historian David Padgham into early coaches operated and fleet list records, to Jean Tomsett for assistance in editing, Nicholas King, Kevin Boorman, Mr Tracey Kennett, John Fowle and to Dr Helen Wicker of the Kent History & Library Centre.

As the reader will discover throughout the pages of this book, I wanted to ensure that a large selection of photographs would assist in bringing stories from the earlier years back to life with a wonderful selection of images to compliment the diverse vehicles operated. Not only has Colin

Rowland provided some magical photographs from his own personal collection these have been supplemented by a number of photographers including the author, David Padgham, Bob Cook, Paul Gainsbury, Andrew Gainsbury, Don Vincent (courtesy of the M&D and East Kent Bus Club) Terry Blackman, Derek Jones, Paul Green, Rob Crouch, Philip Cattermole, Keith Page (courtesy of the Southdown Enthusiasts Club) Alan Snatt, John Grubb, Joshua Dine, Richard Stedall and J T Wilson, with individual photo accreditations to acknowledge their individual skills behind the camera lens.

My books have always been blessed with eye catching jacket designs to provide the first visual excitement of what awaits, my thanks as always to Cliff Brooker.

Finally, my biggest thank you is to Colin Rowland, former proprietor of Rambler Coaches, who has provided the use of his archive of company information and even more importantly, has retained decades of personal knowledge and memoirs. We have spent many hours in discussion, thus enabling me to write the history of Rambler Coaches – The Rowland Years.

Dick Rowland – Motor coach proprietor. (Colin Rowland collection)

Chapter 1

The early years

Our story begins with the birth of Frederick William Stock on the 22nd April 1904 in Basford, a northern suburb of Nottingham, to parents Annie and Charles Stock, who was in employment as a railway signalman. Their son will eventually become known in our story as Dick Rowland, although perhaps confusingly, in his younger years he collects reference by using a number of differing names. Please do use your imagination and focus to follow these early years of the story!

Much of Frederick's early years are unknown, living in different locations and attending numerous schools up until the age of twelve. By his early teens Frederick was said to have a connection to fairgrounds and slot machines including the arcade on top of the Blackpool Tower. By the age of 16 and now living many miles further south at the coastal seaside resort of Margate in Kent, he would be engaged in driving a charabanc for a man known to be his stepfather, a George Robinson, proprietor of a local operator by the name of Red Rambler with whom Frederick's mother was now living at the time. In 1923 his mother was thought to have fallen out with Mr Robinson and on leaving Margate she encouraged the young Frederick to move with her to Hastings located further around the south coast into East Sussex, with the intention for him to be able to run his own coach from this popular tourist destination, with Frederick joining his mother at the end of that year.

By now Frederick may well have been known as Albert George with a surname of White, with an alias of Richard George Rowland, also becoming well known in his new home town as Dicky White and entering into the world of business himself by acquiring a small coach, starting out on Good Friday, 18th April 1924. The local licensing system required him to apply to Hastings Borough Council for a vehicle test and a numbered license plate that would be affixed to the rear of the vehicle enabling him to operate excursions and ply for hire from Warrior Square on the St Leonards Seafront and soon afterwards at Caroline Place just one mile away further along the seafront in adjoining Hastings, the two towns being connected to each other.

Details of early vehicles operated are scarce, the first coach recorded was a 1920 built vehicle, a Lancia Z originally registered in Lancashire as TB 1227 with a 17 seat body. It was soon joined by a French built Unic 13 seat Charabanc dating from 1924. This vehicle had entrance doors both sides and a full length folding back canvas hood. These coaches were first recorded in operation with Dick (licensed as A. G. White) by the July of 1926 although separate licenses were held in the name of both White and R. G. Rowland between April 1928 and July 1930. Both vehicles carried the local Hastings Corporation license plates numbered 142 and 118 respectively and had probably left Dicks ownership by 1930. The Unic was thought to have been named 'The Green Emerald' as its running name; such was the popular trend in the 1920's & 30's of scripts with popular names being applied to the sides of some coaches.

It was said to have been quoted as being a 'lucky bug' for Dick and gave him little trouble when in service.

At the start of the 1928 season a coach of unknown make registered as KE 8836 and seating 13 that had been new to L Myers of Cliftonville, Margate, Kent in 1922 arrived, followed by a 14 seat Unic new to a Mr Robinson in Worthing in August 1922, having been acquired from Overton in Goring, West Sussex. These vehicles carrying the license plates of 208 and 151. The vehicle previously operated by Mr Myers may not have been a co-incidental purchase as Dick having previously worked out of the Margate area not long before moving to Hastings,

This evocative image of the Unic (KK 9777) was taken in the company of two East Kent Road Car Coaches, before its purchase by Dick Rowland. (Derek Jones collection)

may well have known Mr Myers. A certain replacement for at least one of them was RO 9427, a 20 seat Lancia first registered as such in March 1928 although its chassis is thought to have originally dated from 1914, arriving with Dick by July 1930 and was probably the last vehicle owned to be issued with a local Corporation license number (335) under the outgoing system.

Showing the diversity of chassis manufacturers represented by vehicles bought and sold in the inter-war period, a 1926 Birmingham registered Lancia of Italian manufacture was purchased from Pritchard in London in the early 1930's (not shown in fleet list), followed by another example dating from 1925 (with a folding canvas hood) that had operated for a time with Southern National and had arrived from a W H Smith in Buntingford in August 1932. By the mid 1930's a Bean had also joined

The Unic (KK 9777) is awaiting the return of its passengers, no doubt from a local hostelry, in a location thought to be in the village of Sedlescombe. (Bob Cook collection)

the fleet in replacing slightly older vehicles, although it has not been possible to trace any information on the vehicle, it would have likely been a light commercial, with seating accommodation of around 14 to a maximum of 20 passengers likely. Bean also manufactured cars but had diversified into building commercial vehicles at their Tipton factory in the West Midlands between late 1924 until 1931.

A number of coaches owned would carry scripted names sign-written on their coachwork, with one noted as 'Felix' and another 'The Lancia', although it was not actually on a Lancia chassis! A name with a lasting legacy on one particular coach was of 'Unique Rambler'. It was probable in some instances that when a coach was purchased it may have already had the name on it and, having arrived from an area not too close to where it would now operate, it would not have mattered for the coach

The Kent registered coach (KE 8836) is seen at an unknown location and date for the all-important group photograph before its excursion will soon depart. (Bob Cook collection)

In this period postcard by Weekes Pearson, taken on the seafront near to the Queens Hotel in Hastings, a fully laden Leyland coach is seen in what is thought to be a local independent conductors outing, with a number of drivers present too. The man standing inside the coach leaning on the windscreen is believed to be George Robinson, proprietor of Margate based Red Rambler. Second from the left of the group is a Mr Mc Cloud, a partner in the local operator Scout and fourth from the left is Mr Brown, who traded as Premier in the town. (Weekes Pearson – Colin Rowland collection)

to continue to run with its existing names on. The name Rambler Coaches was known to be in use by the late 1930's.

When the 1930 Road Traffic Act was passed in law it would introduce much needed change on legislation for motorists across the country for both private and commercial road users alike, due to the ever-increasing number of vehicles now using them. Before this the regulations for buses and coaches that had been in force dated back to the Stage Carriage Act of 1832 and Town Police Clauses Acts of 1847 and 1889 with a system that originally applied for horse-drawn vehicles and only within that authorities' boundaries. These were perhaps as one could imagine slightly out of date in the 20th century for the faster moving times of the 'roaring twenties'. Under the latter Act, the different local authorities until this time, had been responsible for licensing operators could vary in how they interpreted things were run, with not all towns around the country exercising the right to control the operation of buses and charabancs. Motor powered buses and charabancs had first been seen on Britain's roads not long after the turn of the 20th century, so the legislation was in much need of overhaul.

The changes that came into force for bus and coach operators across the country through the new Act, meant that England and Wales were now divided up into eleven (and from 1933 ten) new traffic areas. Newly appointed Traffic Commissioners would be responsible for issuing certificates of fitness for the actual vehicle's roadworthiness as well as licensing for excursions and services operated. Dick may well have been considered an established operator, already being licensed through the long running system of Omnibus licences issued by Hastings Corporation for excursions from the seafront. Dick's first RAC issued driving license was noted as in the name of Rowland, although when renewed it was intriguingly under the name of Robinson. It was not unusual for local coach operators, normally running only perhaps one or two vehicles to licence their vehicles under their own name rather than the trading name they had given themselves and they would be known as to their customers.

On the issue of Dick's first Public Service Vehicle (PSV) drivers' badge, something required to be worn when on duty at all times for identification purposes by the Ministry of Transport, he was allocated the local traffic area issue number of KK304. Sadly, this badge was lost

The popular practise of local photographers taking a group picture in advance of an excursion's departure to sell to passengers as quickly produced postcards after their return, captures the 'Unique Rambler' before leaving on an excursion to Winchelsea and Rye from Hastings seafront. (Weekes Pearson - Colin Rowland collection)

some years later and as was normal industry practice the number would not be re-issued again. A new number within the then current sequence would normally be given as a replacement. From 1931 at the discretion of the Traffic commissioners coach and bus drivers would by now also be required to take their PSV driving tests if requested and with the issues of badges ever increasing, for Dick this would now mean a much higher badge number being allocated. On applying for his replacement one he was given the new number of KK6304, exactly six-thousand issues on, by fortunate coincidence. As Dick had already been driving a number of years before the eventual introduction of driving tests in 1935 he never actually undertook a driving test of any category himself.

When the summer season tourist trade would eventually cease in the late Autumn periods, Dick would find alternative work as an electrician for his winter employment, engaged for a number of years for a small family run company Westbrooks that were based in nearby Cross Street in the town. One winter Dick was charged with the task of re-wiring the nearby Adelphi Hotel in Warrior Square, a substantial Victorian building with many bedrooms and vast open spaces inside, on his own. Dicks own transport for his tools and cable for the huge task was just his bicycle. Other examples of his work could be found in the masses of lead

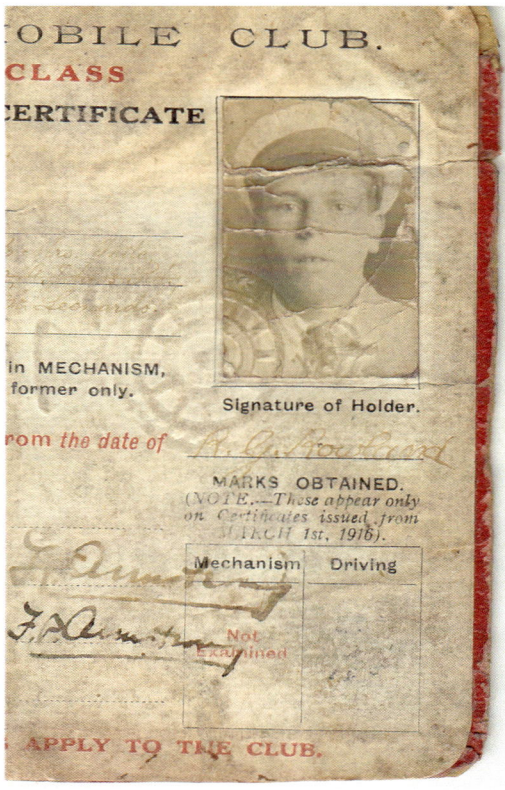

A surviving section of an early driving licence for a young
'R.G. Rowland'. (Colin Rowland collection)

covered cables in the operating theatre of St Helens Hospital for many years, which were still to be found and admired neatly in place decades later when the building was demolished in 1996.

With Dick's interest in all things electrical he became a member of the Hastings Radio Club when first living in the town and got to know his fellow members well, including a certain John Logie Baird, who was soon to create a breakthrough by transmitting flickering images a few feet through his home made apparatus, to eventually become the inventor of the television.

Dick would also work on occasions as a projectionist at the Elite Cinema in Royal Terrace in Warrior Square and in February 1930 took part in the screening of the first 'talking picture' to be shown in the town.

Dick married his first wife Quinine Quinnell, known as Queenie, in 1928, his name at this time being recorded as Richard George Robinson and they were blessed with a son Peter Robinson who was born on 22nd April 1929, the same day as Dicks 24th birthday. A daughter Janet would follow, although his marriage to Queenie only lasted into the 1930's.

The coach business was prospering and in a summary of operations for 1936, a surviving ledger shows a fleet of three vehicles running from June until September that season. With more than one coach Dick would obviously have drivers; Russell Hart was an early driver for the business and a gentleman named George, whose surname has sadly been lost in time.

Around 1935 Dick moved from being a sole coach proprietor to having a new business partner by the name of Bertram Bernard Greenslade, known as Curly, noted as living (along with Curly's mother and her partner) at an apartment in a large property in 13 Carisbrooke Road in St Leonards on Sea. It may well have been that

Dick (or his mother) also lived at this same address at some stage. In 1932 the local street directories noted a 'F.D. Robinson' and in the 1932 to 1935 editions a 'F.R. Robinson' at the same address although this may be a possible coincidence.

A booking clerk was employed named Montague, more popularly known as Monty, to both tout and sell a range of excursions to potential customers from where the coaches were parked on the seafront with advertising in place, Monty becoming a familiar face for many years as part of the Rambler family.

Hastings, like many seaside towns around the country, was hugely popular in the 1930's for both day visitors and extended holidaymakers

Looking very dapper in his smart suit, Dick Rowland poses by his Standard Nine, the only car he would ever own. (Colin Rowland collection)

alike, the town having hundreds of guest houses and hotels to accommodate the thousands flocking to enjoy what the local area had to offer, which of course included coach excursions. The town had a number of potentially lucrative parking areas on the seafront where local coaches and charabanc operators would base themselves in order to sell excursions for these day trips which had structured parking arrangements in place to accommodate the numbers of licenced vehicles. This is something in subsequent years that has become history. Between the wars, there were numerous operators all plying for hire and competition was brisk as the town would be busy with visitors over the summer months.

In 1936 Hastings Corporation were looking to reduce the number of coach stands available in these different locations for operators to ply for their business, as at the start of the 1930's both the Hastings and adjoining St Leonards on Sea promenades were being transformed and modernised by the Borough Engineer, Mr Sidney Little. He became known as 'The Concrete King' for the extensive use of this material in the construction process of reinforced concrete in order to create new and much modernised facilities for the townspeople and visitors alike. Of the many works being undertaken they included widening of the seafront roads, a linking up of road on the seafront by the Queens Hotel, which before then was unpassable by road transport from East to West. A complete re-construction of the Victorian underground White Rock Public and Private Baths, new covered lower promenades between Hastings Pier and Warrior Square and a huge underground car park on the seafront. This was created by reclaiming beach area that was said to have been the first public underground car park in the United Kingdom. These were truly visionary ideas overseen by Mr Little that as his legacy can still be seen today.

Up until this time, coaches could be stationed under a fee paid license system to the Corporation, in locations such as Caroline Parade, Harold Place, Carlisle Parade, Verulam Place and Breeds Place, as well as Warrior Square, slightly further away westwards beyond Hastings Pier. The project would create large physical infrastructure changes and it was inevitable that coach stands would be lost. Between 1930 and 1932 there had been thirty-six coach stands, with fourteen of them at Carlisle Parade alone, this being considered the key location for the best trade. After completion of the works a number had already been lost, although the Corporation wanted a further reduction still.

An order by Hastings Corporation was submitted to the Ministry of Transport on 31st July 1936 for a reduction of the Caroline Place stands

CAROLINE PARADE, HASTINGS. 101

A general view of The Oak coach stand located on Caroline Parade in Hastings, that had taken its name from the Royal Oak Hotel opposite. Although much of the local scene is still familiar today all of the buildings in the foreground of this postcard have long since been demolished. (Colin Rowland collection)

In this 1930's postcard the local scene is viewed looking towards
the coach stand. Smartly uniformed staff are waiting ahead of the
days excursion departures, with an eye to encourage passing visitors
to book seats for an excursion. (Colin Rowland collection)

from fifteen to just seven coach stands and to abolish the five stands at
Harold Place completely. Coaches would also not be allowed to stand
at Breeds Place and Harold Place for more than one hour, in effect
thirteen stands overall would be lost. There were twenty objections to
the proposals with coach operators stating they would suffer a loss of
trade with facilities considerably reduced and that the council had not
considered their position. A local solicitor, Mr Percy Idle represented
seven of the local coach operators affected for the Ministry of Transport
enquiry. These being noted in a local newspaper story as, Scout Motor
Coaches, the Empress, Queen of the Glens, the Lancia Coaches, Messrs.
Skinners, Star Comfy Coaches and the Maidstone & District Motor

Services. As one might deduce, 'the Lancia Coaches' would have no doubt been Dick, using one of his running names to represent his business.

The inquiry, held in January 1937, was concluded after Mr Idle, on behalf of the operators had submitted that had the Council not encroached on the highway at Harold Place the situation would not have arisen. The solution now would be to place the coach stands at Carlisle Parade. To give an idea of the effectiveness of local operators selling excursions from the seafront, Mr Thomas Marsh, Traffic Manager for Maidstone & District stated that although they had three local booking offices, 60% of their business came direct from the coach stands.

Mr George Pearce on behalf of Skinners stated that even with some operators having a booking office or a kiosk, he found that people wanted to see the coaches before making a booking, so coaches had to be put on the stand. His firm used the stand in St Leonards on Sea but did very little business there. The matter of a rota system also came up in the meeting in order for coaches to all have an equal turn to be at the front of the tightly parked coaches on departure. This system, which was eventually implemented assisted all operators to have equal chances to tout for potential customers passing by. This was normally in the direction from where the front of the parked coaches were, thus enabling a fairer system of spreading operators being able to gain their loadings for trips. Dick had also been using the coach stands to sell his excursions further along the seafront at Warrior Square. Sadly, in just over three years, with the outbreak of the Second World War in September 1939, not all of the represented operators would be seen again. It would be some six years later when the chance of resuming operations back on the coach stands would again take place.

Surviving records from a ledger of the 1938 season, show that the mainstay of Dick's business was very much from the seafront excursion trade. The most popular destinations would be to Bodiam, taking in the Castle ruins, also to the nearby villages of Crowhurst, Ninfield, Sedlescombe and Westfield and towns including Rye and Battle, noted for its Abbey and of course where the famous Battle of Hastings had been fought on 14th October 1066. Although private hire bookings were more limited, Beano's always achieved healthy passenger loadings to mainly Bodiam and Rye. For the reader who may not know what the traditional meaning of a 'Beano' was, it would normally consist of either all male, or all female parties taking a well earned day off from their work places to take a privately booked coach outing to travel in a little scenery, whether to the coast or through the countryside, usually with liberal amounts of refreshment, with, no doubt a sing-a-long on the way back home when high spirits would be at their best. The motor coach provided an important part of the group's day, usually booked by the organiser from a local club, pub, or a workplace. Records do show a small handful of private charters to destinations such as Margate, Maidstone, London, Alfriston and nearby Pett Village being taken. The Bannow Blind Home in Quarry Hill, St Leonards was a regular customer, giving their residents some much needed time out from their normal surroundings. This customer was still a regular hirer into the 1970's.

For commercial drivers the understanding of the handling and limitations of the buses, coaches and charabancs they drove was important to ensure any potential accidents were kept to a minimum. The top speed of a coach in comparison to its modern day counterparts was very modest, although the comparatively poor braking of vehicles was something that required the driver's concentration and perhaps what would be considered a degree of skill in order minimalise any incidents. Dick's own skills were indeed tested on one excursion when descending the long and steep Dover Hill from Capel le Ferne heading into Folkestone as the brakes unexpectedly failed on his coach. Fortunately, with the use of his gears, the handbrake (usually slightly more effective in brief application than the foot brake in an emergency) and by running the coach's wheels into the kerb he was able to bring it to a stop at the bottom of the hill. Dick advised his party that he would have to 'sort it out' before continuing homeward bound although the passengers themselves replied back to him 'well, you got it down that hill, it's pretty flat now from here on home' so with their encouragement he decided to carry on back to Hastings with repairs to the braking system taking place afterwards. On another excursion which took Dick through the narrow medieval streets of historic Canterbury in Kent, he came across a parked vehicle that he could not pass in the High Street near to the Cathedral. Not wishing to cause an obstruction Dick carefully drove over the pavement but had been spotted by a keen police constable who, after requesting his name, address details and driving certificate, then served him with a summons to appear before the local magistrate for his offence. When the case was heard Dick took along a number of the passengers who had been on the excursion in question as witnesses to collaborate the fact that he had made the decision not to block traffic flow in the High Street and were more than happy to attend the hearing. Should the charge have been made under the Road Traffic Act of 1930, for example, section twelve, Dick could have faced a hefty fine of up to fifty pounds or even disqualification from driving. Fortunately, the case was dismissed.

Dick was certainly not shy of buying and selling vehicles in these busy and competitive years. As younger coaches became available on the second hand market with the appeal of offering larger seating capacities in comparison to earlier models operated, newer stock would meet the demand for passenger loadings as acquisitions were made.

Vehicles purchased were not painted into any specific livery in the early years, normally continuing in the colours they came. The first recorded livery of an operational coach was of a 1928 Studebaker (KD 2343) with 20 seats in cream and blue that had first operated with Imperial in Liverpool until 1934 but was purchased from nearby J Pearson & Son in 1935, who had not actually operated it themselves. Some later coaches were reported brown & cream as it may have been those colours that took Dick's fancy. The Studebaker's engine was an impressive eight cylinders in-line petrol unit, a powerful vehicle, which Dick would upset the local taxi drivers by easily overtaking them up the long uphill incline of Old London Road when leaving the Old Town in Hastings on excursions, fully laden with passengers on board.

This enlargement of a photograph taken in 1939 shows off an attractive view of one of Dick's pre-war fleet, the signwriting on its sides reading Rambler Coaches. Tantalisingly, the person seen looking away from the coach, wearing a white cap and drivers' jacket, may well have been Dick Rowland himself. (Colin Rowland collection)

Towards the end of the decade the last three coaches to be representing the business would be the Studebaker, joined in July 1938 by a 1929 26 seat Star Flyer, which carried a 'WM' Southport issued number plate, normally driven by Curly. The last coach purchased quite late into the season in August of 1939 was a 32 seat Gilford, thought to have been acquired from the South London area, which was the only half cab coach ever owned, and sported the added comfort of Gruss air springs. It was also in the late 1930's that Dick would meet his future wife Muriel Maisie French, known by her own family as Mary, when working in a sweet & tobacconists shop at Harold Place in Hastings near to the location of the local coach stands.

The onset of the Second World War, when declared in September 1939, would alter everything for the business. It would be a long time before normality would be seen again, not returning in the way things had been up until this time. Dick's business partner Curly Greenslade had decided to move up to London due to the obvious downturn in work as excursion trade would now cease and sadly their partnership never reformed again. Dick and Muriel also decided to move up to London to live with his mother in Chiswick as general work in Hastings had become difficult to find. During these war years Dick worked for the de Havilland aircraft factory on the Great West Road soon becoming a charge hand, with Muriel taking on work for nearby Bush Radio, building mainly radios for aircraft. Dick would volunteer for fire watching duties at night due to air raids, regularly covering other people's shifts too as some would not arrive for their allocated shift, which was of course a vital seven day a week commitment. One night the couple couldn't find their way back home after work due to one of the City's regular thick smogs, often referred to as pea supers due to the denseness of the fog descending on the streets. They were relieved when a passer-by was able to take them exactly where they wanted to go without hesitation, even though he was blind. On another occasion they missed being able to catch a bus home one night so had to walk the entire journey instead which turned out to be lucky fate. They eventually came across the bus they should have caught; a bomb had exploded ahead of it on the road and it had unavoidably gone down the crater that opened up in the blast.

In 1940 Dick made an early visit back to Hastings and to his horror discovered that his coaches were missing from their storage, soon finding out they had been requisitioned by the local Fire Brigade, having arrived unannounced at the garage and in his absence broken the lock off the door and commandeered them. The newest of the coaches, the half cab Gilford, was by now converted into a mobile canteen and would be based at the Fire Station at Seaside near to the beach at West St Leonards. Apparently, in only its first day of use it took a direct hit, destroying the coach with all its occupants inside, including the Fire Chief. Although no records have been found to verify the incident, it may well have been that this information was held back from public knowledge due to its sensitive nature.

The powerful Studebaker first went to Tunbridge Wells Fire Brigade as a Fire Tender, reported in this role by October 1940. Then onto the Home Office under the National Fire Service in September 1941, last noted with the Ministry of Supply in April 1943.

The Star Flyer was thought to have gone to Hastings Fire Service with its use unknown. As Dick had not been present when the coaches were taken, he did not receive an issued certificate from what was thought to be the now deceased Fire Chief for each of his requisitioned coaches, thus losing a preference on replacing the vehicles after the war had ended. The future compensation for his loss would be £25 per coach. In the event of peacetime he would have been in a better position to purchase something after the war, but did not have the written proof required. To compound the loss of the vehicles, when they were parked up in storage the luggage boot of the Gilford had been packed with Dick's tools and thousands of photographs. These had been taken over a number of years, mainly on occasions when local photographers would take official group photographs for holidaymakers in happier pre-war days ahead of an outing from the seafront coach stand. One was normally given to the driver on occasions for which Dick had saved in his large collection of mementos. Both tools and photographs were never seen again.

When working in London for the war effort Dick recalled how poor the quality of workmanship was by a small minority of staff at de Havilland at times. One day an aircraft wing that was being built just disappeared out of the factory after a shift. It could not be found but was later discovered in the local canal, sheepishly thrown in by unidentified 'persons' as the quality of work had been so poor. Sometimes Dick would go back to work at night to try and put right some of the other employees' poor work such was his own standards. He had a natural gift for electronics and the understanding of its complexities and recalled that the factory had an example of a German built aeroplane inside, thought to be a crashed model retrieved for evaluation purposes. He noted it was perfect to view in its workmanship. The British products being constructed were noted by Dick in comparison as a right lash up, wiring all over the place and nowhere near to the standard of the German built one.

Chapter 2

Post-war coaching 1946–1966

After nearly six years of the ravages of the Second World War, in May 1945 peace was declared in Europe and Dick was already thinking about what this new era could offer him as he still held his coach excursion licenses back in Hastings. It was these licences that would draw him to restart his business again. It was thought some two hundred licenses were held for a wide selection of destinations, previously set up each for each season's trips under the regulated system excursions were licensed, although in reality around twenty licensed destinations were used in operation.

Dick was still employed as a charge hand at de Havilland in London and waited patiently until early 1946 to be released from duty before he could look to get started again in business. Whilst waiting for discharge in Chiswick he would now be looking for a coach as his pre-war vehicles were sadly lost to the war effort. Vehicles were in short supply at wars end; Dick was the first man in his local newsagents' shop to buy a copy of the Commercial Motor magazine looking for any coach that might be available for sale. Reading would be thin with perhaps just one vehicle advertised, usually with missing parts or glass, but with perseverance he did eventually find a vehicle, a 1929 BAT Cruiser with Lycoming engine and 20 seat Eaton body. It had originally been new to a Scottish owner who had been taken over by SMT, then onto to Bristol (where it was actually built) and finally in use with Sydenham Coaches in London. After the ravages of war use it was complete but in poor condition. Dick initially parked his new purchase in the street where they were living, with Muriel and his mother re-trimming the seats and fitting new headlining material using thousands of tin tacks. Dick found a small yard nearby where he could fit a replacement engine, thought to

With popular destinations on display to book, Dick and Muriel Rowland are pictured with a customer c 1956. (Colin Rowland collection)

be a Reo Gold Crown unit. To get the old engine out and new unit in required the help of neighbours and became a team effort. To finish, the BAT, in a brown and cream livery, was given fleet Number 1 and with car ownership low and demand for coach trips high, Dick and Muriel were very much back in business again for the 1946 season in Hastings, giving war weary customers their first tastes of a peacetime break. A ledger was kept recording every trip with passengers carried (including the children's half fares) and costs.

Dick and Muriel finally married in 1947 at Battle Registry Office, the ceremony taking place in the late morning, as in the afternoon Dick would be out collecting a group of holidaymakers to take to Bodiam Castle. A wedding celebration latterly took place at Muriel's family home of Hollingrove in the village of Brightling. Dick's new father-in-law, Chester French had produced some home-made elderberry wine which Dick sampled for the first time, and it turned out to be much stronger than Dick had realised. After becoming, one might say, unwell, Dick never touched an alcoholic drink for the rest of his life.

The newlyweds first lived together at East Hill House, Tackleway, in the Old Town of Hastings using the telephone number 4146, with surviving headed paper proudly displaying the business name of R. Rowland – Rambler Coaches at this address. Their next home around 1949 would be a move to 150 Marine Court, a small flat at the rear of the building which was, (and still is) an impressive Art Deco style block of flats over fourteen floors, styled to the lines inspired by the Cunard ocean liner 'Queen Mary' and completed in 1938 on the St Leonards on Sea promenade, providing them with a new telephone number of 1266.

A surviving ledger from 1947 indicates that the new peacetime seafront excursion trade was buoyant. Many of the pre-war registered destinations were back on the advertising boards again boldly chalked up

Early post-war headed paper showing Dick and Muriel's new address, having moved back to the coast from London, as East Hill House in the Old Town of Hastings. (Colin Rowland collection)

by hand, tempting potential passers-by to the delights of Rye, Eastbourne, Hawkhurst and Dover & Folkestone, with tours to the Rother Valley and Bodiam being the most popular trips out of all. This first full season lasted until October with a final afternoon trip to Bodiam signalling the end of a much needed good year of trading under their belt.

Dicks pre-war business partner Curly Greenslade remained in London after the war and was by now working for Banfield's Coaches in Peckham, seen as a regular driver on the Banfield daily seasonal express service down to Eastbourne and Hastings, until he passed away in 1967 at the age of sixty-seven years. New drivers would be required as the Rambler

25

Smartly dressed booking clerk Monty stands alongside the
BAT Cruiser (GE 7766) whilst working at The Oak coach stand
in the early post war period. (Colin Rowland collection)

business re-established itself again. Fred Andrews became a regular driver
with assistance from Russell Hart with booking clerk Monty back again
to meet the demand of the new season ahead in touting the company's
excursions and selling tickets from the coach stand.

The winter months remained traditionally quieter although a small
handful of private hire bookings were taken in the local area, with some
regular fixtures for a local football club helping to cover costs. A booking
to Ninfield took place on Christmas Day and the following day, Boxing
Day, another trip for a football match and a separate trip to Battle took
place, no doubt for the party to join in seeing off the traditional fox hunt

meet departing from Battle Green near to the historic Battle Abbey. The Boxing Day drive to Battle continued over the years as a regular feature, although one particular year Dick had collected his party from the town after the meet set off from the Abbey at the same time the meet accessed nearby fields in order to find a fox to chase and hunt down. Dick had just turned into nearby Powdermill Lane, travelling on the road that cut through what was considered part of the ancient Battlefield site to continue the drive, he could see the foxhounds chasing down across the fields with men on horseback closely following but was startled by the sudden sight of the fox itself which unavoidably ran out from a hedgerow and into the path of the moving coach and was regretfully run over. A slightly tricky situation that would have curtailed the immediate intentions. . .

As the year turned 1948, regular football match bookings continued every weekend and in January the BAT was joined by two coaches acquired from Newmans of Hythe, just along the coast in East Kent, being a 1937 Dodge with Real 26 seat body and a 1935 Commer Greyhound with Waveney coachwork, becoming fleet numbers two and three respectively. Both coaches retained their green and cream colours of Newmans. The Commer would receive a replacement Bedford engine (petrol of course) which was considered to be an improvement on its original unit. In late June the Dodge had suffered a serious mechanical failure when on an excursion as the not inconsequential sum of £17 18 shillings and 10 pence had to be found for parts and spares to rebuild its engine. Local operator Skinners was hired in at a cost of £1 for a replacement coach to return the stranded passengers from their outing and a further outlay of 12 shillings in telephone calls associated with the breakdown was certainly unwelcome at what would be another busy year of trading. The fleet was working hard though with excursions the

The BAT Cruiser has been captured on film by a private photographer on a day trip out in the late 1940's. Sadly, the locations and dates are unknown also the name (who was thought to have lived in the Hastings area) who presented these rare images to the company many years later. (Unknown – Colin Rowland collection)

mainstay of business and private hire bookings a growing part of the seasons work too. In one month alone three charters to Margate and two to Epsom & London took place. The season turned out to be productive with Monty not standing down from his duties on the coach stand until late into the season at the end of October.

On 10th May 1949 Dick and Muriel were blessed with the arrival of a son of their own, Colin, who as the reader will discover would later go on to take the family business to new heights. By the end of this season the BAT that had restarted the business was now retired at twenty years of age, finding a new home as a static store for Bartlett's Motor Works on The Ridge in Hastings, where it would end its days.

Dick's sister Nellie was keen for her husband William 'Bill' Pocklington to join her brother in his coach business and around 1950, with an

The 1935 Commer Greyhound with 25 seat Waveney coachwork (CKE 23) is seen when new with its first owner, Newman's in Hythe. (Courtesy of M&D and East Kent Bus Club)

Dick enjoys a break whilst sitting on the bumper of his 1937
Dodge (RD 9779) on an excursion to Walden Heath Tea Gardens
in Amberstone around 1948. (Colin Rowland collection)

investment of what was thought to be fifty pounds, Dick would again
have a business partner, the capital no doubt assisting to finance the
previous purchase of the two coaches from Newmans. Bill's involvement
would provide the company a London address on its headed paper of
'100 High Street, Colliers Wood' which was Bill's high class tool shop.
He would remain a sleeping partner in the business up until his death
in May 1962 where, with Dick's sister having passed away before Bill,
their son-in-law now inherited his half of the Rambler Coaches business.

With him having no interest in coach operation his newly inherited half share was offered to be sold to Dick, which of course he sensibly accepted.

Colin recalled as a young boy visiting his Uncle Bill with his father, on walking down a particular street in the area his father pointed out to him that his uncle owned the whole street of terrace houses as far as the eye could see. On the uncle's death the will showed just ownership of a hardware shop and part ownership of Rambler Coaches, nothing else.

Dick was keen to continue to invest in newer vehicles with many pre-war coaches having endured the harder operating conditions of the Second World War. In May 1950 the biggest investment as yet came when a 1949 Bedford OB Duple with 29 seat coachwork was purchased from Unique Coaches in Brighton. It wore a two-tone green livery with

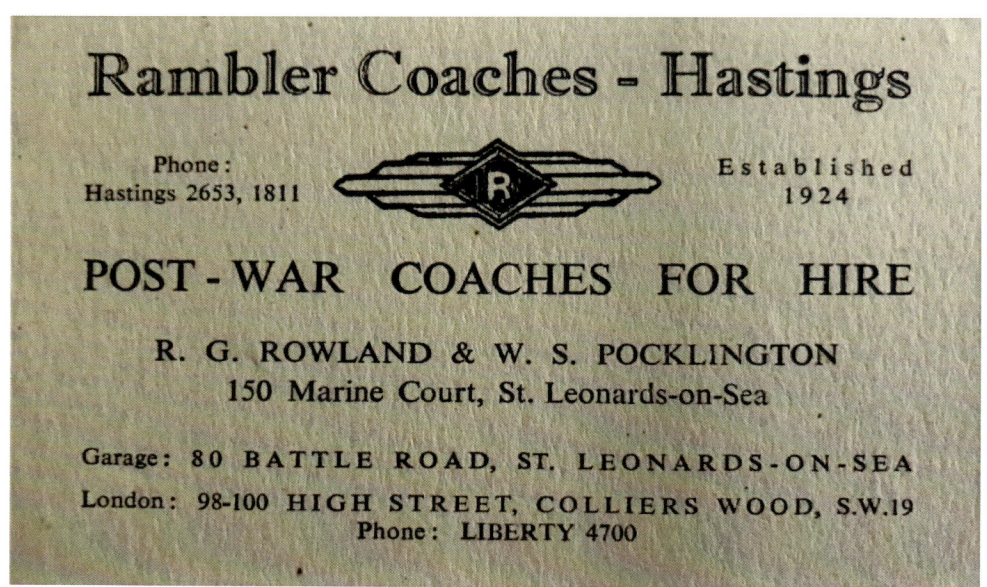

This impressive calling card for Rambler Coaches now boasts the joint owners of 'R G Rowland and W S Pocklington' for both St Leonards on Sea and Colliers Wood in London. (Colin Rowland collection)

Dick adding a cream relief to enhance its looks. This coach at just a year old would have certainly been in very good condition. It was likely that it would not even operated for a full years use, no doubt been stored over the previous winter months as Unique's season had drawn to a close. The following March in 1951 Dick returned to the same operator for a similar 1948 model, with the Dodge sold in July 1951 to Edward (Ted) Waterhouse of Burwash, laying the foundations of Waterhouse Coaches, the company eventually moving to Polegate with much of their business taking place from the Eastbourne area. There was probably no sentiment in the coach's sale as it was noted as being top-heavy to drive and leaked badly even after its body had been refurbished. Its former running mate, the Commer Greyhound, was sold in June 1952, becoming a mobile shop in Tonbridge, Kent. It was last seen by Colin parked near to the local railway station there in the mid 1960's.

It was known that by the early 1950's a lock-up garage was rented underneath the rear of Mr Deal's shop at 80 Battle Road in St Leonards on Sea, with access being from a small track at the rear of the parade of shops. Although compact in size it could house the coaches comfortably until the arrival of the newer Bedford OB models, the roof clearance not quite high enough for them to fit inside. Dick dug out, by hand, the entire floor space by around eighteen inches, digging out an inspection pit at the same time so that the vehicles could fit snugly inside behind locked doors. All maintenance was done in house with assistance when required by local mechanic Claude Jury. For a time, the coaches carried the local shop phone number of '2653' along with their address sign written on the rear of the coaches, whose owner was happy to take calls on Dick's behalf. By 1951 driver Fred Andrews would now have a Mr Page working with him, assisted at times by a Mr Barrett amongst others. Some regular customers in the slowly growing private hire bookings were

Seen on Hastings seafront we find the Commer Greyhound (CKE 23)
between hires. (Courtesy of M&D and East Kent Bus Club)

International Stores, the Dental Board, Seagull Swimming Club and a number of local Public Houses including The Bull Inn (Bexhill Road) Old England, North Star, The Plough and Yorkshire Grey. The season's excursion programme was also having a few changes too to freshen up the offerings with destinations now added such as Wannock Gardens, Hawkhurst Moor, Ashburnham and Pevensey, where the customers could take in the ruins of the Roman Castle and the Old Mint House.

In May 1953 a third Bedford OB Duple Vista (DCK 565) was acquired from Premier Coaches of Preston making the fleet its most uniform it would ever be, with all three vehicles of the same make, body and seating capacity, albeit the third coach retaining its livery of two blues from its former operator. This coach also had curved roof quarter light glazing above its windows both sides.

It's Whitsun 27th May 1950 and a selection of local operators are on the coach stand. On the left is Dick Rowland's Bedford OB Duple (JCD 176) acquired in the March, with Harry Phillips (Empress Coaches) Bedford OB Plaxton (EDY 44) itself just one year old, Dick's Dodge (RD 9779) now in its last season, finally a Bedford WTB (EXT 612) of Scout. (David Padgham)

A number of memorable drivers have been employed by the company over the years and although it's not been possible to mention all their individual names within this book, one man from the early post war years that remained vivid in Colin's memory was a driver known just as Glaxo (his surname was actually Page). He regularly drove one of the Bedford OB's and was a man described as being of larger proportions. In order for him to drive his particular allocated coach Dick had to move the driver's seat further back to accommodate him comfortably when sitting behind the steering wheel. This also meant Dick having to move a number of the interior seats back slightly on the offside of the coach by re-drilling new holes in the floor. Glaxo was amazingly persuasive in his salesmanship in order to get potential day trippers to book an outing with him and could easily fill his coach with passengers quickly.

One day Dick noted what seemed to be pin holes in the wood inside of the coach at the front and thought it was potentially wood worm but unsure. It was only on one occasion when the head gasket blew on the coach's engine a few miles outside of Hastings at Cripps Corner that the mystery was solved. As Dick arrived with a replacement coach, Glaxo (probably uncomfortably) now took the passengers back home in the replacement vehicle. Dick soon discovered what the holes were for. . . Comfy Knit was a plastic ball that could be used to wrap wool as part of the knitting process, available normally for something like a shilling. Glaxo had examples for sale pinned to the inside of the coach on the pillar for double the normal shop retail price for the customers on board to purchase!

Colin recalled once that he had accompanied his father on a trip to Dover where they went to their usual café on arrival. The female proprietor there was livid and wanted to know where Glaxo was. He had

In this close up view of Bedford OB Duple (JCD 176) the popular driver 'Glaxo' is seen wearing his trademark beret standing near to the rear of the coach. The gentleman with his back to the photographer is thought to be driver Fred Andrews. (Colin Rowland collection)

sold her a box of Comfy Knit ball of wool holders for 1/6 each, for her to sell on at 2/- each. She soon discovered afterwards they could be bought anywhere for 1 shilling!

Glaxo's nickname had come about due to a large advertising sign that at one stage was next to the location where he would sell tickets. It boldly advertised 'Glaxo for Babies' which to amusement of his fellow colleagues earnt him the title of Glaxo. Always noted for wearing his trademark plimsoll shoes; in later life when he had by now retired from driving coaches, he could still be found locally selling papers at Maynard's on the Hastings seafront at White Rock near Robertson Street. Still hankering the desire to be able to drive coaches once again, he once said to Colin, on meeting him in retirement, 'Eh boy, can't you get me a little 29 seater'.

A young Colin Rowland with his cousin Peter Brann enjoy a photograph with Bedford OB (JUF 637). Note both the AA (Automobile Association) and BDC (Bedford Driver's Club) badges on the coach's radiator. (Colin Rowland collection)

Bedford OB Duple (DCK 565) is seen on 2nd April 1956 in the company of two Maidstone & District coaches on the local coach stand. This particular vehicle remained in its previous operator's livery of two tone blue whilst in Rambler ownership. (David Padgham)

Excursions from the seafront continued in popularity throughout the 1950's and 1960's. The season traditionally starting on Good Friday with Sunday trips out if the weather was fair, with busy summer schedules running on through until the end of October. Hastings and St Leonards on Sea was a popular choice of destination for holidaymakers, especially visitors from London, being just seventy miles or so away to journey to, with a variety of Hotels and Guest Houses offering good accommodation. With the combination of nice sunny beaches which were sandy at low tide, outdoor and indoor public swimming pools, a large Pavilion, Pier and endless hostelries, before one even looked at the charm of the Old Town, Castle ruins, Smugglers Caves and the 1066 connections it was (and still is) a destination of popular choice.

A coach stand rota had been in place for some time on an agreed rolling order for the local coach operators to park in the line on arrival in the mornings on the seafront, with an arrangement for the first visible coach touting for excursions to be the first departure of the day, each operator having a number. The largest operator however, Maidstone & District Motor Services, would use their allocation of three coaches by arriving with all three vehicles at the same time, parking the first up at the head of the queue with the advertising boards against its sides (as was normal practice to promote the ranges of excursions on offer) but then leave the next two coaches with no visible boards on display for them to gain a potential booking advantage. With the other operators being parked further down the line it gave the impression of the lead coach being *the* booking place. With both Dick and Harry Phillips own coaches usually not so visible, holidaymakers might sometimes only see the first boards in close proximity without looking further on.

A large proportion of this trade would come from the direction of Hastings Pier as tourists would be enjoying a walk along the seafront from their accommodation before coming across the parked coaches with the initial hub of activity at the first coach. The Maidstone & District also had the advantage of having a local booking office at Palace Chambers, opposite the public swimming baths near to Hastings Pier and a coach station on ground (that had been leased since 1932) alongside the Town Hall and Central Cricket Ground as a further visible outlet for bookings. The company even had a telephone in a lockable box on a lamp post at Warrior Square so their own staff could communicate bookings and enquires from this coach stand. A gentleman's agreement had been in place between the operators on who would take turns in line so that in theory everyone would have a turn on the top stand, all vehicles had to be present on location to gain their allocated slot by 09.30 in the morning. If Maidstone & District were late arriving (which could occasionally happen) the other operators would quickly pull forward into the prime spaces as there could be up to ten coaches present, all plying for the day's trade.

An annual meeting would be arranged between operators using the coach stand to discuss the excursions licences, what fares may require a future increase or changes to be made, mutually between them ahead of each operator submitting their individual requests to the Traffic Commissioner for consideration. It must be remembered that all excursions had set licensed routes and operators had the right to object

The Bedford OB Duple Vista (DCK 565) clearly shows off the attractive lines of its coachwork when parked on The Oak coach stand. (Colin Rowland collection)

to changes being proposed by another, in turn an application could be declined. Operators such as Maidstone & District, Harry Phillips of Empress Coaches (and in earlier years companies such as Skinners Coaches and Mr Bingham from Scout) and Rambler Coaches all attended. Latterly when these annual meetings took place there would be an offer put forward to Dick afterwards by a representative of Maidstone & District to purchase his business which was always declined.

Maidstone & District's presence and share of the excursion business in the local area had been increased with take overs of the operations of both Scout on 9th May 1951 and Skinners on 15th August 1953. The company would continue to operate some vehicles in the former company's liveries of an attractive blue for Skinners and the cream with red relief livery for Scout until the end of the 1960's. The Scout name would disappear in June 1969, followed by the last liveried Skinners coach being re-painted out of its traditional colours at the end of the same season in the November, with the town's oldest name in transportation for over one hundred years finally consigned to history. With Maidstone & District and both Skinners and Scout now being part of a much larger company, The British Electric Traction Group, or BET group as it was more commonly known, there was a little more friendly rivalry locally as both Dick and Harry Phillips were slightly marginalised in their presence on the coach stand. It would be rarer due to the system of taking turn in the rota order for either of them to actually be at the most lucrative position at the front of the row. Dick and Harry nicknamed the Maidstone & District 'The Combine' as a general term when referring to them and their activities. Dick got on well with Harry, both having mutual respect for each other, it was not unusual for them to cover each other's bookings should the need arise, Dick sometimes running a coach for Harry's Hellingly Hospital service near to Hailsham

These five photographs of the three Duple bodied Bedford OB
coaches were taken at the same time outside the garage behind
Battle Road in St Leonards on Sea. (Colin Rowland collection)

in order for Harry to operate an excursion to a race meeting. Harry had operated his twice weekly service to Hellingly since the early 1930's. Dick's personal feelings on using public transport were remembered by his young son Colin that when waiting to catch a public service bus with his father, should a Maidstone & District vehicle come into sight Dick would stand back to let it pass, as his bus of choice would soon arrive not far behind it, Dengates of Beckley. Such was his preference for using an independent operator.

A notable occasion was the arrival of Dick's first new coach in August 1954, GDY 888, a 'Big Bedford' SBG Duple Vega model with 36 seat coachwork, with Monty the booking clerk refusing to allow the first Maidstone & District driver arriving on the coach stand that morning to park his vehicle in first position so that Rambler's new coach could be seen in pride of place on its first day in service. It would head up what was still at the time a selection of traditional style bonneted and half cab type coaches that made the other vehicles in the stand line-up look slightly out of date now. On its first trip to Rushlake Green it had only reached Battle when it broke down with the passengers on-board having their fares returned. The fault was later discovered to be a set of burnt out points on its 290 cu in (4.8 litres) petrol engine. On its next outing the following day, most of the passengers travelling consisted of the previous day's ones, determined to get their trip out on this new coach. The placing of the order to actual delivery time of this coach was impressive. Dick placed the confirmation to build it with Coaches and Components in early August to his own specification, the completed coach was ready for delivery towards the end of the same month. One has to remember that the normal construction process of building a coach by hand with the frame in timber and everything hand assembled it would normally take far longer. With a Bedford chassis available to start the building of coachwork by Duple's Hendon coachworks in London and the factory quieter as most coach operators were now busy with their early season's new purchases already in operation, staffing skills were fully available to build this coach in a very respectable timeframe. One of the Bedford OB's JCD 176, was taken in by Coaches and Components as a part exchange with its last booking for an evening drive to Hawkhurst taking place on 22nd August before its final departure, where it would find a new home with an operator in Thirsk.

The new coach would be too big to fit inside the Battle Road garage, even after the tyres were taken off the rims in an effort to see if parking it inside could be achieved in the winter months when not in use, so initially there was no option than to park it outside. A suitable large lock-up garage was soon rented in North Street, St Leonards on Sea,

On Boxing Day on 26th December 1956 we find Bedford OB Duple Vista (JUF 637) touting for business on the coach stand at Warrior Square on the St Leonards on Sea seafront. Festive tourists staying locally will no doubt be enjoying a stroll to enjoy some fresh air and to potentially book a trip out. (David Padgham)

Seen when new is the company's first 'Big Bedford', a 36 seat SBG
Duple Vega (GDY 888). (G E Gregory – Colin Rowland collection)

Photographed around 1954 a young Colin Rowland stands
alongside the new Bedford SBG Duple Vega (GDY 888) with
booking clerk Monty. (Colin Rowland collection)

44

in January 1955 from Dengate's Fruiters in part of a larger premises for the sum of 15 shillings per week. Incidentally, the building had formerly garaged a number of the Skinners Coaches fleet. One of its more unusual stablemates was a combine harvester, not such a particularly common sight in a coastal town location.

Later in its service life GDY 888 suffered an accident when travelling through Peasmarsh and went into a ditch, regretfully at a point where the ditch channelled into a concrete pipe casing causing heavy damage to the coach's near side front. It was recovered to a local garage and mechanical repairs were undertaken by Coombs Motors in order for the coach to be driveable again. It was then taken to the dealer E J Baker at Farnham for the body damage repairs to take place. Once the work was completed and it was back in use Dick noticed that the steering lock was lacking on one side when manoeuvring to use a full turning circle. Investigation soon found that due to the accident and the impact sustained the main steering shaft in the box had twisted by 2-3 splines, with the steering drop arm not now able to complete its movement one way, but this was soon rectified.

The 1956 season was particularly good due to the fact that staff from Maidstone & District had gone on strike. Customers who would traditionally book trips individually and usually on the morning of an excursion after having first looked at the variety of destinations different operators could offer, were now rushing to book with Rambler and for tickets over the entire week to ensure they could get their trips out. A regular seasonal driver at the time was Danny Agombar, who worked for twelve seasons for Rambler until around 1968. He had his own regular customers throughout the season who travelled with him on what was sometimes the same trips out every night. A favourite destination for Dan was the New Inn Public House in the nearby village of Westfield,

Surviving company headed paper with a written quotation on
8th March 1956 for a Mr Brann, offering quotations for both
29 and 36 seat coaches. (Colin Rowland collection)

where after passengers had disembarked the coach to enjoy refreshments
in and around the public bar, they would then enjoy the sound of Dan
striking up on the chords of the piano to entertain them all too. Dan's
brother-in-law, Len Aukett would drive on occasions as well. There were
no full time staff as such at this time just seasonal men with only the
odd private hire booking available in the quieter off season months for
customers such as The Whitefriars and The Bull Inn Public Houses.

46

In this lively photograph taken on Hastings seafront, drivers Dan, Dick and Cyril 'Taffy' Beynon are pictured on the left of the image with happy passengers that have booked their coach excursions, whilst the continuing strike at the Maidstone & District Motor Services renders their coaching fleet out of use. (Hastings Observer)

In December 1956 petrol rationing was reintroduced in the UK due to the Suez crisis that was unfolding. The restrictions on the supply of fuel to the country would create panic buying by motorists due to the set quantities of fuel that could be purchased at garages. For the seasonal coach trade in East Sussex this was something that could be managed by local operators, although the consumption of the petrol engine vehicles could be an issue when hires of longer distances were undertaken and re-fuelling required. Garages were now having to place an upper limit on the amount of fuel they could provide per vehicle, creating a new problem for many commercial operators including Dick. An example of one particular trip to London, after Dick's passengers had disembarked it was a slow process of driving about in the city, making stops to join queues at different filling stations in order to buy small quantities of petrol allowed at each one until he was satisfied that he would have enough in his fuel tank to get the coach back home again. Fuel rationing was eventually lifted in May 1957 as the new season was getting underway.

This coincided with the purchase of another Bedford SB Duple (LFJ 737) an early example of this model dating from 1951 seating 33, in the May of 1957. Unlike a number of later Duple models this coach did not have a pair of passenger seats opposite the driver's seat in between the engine cover, but had a small seat that was inaccessible for passengers to sit on. As it had no heaters (this would still have been an optional extra for some years to come) Dick got around this slight discomfort on colder

On a glorious afternoon on 14th June 1958, Bedford OB Duple (JUF 637) is seen on Hastings seafront ready for its next excursion. In June 1960 it would be the final of the trio of OB models to be sold. The man standing near to the coach in the white jacket is believed to be driver Roy Corbin. (Don Vincent - courtesy of the M&D and East Kent Bus Club)

days by fitting up a paraffin heater on the bulkhead at the front of the coach behind the driver. This worked quite well with the only noted incident of an unhappy passenger on one occasion. A group travelling to London to attend the Cruft's Dog Show at Olympia, many with their dogs entered in the show too, regretfully one inquisitive dog burnt the hair on the end of its nose from the heater so it couldn't be shown at the event by its now disgruntled owner.

On the subject of dogs, Dick's elder son Peter and his wife Daphne had been on a trip to Maidstone Market in Kent one day enjoying looking around at the many choices of things one might be tempted to buy. Towards the end of the day, they were walking back through the stalls and noticed that one of the market traders, a puppy seller, had just one animal left, a cross cairn terrier & poodle breed and was packing up trade for the day. Peter enquired 'what will happen to this dog'. The trader replied 'he hasn't sold so he will be thrown in the river'. Peter managed to find the two shillings and six pence required to buy the puppy, which was named Candy, returning home with them and becoming part of the Rowland family. Within a short space of time though with Candy being at home in a small flat whilst the couple were at work it proved not ideal, so Dick now took the dog on, becoming a regular companion on excursions with him, sitting comfortably up on the coach's engine cover nestled below the front windscreen. As a young puppy Dick would place Candy inside his buttoned jacket placidly looking out, when he was on the coach stand touting for bookings which became an attraction in itself.

With the arrival of Bedford SB (LFJ 737) it would initially be parked most nights on the main entrance forecourt of nearby Coombs Motors premises by arrangement and moved in the mornings onto the street before staff would arrive for work, until a garage was found that had

Dick Rowland (standing inside the passenger door of GDY 888) is seen
with Cyril 'Taffy' Beynon and Roy Corbin. (Colin Rowland collection)

previously been the paint shop for Skinners Motor Engineers in
Western Road who had once owned the coach firm of the same name.
The building could accommodate two coaches with two large doors that
opened out across Western Road, although not ideal for the buildings
new use in housing coaches, these were soon replaced by three new
sliding doors. Colin recalled as a boy exploring one of the now out
of use former Skinner's buildings of which there were a number in
Western Road, one being five or six storeys high complete with a
courtyard and the spaces still evident to take carriages for horses from
times gone by.

A young Colin Rowland stands alongside Bedford SB Duple
(GDY 888) on Hastings Seafront. (Colin Rowland collection)

Parking the coaches in the new garage would require them to be driven onto the Skinners garage forecourt opposite their new premises in order to reverse inside at the end of the days duties. The arrangement worked well until the 1960's when Western Road was made a one-way street. Coaches until that time would normally turn from Norman Road (near to the seafront), into Western Road. It would now technically require driving up nearby Warrior Square to access the other end of Western Road which was more inconvenient. To start with the coaches would be discreetly reversed backwards down Western Road to the garage as traffic usage was quiet until one day a Policeman on his beat noticed

In this photograph taken by Don Vincent on 14th June 1958, we find Bedford SBG Duple Vega (LFJ 737) parked on Hastings seafront, ahead of an excursion that is soon to take place. (Don Vincent – courtesy of the M&D and East Kent Bus Club)

what was happening and said that it could no longer be done. From then on a key to the gate of the filling station was provided by Skinners so the coaches could have better access when manoeuvring into the garage.

In September 1958 Dick's mother Annie whom he had followed in moving to Hastings back in late 1923, when looking to start his new coach business, passed away locally in St Leonards on Sea at the age of eighty-six years with her son at her side. Annie would no doubt have been proud to have seen her son's achievement in the business of running coaches.

The origins of what became Rambler's now well-known livery came about in 1959 when Dick noticed a coach operated by Robinsons of

Great Harwood in Lancashire parked at the Queens Hotel on the seafront having arrived on tour for the week. He liked Robinsons own shades of green being similar to his own coaches, also the Robinson's coach sporting the addition of black as part of the livery. Within a week the Bedford SB Duple GDY 888 was now seen in green with the addition of black too (along with Dicks own cream relief) enhancing its looks. Normally the coaches would receive a repaint every two years or so to freshen them up, always brush painted in Dulux coach finish to maintain a smart appearance.

Father and son. Dick and Colin Rowland are photographed together near to Longport Coach Park in Canterbury, Kent. (Colin Rowland collection)

In 1959 the Rowland family moved from Marine Court to a new home at 22 Western Road, St Leonards on Sea for the sum of £800. Dick had liked a house in nearby St Johns Road, but at £880 the price was out of reach for him to be able to afford. The front room of the three-story property became a booking office with a separate front room, kitchen, scullery and bedrooms upstairs, remaining the Rowland residence up until 1980. A sign with the name 'Rambler' was proudly affixed on the front of the building with both house and workshop telephone numbers on it for those customers wishing to call. In the early days of the office in Western Road it was not unknown that if nobody was available at home, regular customers could let themselves in and leave their money on the office desk with a note for the trip they had booked. Candy the dog was in attendance and would just happily sit there, sometimes with two or more amounts of money left with notes by customers. The office telephone number 1266 was retained from the former family address at Marine Court. Muriel herself though was not too far away though working next door at number 21, which was Sutch's Grocers shop.

As the new decade of the 1960's got underway the 1960 season was marked with the opening of a new coach stand at Breeds Place along with changes to the A259 coastal road layout, seeing the traditional Caroline Parade stands removed. A number of vacant Victorian buildings at this location had previously been demolished and a block of new maisonettes with shops below constructed. An attractively designed two story Italian restaurant at the end of the new development 'Iorio di Maschio', (known from 1978 until 2022 as The Italian Way) was now under completion to grace the local scene, looking across at a new roundabout complete with an illuminated feature water fountain and coach stands on the opposite side of the road running alongside the promenade. Normally up to eight coaches could be accommodated to sell their excursions from this fine location.

The purchase of the company's second brand new coach came in June 1960 as a Bedford SB3 Duple Super Vega (ODY 544) ordered through the dealer Bakers; at 41 seats it was also the largest coach to date to be operated. Its specification had the additions of a Radiomobile receiver with public address system at a cost of £70, an extra £2 for moquette trim over the engine cover and a further £22 for having the backs of the seats in moquette as well. The total purchase price being some £3,900.

When under construction at Duple's Hendon factory in London for what was anticipated to be an Easter delivery, Dick accompanied by a young Colin made a visit in March to see how work was progressing ahead of the summer trade. They were taken of a tour of the factory to see an array of coaches in build including their own in its advanced stages of completion, but to the embarrassment of a Duple representative their coach could not be found. After a chassis number search the coach was discovered in one of the paint shops but to their surprise it was on 7 feet 6 inch wide body, not 8 feet wide as ordered and painted in blue with cream livery. After some initial confusion the matter was resolved when their coach was fortunately discovered in a different location and was being built as per their order. At an early stage the names Rambler and Blue Rambler of Cliftonville in Kent had become mixed up, so Blue Rambler's coach would now be completed for Easter instead of its planned June delivery, with Dick having to wait a further two months before his new coach would be ready for the busy summer season. This was the first vehicle ordered new to arrive in the now standard livery of green, black and cream relief.

Dick would always enjoy moments of amusement with his passengers on excursions and when an unplanned situation could arise, Dick's quick-witted humour always gave his customers a laugh. In 1959 new double white line road markings were gradually being applied around

The new Bedford SB3 Duple Super Vega (ODY 544) is seen having returned from an afternoon drive to the newly constructed Breeds Place coach stand on Hastings seafront. (Colin Rowland collection)

the country to discourage overtaking on sections deemed narrow or unsuitable to overtake other vehicles in an effort to improve road safety. When new double white lines were painted on a section of road between the towns of Tenterden and Ashford in Kent, Dick was driving with passengers on board and had spotted a Policeman on his bicycle coming towards him in the opposite direction. He also noted a parked vehicle on his side of the road which would mean crossing these new double white lines in order to pass it. Dick stopped the coach and flagged the Policeman down asking with a straight face 'what am I to do? I have to cross this double white line as there is a van parked outside this house delivering but with the double white line alongside it?' The policeman after careful thought about the predicament said, 'I'll tell you what, I'll get back on my bicycle and cycle down the road out of sight, then you just go over the lines!'.

The Bedford SB was complimented in March 1962 by a similar three-year-old Bedford SB (UOT 585), again with 41 seat Duple coachwork and dating from 1959 that had been new to Coliseum Coaches in Southampton. It replaced the earlier Bedford SB (LFJ 737) that moved

Driver Don Fenn stands beside Bedford SB3 Duple Super Vega (ODY 544) at Breeds Place around 1964. In the early 1970's the stylish Rougemont Hotel seen behind the coach will be demolished to make way for a new development of offices known as Aquila House, renamed in later years as Muriel Matters House. (Colin Rowland collection)

onto H R Richmond, trading as Epsom Coaches in Surrey, which incidentally was the last coach owned that had not worn the addition of black to its Brunswick green and cream livery. After running this latest purchase for a time, one winter, Dick decided to treat it to a reconditioned Bedford engine. In order to undertake this task at his lock-up garage Dick built a sturdy frame that would be two inches higher than the front mounted engine itself when ready for the frame to be positioned to remove it. With ancillaries unbolted and the engine free, Dick then jacked up the coach from the ground, put the stand underneath then lowered the coach slightly for the engine to rest on the frame. By pushing the coach back a few feet it would expose the engine from the front of the vehicle for local man Claude Jury to assist in using his Land Rover fitted with a crane to swap the engines over in Dick's homemade frame ready for the exchange to be completed.

Established 1924   Phone HASTINGS 1266

RAMBLER COACHES

22 WESTERN ROAD
ST. LEONARDS-ON-SEA, SUSSEX

Coaches for Hire up to 41 seats

NO CONNECTION WITH ANY OTHER COACH OPERATORS

Calling Card c 1960's. (Colin Rowland collection)

From a young age Colin would already be getting to know other local coach operators when in turn as local coaches had departed from Hastings seafront on their excursions, others from outside the area would arrive to drop their passengers off. One such person was Eric Cole from Berkeley Coaches in Eastbourne, who after parking up would say 'come on then, let's go and get a cuppa' and walk around to the boot of his coach, open the unlocked handle of the door, take some cash from the takings inside and on closing the boot again, walk across the road with Colin to Tilley Demarco's café in nearby Pelham Arcade. Dick had decided one day that he would cut down from his normal daily intake of eighty cigarettes to just five. He would go over to Tilley to buy smaller packets which Colin suspected was Tilley splitting larger packets into small 'fives' in order to service Dick's requirements!

Men called upon to drive would still be seasonal employees in the 1960's and included Don Fenn who had previously been an aerial photographer. A useful regular additional off-season job for Don came up late in 1962, driving Hastings based staff for the Richmond Sausage Factory up to another factory in Tunbridge Wells to cover additional pre-Christmas production capacity. This was enhanced personally for Don

Driver Dan Agombar stands with Bedford SB3 Duple Super Vega (UOT 585) at Bodiam Castle. This coach was purchased from Coliseum Coaches in Southampton when just three years old in April 1962. (Colin Rowland collection)

In this fine image Bedford SB3 (UOT 585) is found at Folkestone coach park on the Kent coast, opposite the Rotunda amusements. (Colin Rowland collection)

by finding part time work at the same factory itself between dropping and collecting the workforce for their return journey home to assist increasing his own wages.

The start of the 1963 season would be remembered as one of the coldest winters on record for over two hundred years. Heavy blizzards, snow drifts and ice, with rivers and even the sea freezing over in some parts of the country. The temperature in some areas dropped to below –20 degrees centigrade with conditions becoming known as 'the big freeze'. Operations of a few private hire bookings had continued to take place right up until the 30th December in 1962 although by now snowfall had been heavy and everything had to be cancelled. No initial bookings starting again until just a tentative few from 19th January early in the year. February remained quiet with just a few brave souls venturing out on hires and it would not be until the following month the worst was over for business to pick up. Towards the end of the year in November the Bedford SBG Duple (GDY 888) Dick's first ever new purchase back in August 1954 was now sold, showing some 250,000 miles of service to the company which was considered quite high mileage at the time for a seasonal excursion coach. Still in excellent condition it was sold through the dealer E J Baker in part exchange for a yet to arrive brand new 41 seat Bedford SB Duple Bella Vega for the 1964 season. GDY 888 now found a new use with the contractor Croad in Portsmouth. When its relatively brief working time with them was now at an end it returned for the last time to the same dealer, no doubt as a part exchange for another coach and was broken up on site in 1965.

The new Bedford SB (VDY 207) was the first diesel engine coach purchased and was collected from E J Baker on 13th April at a cost of £3,257.0.0. reflecting Dick's continued faith in investing in a new fleet. He had specified the previous season's 1963 style side flash moulding which provided an eye-catching way of using the company's green and black with cream relief livery to good effect. Dick ordered the coach to be 8 feet 2 ½ inches in width, at the time Duple would also build coachwork to specifications of 8 feet and the narrower dimensions 7 feet 6 inches. This was a popular choice for some UK operators needing to regularly use narrow lanes in service and in the Channel Islands of Jersey and Guernsey which had restrictions of this width for the same reasons.

Further personal additions by Dick included a reel-to-reel tape deck equipment being installed to be able to play recorded music to passengers (Colin thought possibly the first for use on a coach) and a 'nodding cat' mascot on the dashboard for the ultimate personalisation. A diesel power would have been for improved fuel economy in comparison to a contemporary petrol engine coach. Dick would not be hurried when driving, so respectable consumption figures of ten to eleven miles per gallon with the petrol engines would normally be achieved with diesel consumption figures even better.

Looking resplendent in the afternoon sunshine on 15th May 1966 we
find Bedford SB5 Duple Bella Vega (VDY 207) on Hastings seafront.
(Keith Page – courtesy of the Southdown Enthusiasts Club)

Colin recalled the process of viewing and then purchasing a new
coach, was so different in his formative years when accompanying his
father, compared to decades later when he would be buying numerous
new coaches himself. For example, when visiting Yeates with his father
for the dealers 'show times' events normally staged at the end of the
summer season, a representative dressed in a clean white overcoat would
actually take a requested brand-new demonstrator coach out for a drive
for clients including a demonstration on how the coach should be
correctly driven too. Colin vividly remembers the delight of a run out in
a brand-new Bedford VAL Duple Vega Major twin steer 52 seat coach.

The 1964 season was noted as being hot, especially over the months
of July and August. A rainstorm on 21st August finally broke the cycle
(and a loss in the healthy passenger bookings for that day), although the

following day it was back to glorious weather and ticket sales back up to their normal full capacity. It was also this month that a skirmish that became dubbed by the press as 'The Second Battle of Hastings' took place, when crowds of young people descended on the town to swell the thousands of holidaymakers over the Bank Holiday weekend. Large groups of 'rival' 'Mods and Rockers' had been arriving on scooters and motorcycles respectively and with it conflict and then violence would eventually erupt in the town. Much of the fighting between the hundreds

Dick Rowland is on duty touting for customers bookings on Breeds Place Coach Stand with his faithful dog Candy in his arms. The coach behind is Bedford SB3 (ODY 544) displaying an excellent choice of excursions available to book. (Colin Rowland collection)

of numbers in the two groups took place on the beaches and on the seafront very close to where the coaches were parked on the stands as both horrified holidaymakers and locals alike watched. Dick refused to relegate himself into making a hasty retreat from the coach stand as he was still taking enquiries and bookings. A stray object that had been thrown from amongst the fighting crowds did bounce onto the roof on his brand-new Bella Vega coach though fortunately not causing any damage. Dick remained by the front passenger door of the coach with the vehicles' heavy cast metal wheel brace on the step inside, for defence, just in case. The Police, both local and officers drafted in from other areas, would gradually disperse the mass crowds and arrested those taking part in the scuffles with large numbers of youths being physically marched out of the town on foot.

Private hire customers would continue to grow throughout the 1960's with hires from Rediffusion, Crowhurst WVS, Randolph Hotel, Hastingleigh Reform Club and Public Houses such as Warrior Gate, Silverhill Tavern and the Bull Inn. Another aptly named customer being The Rambling Club. Regular business would come from the Adelphi Hotel in Warrior Square for the guests who would book their excursions through the hotel reception, with the required passenger seats on trips telephoned through to the Rambler office in advance of an outing. Sometimes up to three coaches could be required in the peak season for these trips out.

For touring coaches having arrived in the town for a week's stay, they could not technically operate local day excursions unless they were specifically licenced to do so. Once these vehicles were parked up, local coach operators would then have the day excursion business for the eager holidaymakers keen to see the local area. Other hotels such as The Alexandra, Queens, Randolf, Warrior and Invergordon were repeat customers throughout the 1950's and 1960's for groups arriving with tour operators such as Beeline from West Hartlepool (normally with two regular drivers both called Bob) Monks-Hutchinson from Leigh and Leeds based Wallace Arnold in their Bedford VAL twin steer coaches. If Dick's own coaches were in short supply to assist tour operators at the height of the summer season, Dick was known to place an 'on hire' poster in the windscreen of the visiting coach itself by arrangement and take the group out himself. Dick enjoyed taking out a nearly new Monks-Hutchinson Bedford VAL 52 seat twin steer coach for an excursion on one of these occasions. A rare visitor to the south coast from the Monks fleet in 1965 was a 1963 AEC Reliance with Duple Astrocoach body (BTU 200B). From the vehicles waist to the top of the roof quarters on both sides the coach was continuously glazed, supported by steel pillars with composite construction for the rest of the frame. It had first been operated new for a short time from April 1964 by Smiths of Wigan passing in the July of the same year to Monks and regularly driven by Jimmy Crook. A young Colin was impressed with its light and airy design on what turned out to be the only example of its type ever built.

Amongst popular day trip destinations on offer such as Beachy Head near Eastbourne and Canterbury and Dover, groups could also visit the Pestalozzi Children's Village at nearby Sedlescombe. Parties would be invited in to learn more on the cultures of the students living there from countries such as Tibet and Nepal as well other European Countries.

On regular excursions Dick would personally enjoy driving to Wannock Gardens on Mondays, Wednesdays and Sundays, costing passenger's five shillings and threepence for the experience. On Sundays a Beachy Head tour became part of the excursion too for a slightly higher price of six shillings. At the coastal landscape's peak it was some five hundred and thirty-four feet above sea level, offering excellent views

Dick Rowland 'coach proprietor' with his new Bedford SB5 Duple Bella
Vega (VDY 207) at Dover coach park. (Colin Rowland collection)

over the surrounding downlands near to Eastbourne. On Tuesdays
and Thursdays Dick normally drove the Kent Circular Tour taking in
Canterbury, Dover and Folkestone, the price being set at ten shillings
for many years. This particular excursion was not offered in competition
from Maidstone & District, who operated a Canterbury and Margate
excursion instead. The Kent circular tour was firmly established in each
season's offerings by the 1930's and continued after the war years into
the 1970's. This excursion on departing Hastings would then head out
through the village of Westfield and continue on the A28 road making
its first stop at Tenterden in Kent. The local 'Ye Olde Cellars' Public

House was a favourite morning break for half an hour and from then on it would journey to Canterbury for a two hour stop before continuing to Dover for around one and a half hours and onto nearby Folkestone for another hour break. Should passengers be able to keep to time when returning to the coach after each stop an option for the last homeward bound part of the tour would be to stop in Hythe, to board one of the miniature 1/3rd size 15 inch gauge steam trains in operation at the Romney, Hythe and Dymchurch Railway, with customers being collected again at a station further down the line. To complete the enjoyment of the day, one last stop would be made in Brookland just a few miles from the border of Kent and East Sussex, where the option of half an hour to enjoy a drink in the local pub The Royal Oak (closed since 2017) could be taken. There was also an arrangement with the local post office to be able to borrow the key to the delightful 13th Century Church of St Augustine next door to the pub. The driver himself could open up for customers to take a look inside the sixty feet tall church bell tower that was unusually built alongside the church itself.

Chapter 3

Mother & Son

As soon as Colin was old enough to leave education at the Grove School in St Leonards on Sea in 1965, he joined the local branch of Rediffusion, based in a small workshop in Beaufort Road, Silverhill which was co-incidentally part of the local Maidstone & District Silverhill bus depot site. His new work was to convert customers' existing Rediffusion Mk 8 television sets from their 405 lines to 625 lines for the then new television channel BBC2 that had been launched in the previous April of 1964. Incidentally, it became Europe's first television channel to be regularly broadcast in colour from July 1967. Colin would also undertake other work on occasions for Skinners in Western Road, driving their Austin Princess and Sheerline limousines and hearses. The wage of five shillings for driving was enhanced to ten shillings if he took part in assisting to carry the coffin as a pallbearer. For three successive Christmas periods in a row Colin also assisted by driving a van for Ellis, Son & Vidler a local wine merchant on deliveries. On one particular delivery he drove the company Standard Atlas van all the way to Berkshire to deliver just

Mother and son. A young Colin and his mother Muriel stand by the brand-new Bedford VAM Duple at the 1967 Brighton Coach Rally. (Colin Rowland)

one bottle of fine wine. The journey being noted as slow and noisy due to the vans loud running diesel engine. The company eventually sold the Standard for a Ford Transit van with 2 litre petrol engine which was considered by Colin a much better proposition to drive.

One particular day in August 1965 Dick was due to take a party of passengers out on an excursion from Hastings seafront but was taken ill just ahead of the scheduled departure. Colin recalled his father leaning against some railings not far from his coach which already had its passengers on board. Dick appeared to lose feeling down one side of his body and felt weak, but with Colin still too young to legally drive

Photographed when in the capable hands of a young Colin Rowland, this Austin Princess limousine (CLL 659B) is seen at The Green in St Leonards on Sea. (Colin Rowland)

to be able take his place and no other drivers on-hand to cover, there was no alternative but to have to cancel the outing with the concerned passengers being re-funded. Dick later regained feeling again and with symptoms as yet undiagnosed, once he felt better, he would eventually be back at work, with a hospital appointment booked in October for further investigation. Later towards the end of the 1965 season Dick placed an order for another new coach for early delivery the next season. This time it would be on the brand-new Bedford VAM chassis. This would be the first time an order was placed with coachbuilders Plaxton to body it with 45 seat Panorama coachwork. (*Plaxton at the time badged its coachwork on its sides with the cast script 'VAM' with the larger Bedford model as 'VAL').*

Dick and Colin had visited a trade show being held at the coach dealer E J Baker for the launch of the new VAM chassis and to see on display an unbodied example that was especially prepared in a black gloss finish to showcase it. Eric Cole from Berkeley Coaches in Eastbourne had also attended the event and liking the VAM concept placed an order for a new coach. He mentioned to Dick that the dealer had thought an order from them might also be the case, although at the time he hadn't done so. Eric went on to say that they only had one chassis left at that time, Dick quickly making contact and purchasing the actual show chassis itself. It later turned out that the pre-preparation of this chassis before applying the gloss finish had not received the level of care on it beforehand and eventually encouraged rust which in time became apparent.

Dick's health was showing signs of worsening though and with this, bookings taken in November and December were far fewer than in previous years. In January 1966 just four bookings had been taken early in the month and with Dick now gravely ill he was admitted to

Seen on Hastings seafront standing by Bedford SB Duple (UOT 585) are a young Colin Rowland, booking clerk Jack and driver Dan. (Colin Rowland)

Hurstwood Park Neurological Hospital near to Haywards Heath, where in the operating theatre a brain tumour was discovered. Dick sadly passed away there on the 22nd January at the age of sixty-one years. A small handwritten note was later found with his personal belongings where Dick had written 'God Bless Peter, Colin and Candy'.

Muriel felt that with Dicks passing it was time to call it a day with the coach business. Colin however persuaded his mother that they should carry on through this difficult time. The brand-new Bedford VAM 5 Plaxton (DDY 250D) that Dick had ordered for delivery ready for the 1966 season was due to be collected within weeks from the dealer E J Baker and Muriel received a compassionate telephone call from their representative Ernie Waterman to say that they did not have to go ahead on taking delivery at this difficult time. Both she and Colin decided to collect the coach as would have been Dicks anticipated plans.

In February and March just a small number of bookings were taken whilst Muriel and Colin needed time to start to re-adjust to life without him, the delivery of the new coach would give them the confidence to start the seasons trade again. Its first trip out was on Good Friday 8th April to Beachy Head and Wannock Gardens and unusually there was a dusting of snow that came down just after Easter in the April but after that the weather improved. The coach was also entered in that year's Brighton Coach Rally, just two days after what would have been Dick's sixty-second birthday. Driven by Tony Patten and accompanied by Colin it took part on the Sunday of the two-day weekend event over the 23rd and 24th April, being entered in the Concours de Elegance. Not long after their early arrival on Madeira Drive on Brighton's seafront, a film crew also arriving early asked if they could film a report from on-board the coach itself, with its presenter, who Colin thought was Shaw Taylor.

(Research has revealed that a television crew for the programme Wheelbase hosted by former racing driver Graham Wilkins were indeed filming an 'on the spot report' from the 12th Brighton Rally that would be screened the evening of the following Friday 29th April, on BBC2).

With this particular Bedford VAM 45 seater being fitted with the somewhat underpowered 5.4 litre 330cu.in. Bedford diesel engine also used in the smaller VAS chassis, commonly bodied as 29 seat coaches, there was an option available for the slightly more powerful Leyland unit for this larger model. Dick had specified the Bedford engine although when in operation, with a full load of passengers, it would have to be driven hard on hills, only just managing to get up the steep Battery Hill

With Tony Patten in the driving seat, a young Colin and his mother Muriel Rowland, the Rambler Coaches participants are seen with the brand new Bedford VAM Plaxton (DDY 250D) at the 1966 Brighton Coach Rally. (Colin Rowland)

Taken at the same time as the previous photograph, a relaxed Tony and Colin are seen inside DDY 250D. Note the 'VAM' script next to the side indicator, fitted by the coachbuilder Plaxton on completion of its build. (Colin Rowland)

in Fairlight in first gear when heading back towards Hastings on trips. On the section of the A259 from Rye that runs parallel inland in the same direction back into Hastings, in the location known as Batchelors Bump, with a run at that hill the coach could normally just make it over the top in second gear.

Maidstone & District Motor Services again made contact with Muriel this season to ask if she would sell their business to them, Muriel and Colin declined. It turned out that this would be the last time an offer was put forward. After the purchase of another brand-new coach the following year it put the notion of a potential sale out of the minds of the management of the larger operator for good. Local customers remembered in the 1966 season included The Cricketers Pub, Priory Deaf Club, Women's Voluntary Services and the local Post Office.

A new attraction in Hastings for the 1966 and 1967 seasons was the visiting SRN6 Hovercraft Britannia, operating short pleasure trips from the beach. The craft was based in Dover and would travel along the coast to Hastings, operating in close proximity to the coach stand itself. Small excursions along the coast westwards towards Galley Hill, Bexhill and in the other direction of the Cliffs beyond the Old Town towards Fairlight, proved a popular experience. With seating for thirty-five passengers and being capable of up to fifty-five knots, it was owned by Townsend Car Ferries and operated by P & A Campbell. The company had itself for many years become well known in the UK for operating its fleet of mainly paddle steamer excursion vessels around the country including from Hastings Pier.

On occasions in the busy summer months additional drivers would be called upon for assistance when the fleet of three coaches were fully operational, for which a small pool of people were normally available as well as the regular seasonal drivers. On one occasion extra cover was still needed and Muriel telephoned Mrs Jean Tomsett joint proprietor with her husband Wilf of Cooks Coaches in the nearby village of Westfield. Jean was happy to oblige and drive on an outing using one of the Rambler Coaches. Jean and Wilf's own immaculate fleet of Bedford coaches were all petrol engine examples, something which would only ever be their preference due to their smooth and silent running. When Jean arrived and sat in the driving seat of VDY 207 (the only diesel coach owned by Rambler at the time) Colin recalled the look on Jean's face as she pressed the start button on the coach's dashboard and the nosier diesel engine sprung into life from beneath its engine cover! She was not impressed.

Colin's skills would develop in finding solutions to the little issues that would come up in not only operating coaches but managing drivers' issues. He was now running the business with his mother and was well prepared when a particular driver would regularly complain that the 300ci petrol engine in Bedford SB (ODY 544) wasn't fast enough and lacked power. The obvious checks such as condition of spark plugs the setting of the point's gap on its distributor and suchlike, showed that the coach was in fact running just as it should. With the said driver still complaining, Colin called in to Coombs Motors to look for parts, changing the speedometer drive on the gearbox end for a different housing and gearing ratio on the end of the drive from a different Bedford application. With the discreet

Eager holidaymakers are about to board the new Bedford VAM Duple Viceroy (EDY 565E) outside the Adelphi Hotel in Warrior Square, St Leonards on Sea, for a day excursion as part of their holiday break. (Colin Rowland)

experiment successful, the coach speedo was now geared that as it picked up speed it was now registering a higher reading on the speedometer. The driver was now more than happy that the coach was finally performing better than before, or so he thought. . .

Muriel and Colin's first new purchase of their own since Dick's passing, came the following April of 1967 in the shape of another Bedford VAM, with 45 seat Duple Viceroy coachwork and this was registered as EDY 565E. This time specified with the 0.400 Leyland engine option. Its interior moquette was trimmed in an attractive black with green and red, the same as used in the then well-known Standerwick Leyland Atlantean buses used on express motorway services. It was entered in that year's Brighton Coach Rally event for the whole weekend, again driven by Tony Patten who would also take part in the same coach for the 1968 rally. Tony's actual full time position was as Stores Manager for

Seen just before he is due to take part in the driving test course on Madeira Drive is Tony Patten in EDY 565E. (Colin Rowland)

In this rare close up photograph of the rear of EDY 565E, Tony Patten has just completed his reversing manoeuvre into the tightly marked out bay. A Judge now carefully measures his final parked position on completing the task and points will be awarded for best positioning. A brand-new Bedford VAL Plaxton Panorama from the famous tour operator Wallace Arnold can be seen ahead of the Rambler coach. (Colin Rowland)

Bedford VAM 's DDY 250D and EDY 565E sporting Plaxton and Duple coachwork respectively are seen together when on a private hire booking. (Colin Rowland)

Coombs Motors and he would drive part time on occasions. In July 1971 he went on to purchase Empress Coaches from Harry Phillips junior, successfully running it until selling the business in 1998 to take a well-earned retirement.

EDY 565E did have a mishap in its first season in service when less than two months old, providing some unwanted local publicity. Driver Don Fenn had taken a group out on the 28th May from the Hertfordshire Convalescent Home in St Leonards on Sea and would soon be travelling on a pleasant and sedate drive along the Wittersham levels in the neighbouring countryside of East Kent. Here he had to pull over onto the edge of a verge on a narrow stretch of this road in order for another large vehicle to pass him approaching in the opposite direction. With deep ditches on either side, the road surface started to give way and collapse with the coach now slowly falling into the ditch. The passengers could only be evacuated out of the offside emergency exit. Due to the nature of what would become failing day light in this isolated area, the decision was made for the coach to be left overnight until recovery could be better attempted the following day. The shaken passengers were returned home in another coach. The following day an Ashford based recovery firm arrived and would start the process of retrieving the stricken coach, which by now had pretty much settled on its side. Incredibly, once skilfully righted the only minor damage was found to be to lower body panels and lower body frame on the nearside, soon repaired before it was back in service.

Two drivers remembered from the end of the 1960's were Doug Sutch and Gordon Rowlands, who incidentally became Rambler Coaches first full time driver in 1969. (see appendix – memoirs of Gordon Rowlands) Gordon had taken EDY 565E on tour with an American party travelling to John o' Groats in the North of Scotland and then onto Land's End

Taken from a newspaper cutting dated 3rd June 1967, Bedford VAM Duple Viceroy (EDY 565E) has now been evacuated of its passengers and is slowly starting to settle onto its side where it will remain overnight on the Wittersham levels until its recovery can take place the following day. (Bob Cook collection)

in Cornwall. Before he had set off Colin painted the moulded letters Michelin on all of the coach's tyres in blue, white, and red to symbolise the colours of the American flag just for fun. On the coach's return all the colourful wording was still pristine without being marked or scrubbed off the tyres at all, not bad seeing as the coach had literary travelled the entire length of the country including many minor lanes when on tour. On another occasion Colin had taken a replacement mirror and arm to the garage early one morning to fit to the nearside of DDY that had been broken the day before, ahead of Doug setting off for a sightseeing tour of London. Doug had in fact set off before Colin arrived. On his return later in the day Colin showed him the missing mirror to which he replied that he hadn't even noticed it wasn't there! In the winter periods before Colin was old enough to apply for and obtain his PSV driving licence, Doug would also be called upon off season if required, although it would mean Doug having to leave his grocery shop business in order to oblige. A young Colin would then swap roles in order to undertake Doug's deliveries in the local area in his place.

This photograph taken for the Hastings Observer Newspaper shows
Bedford's VDY 207, DDY 250D and EDY 565E, when parked on land
behind Bexhill Road, St Leonards on Sea on a private hire booking.
(William Press official photograph - Colin Rowland collection)

Seen parked outside Skinner's garage in Western Road, St Leonards
on Sea, in readiness to soon depart for the 1968 Brighton Coach
Rally is the Bedford VAM Duple EDY 565E. Keen local readers may
note that the coach is facing in the opposite direction, before Western
Road would be reclassified as a one way street. (Colin Rowland)

After giving many miles of trouble free service, EDY 565E was booked in for an engine re-build at a local company R W Dicker, under the skilled hands of Lionel Croft (Lionel had incidentally attended school with Mrs Rowland). Colin noted that the Leyland unit would cover around only 50,000 miles before needing a set of new piston rings. Colin was present when the rebuilt engine was due to be started up again for the first time by Lionel once his work was completed and was impressed that it fired up 'straight on the button' such was the care and attention to his workmanship.

As the Rambler Coaches story now moves into the 1970's, a young Colin Rowland enjoys an informal photograph with his friend and fellow coach operator, Eric Cole of Berkeley Coaches in Eastbourne standing by the 1968 Bedford VAL Plaxton Panorama 1 (ATU 53F) in 1971.

Chapter 4

Into the 1970's with John Goodwin

By the start of the 1970's cultures were already changing in coach travel, with a gradual decline of the traditional seafront excursion trade by the end of the decade. Ever more affordable package holidays abroad would tempt younger clients to the guaranteed sun of overseas destinations.

The first new coach of the decade to be purchased arrived through the dealer Baker West in April 1970, being a Bedford NJM Dupe Vega 31 (KDY 300H) collected by driver Gordon Rowlands and accompanied by Colin direct from the Duple factory in Blackpool, at a cost of £5,821 and 7 shillings. This model was the type more popularly known as the long running SB5 diesel engine model which had now been re-designated by Bedford as the NJM. Its part exchange was the last coach that was purchased by Colin's late father, the Bedford SB Duple Bella Vega (VDY 207), leaving the small fleet at the end of the previous season in October 1969 before its new replacement would arrive. The striking comparisons

A moment in time is captured of overseas student leaders visiting the UK, when on a day trip for Pat Kelly's language organisation in 1973. The vibrant fashions of the early 1970's make for a colourful picture. (Colin Rowland)

of different body design styles between the two similar Bedford SB / NJM Duple combinations that were only six years apart in age were very much defined by the decades they were built in.

Colin actually drove the coach home on the long return journey to gain further hands on experience ahead of taking his PSV driving test. There was a delay in its completion, so Baker West loaned a second hand vehicle, a Bedford SB Duple which had been new to Cookes of Stoughton near Guildford (BPC 300B), noted as being rather tired. When its engine was up to operating temperature, it tended to stall at traffic lights and liberal amounts of 'easy start' would have to be injected into the coach's air-cleaner by lifting the engine cover inside to coax its engine into running again. Less than ideal when passengers were on board.

When learning to drive Colin would take an available coach out in the evenings with his mother Muriel joining him for the ride. Having grown up with coaches from birth he already knew his way around the vehicles themselves and the craft needed to drive them. After the enjoyment of having the practise of polishing up his skills, Colin turned twenty one years old on 10th May and within the month took his driving test under the watchful eye of the local Ministry man Mr Linton who duly provided him with a first time pass, driving the Bedford VAM Plaxton (DDY 250D) which became his regular vehicle to drive for the 1970 season

Private hire business was continually developing, with trips to London Theatres being popular and event bookings too, for the Ideal Home Exhibition in London, Chessington Zoo, Chelmsford Gang Show and

Seen outside the Duple factory in Blackpool and ready for collection is the brand-new 41 seat Bedford NJM Duple Vega 31 (KDY 300H) in April 1970. (Colin Rowland)

Clarence Pier in Southsea, also a booking to the distant Longleat House in Wiltshire, which incidentally was Colin's second ever booking he drove after passing his PSV driving test.

For rising numbers of young exchange students from Europe and especially Scandinavia travelling to visit the UK's south coast was gaining in popularity, for its culture and close geographical connections to London. This would become a large part of the company's activities in the years ahead. The organisation STS (Student Travel Services) was an early customer followed by EF (Education First) who hired several coaches from the end of May onwards throughout every summer season became a regular feature. Relationships with both organisations endured for many years. Latterly other long-standing companies such as Embassy and Senlac were all still customers into 2018.

Without a doubt, day trips to London were *the* popular destination of choice over the weekends, although other more local venues such as Arlington Stock Car Racing near to Hailsham was popular for an evening's entertainment out with over ten coaches regularly used. Additional vehicle capacity from Fuggles Coaches in Benenden and Cooks Coaches in Westfield would be called upon on occasions. The numbers of students staying in the Hastings area was said to be in the region of around five thousand with EF alone with some two thousand students in nearby Bexhill on Sea.

Colin recalled the hardest day driving he ever experienced was an occasion in EDY 565E. Having departed Hastings with a group for the long journey to Felixstowe Docks in Suffolk for them to catch their ship home and before the advent of the growing motorway network, many journeys would be on A and B roads, still the only routes for many destinations and taking longer than is now usually possible. Colin had already completed one two hundred and fifty mile round trip in EDY

On a warm summer's evening driver Doug Sutch is photographed by Bedford NJM Duple Vega 31 (KDY 300H) on Breeds Place coach stand. (Colin Rowland)

sitting in the heat from not only the large all-round glazing of the coach, but also from the vehicles front positioned engine alongside him and before it was yet be fitted with power steering years later. As he finally arrived back in Hastings, he was immediately asked if he could drive an emergency booking for a student firm that had forgotten to book their return travel home and it was an urgent journey to catch a ferry. Colin asked where to. . . it was to Felixstowe!

Muriel Rowland took some time off on behalf of the company on the 19th June 1970 to attend the funeral of the founder of Empress Coaches, Harry Phillips senior, who had passed away aged seventy-nine years and had been still actively running his business. He was the last of her late husband Dick's contemporary pre-war era fellow operators who were in operation in person, the business continuing with his son also named Harry. At the time both operators were now running three coaches each.

Customers in 1970 included the RAFA Club, Mastins Store, C & C Marshall, 18+ Club and others with the longer titles of the Hastings & Thanet Building Society, Hastings Rangers & Venture Scouts, East Sussex Model Engineers and the Student Nurses Association from Royal East Sussex Hospital in Hastings. For a few weeks another booking took place on a daily basis to provide transport for staff in accommodation locally that were working at Ore Place on The Ridge in the town, the then home of Royal Army Service Corps Records Office.

In the December of 1970 the company finally purchased its first Bedford VAL twin steer coach (ATU 53F) their largest vehicle yet at 52 seats. With student bookings normally demanding highest capacity vehicles available, a decision had been made to sell the 45 seat Bedford VAM (DDY 250D) replacing it with this 1968 coach. It featured a Plaxton

Bedford VAL 70 Plaxton Panorama (ATU 53F) shows off its clean lines and smart livery when parked on a private hire booking. c 1971. (Colin Rowland)

Colin Rowland is photographed in the driving seat of Bedford VAL
70 Plaxton Panorama (ATU 53F) c1971. (Colin Rowland)

Panorama 1 body with the later Bedford 466ci engine at just under three years old. It had just one previous owner, the tour operator Shearings-Pleasureways. Due to its length of over 37 feet it would initially be parked when not in use in nearby Warrior Square. A small piece of ground was soon rented opposite the Prince of Wales Public House in Western Road opposite Cross Street for it to be more conveniently parked overnight. Years later when the site was no longer in use for parking, it was used by local school teacher and owner-coach driver Bob Sloan trading as Bob-a-long. He specialised in 'walking by coach' excursions and holidays for rambling groups with Bob having a strictly non-smoking policy onboard, years before this would eventually become law for coach travel.

In this group photograph the Chairman of the 18+ Club, Martin Harvey,
(with moustache in the centre of the image) is pictured with club members
and the Mayor of Hastings Cllr Edward Nye just before the group depart in
Bedford VAL Plaxton (ATU 53F). A young Colin Rowland is standing behind
the Mayor. c 1971 (Hastings Observer – Colin Rowland collection)

A useful temporary contract was obtained over the quieter winter
months of 1972 into 1973 for a local manufacturer Kolster Brands (KB)
in Hastings, to collect staff early in the morning from the Cable and
Wireless Factory at Foots Cray for work at the KB factory in Hastings,
returning back at teatime. This five day a week commitment meant that
it would make economic sense for the coach to be left up at the Foots
Cray factory every night with its driver (normally in the evenings John
Goodwin) driving back in the company Minivan that had been left there

in order to facilitate a daily relay, thus saving much of the operating costs. A second-hand 1965 Bedford VAL Plaxton Panorama with 52 seats (GPC 58C) was initially purchased for the contract, although with a full complement of staff on board, this already well-travelled coach would show the wear from its Leyland engine on the long inclines on the A21 route, as a haze of engine fumes gradually appeared through its demister vents on the dash. By the time the coach arrived at the end of each journey a film of engine oil mist had built up on the inside of its windscreen. This coach was the first vehicle purchased in the new decimal money system, introduced in the country in February 1971 and had one of the shortest stays in the operational fleet of just two months. Sold to Tony Patten of nearby Empress Coaches, its engine duly received new pistons and piston liners to vastly improve its tired engine.

John Goodwin proudly stands beside Bedford VAL 70 Plaxton Panorama (ATU 53F) on the Breeds Place coach stand. With a full complement of advertising boards on display it heightens the impression of the overall length of the coach. (Colin Rowland)

The long running Bedford VAL chassis first launched in 1962, was reaching its twilight years by the start of the 1970's and would soon be replaced by a completely new underfloor engine design, designated 'YRT' after some ten successful years in production.

On its launch in 1972, it coincided with Duple Coachbuilders also introducing a new range of coachwork designs named 'Dominant' replacing their then current Viceroy and Vista range. With this an order was placed by the company for a 53 seat example to be built at Duple's Blackpool factory, production having ceased at their Hendon factory in London three years earlier. Registered as TDY 494L there would be no older part exchange against this new coach as the fleet was now slowly increasing in size. There were delays in this coach's arrival as being a newly launched chassis, Bedford had not been able to build up enough stock to meet the demand from operators now wanting to order them. A letter from Ernie Waterman of E J Baker in November 1972 made note that he had had a meeting at Duple to discuss the delivery date with a hope of it being in April 1973 due to a recent strike at the factory putting back delivery times for customers. In the event it would not arrive until the season was very much underway in the June. Its eventual arrival was a success as in the February of 1974 yet another Duple Dominant bodied Bedford was purchased (VDY 626M) this time on the new and slightly shorter Bedford YRQ chassis, accommodating 45 seats. Again, there was a delay in receiving it due to this coach being the first model in the range with full air brakes. Bedford had made a number of technical changes creating a small headache at Duple when the new chassis arrived with it being fitted with two large round dash dials on the driver's console. The traditional Bedford oblong shaped speedo having been a familiar sight for many years, Duple did not anticipate the need to redesign their dashboards to accommodate the new style dials.

A Duple promotional brochure for the new Dominant range in 1973. With the Rambler managements eye on how this new model would look in company colours, the picture on this cover has been carefully painted by hand into company livery. (Duple - Colin Rowland collection)

Its February 1974 and the brand new Bedford YRQ Duple Dominant (VDY 626M)
is being collected from Duple Coachbuilders in Blackpool. Passing alongside
is a new Bedford YRQ chassis for bodying, having just arrived direct from
Bedford's Luton factory, driven some 200 miles by a hardy commercial delivery
driver who can be seen sitting on a wooden makeshift seat. (Colin Rowland)

Seen on Eastbourne seafront on 23rd February 1974 is the Bedford YRQ
Duple Dominant (VDY 626M) when on a private hire booking. (Alan Snatt)

Parked at Breeds Place are Bedfords TDY 494L and VDY 626M. In the
background is the impressive Deluxe Leisure Centre that had first opened in
1899 as The Empire Theatre of Varieties, with famous Music Hall singer and
actress Marie Lloyd appearing as top of the bill. In 1910 it became the Royal
Cinema De Luxe, lasting in this guise until 1965 where it would now become
a Bingo Club, retaining its cinema licence until 1970. (Colin Rowland)

Purchasing new vehicles did not render the company immune from
what one would expect of operating coaches with the reliability of no
major breakdowns on a large investment. Some fourteen months after
VDY 626M had been delivered it was on a tour where its 466ci engine
failed spectacularly heading up the M1 motorway. Colin recalled that
he never did find one of the pistons and connecting rods from its six-
cylinder engine that had literary blown up, but there was a lot of oil
on the motorway. Fortunately, they did have another coach parked in
London on a day trip and with a telephone call made to a café in the
capital nearby to where the coach was thought to be parked, its driver

was located and he set off to collect the stranded group on the M1 for their tour to resume, whilst the broken down coach was recovered back to St Leonards on Sea. A brand new engine to replace the expired 466ci unit was sourced directly from Bedford, although it would be a larger 500 engine destined for a TM truck in build at the Luton factory, giving the coach some additional power. This technically made the coach an as yet undesignated 'YMQ' model, before Bedford had even yet to introduce it for their coach chassis in the future.

An interesting booking in 1973 and a little more diverse than the normal type of private hire charters, was to run the cast and crew of the then popular Television show The Goodies out to locations in the local area. A coach actually appeared on screen in what would become

Bedford YRT Duple Dominant (TDY 494L) is seen in St Margaret's Road, St Leonards on Sea, now showing the later application of light green stripes to its lower panels, something that would become a standard addition to future purchases. (Colin Rowland)

the episode 'Camelot'. The cast were based at the Alexandra Hotel on Hastings Seafront with scenes filmed in Chatham and Fairlight Quarry, but mainly taking place at the picturesque Bodiam Castle some eleven miles away from Hastings. Access to the rear of the Castle grounds through gates with stone pillars at the top entrance was indeed tight, the 41 seat Bedford (KDY 300H) was carefully inched through to ensure it didn't tip on the camber of the track against the pillars and by using bricks to keep it level, thus saving the crew a long walk down to the Castle itself. When filming was underway it was interesting for the drivers to have the chance to see the actors in action including Bill Oddie, Graeme Garden and Tim Brooke-Taylor, the final episode also starring Alfie Bass. The coach was clearly seen with driver Gordon Rowlands on screen,

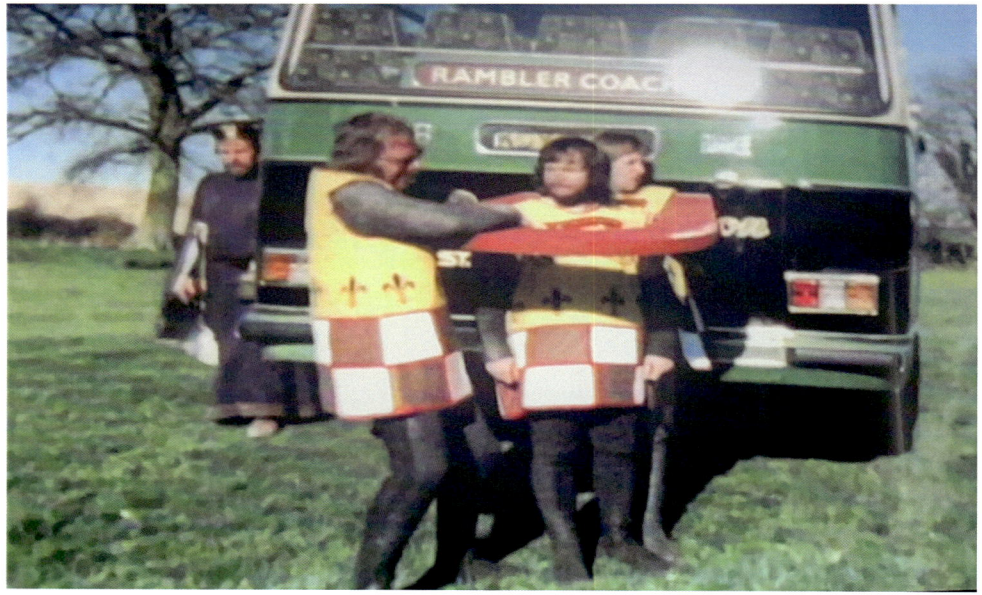

Whilst filming is taking place at Bodiam Castle in East Sussex, The Goodies (left to right) Graeme Garden, Bill Oddie and Tim Brooke-Taylor are seen behind the Bedford NJM Duple (KDY 300H) with giant magnet prop. (Colin Rowland collection)

in some of the filming sequences prominently displaying its company names. Scenes filmed showed passengers boarding, on another scene the coach passes The Goodies at speed which attracts a giant magnet being held up by them (which was actually made from lightweight polystyrene) drawing the trio into the rear of the coach. The episode was broadcast to millions of viewers on BBC television on the 1st December 1973 providing unexpected but welcome advertising for the company.

The British economy in 1973 would suffer from rising inflation with much of the blame accredited to a fuel crisis quadrupling oil prices, leading to what would become high unemployment. Companies would lay off staff and wages were not keeping up with living costs, National strikes further crippling the country. For Rambler business would remain on a fairly even keel although it did create different parallels in costs when coaches were bought and sold at this time. With the collapse

Cautiously emerging from the narrow gates of Bodiam Castle is Bedford NJM Duple (KDY 300H) when engaged on filming for an episode of the television comedy The Goodies in 1973. (Colin Rowland)

of the travel agency and airline of the Luton based Court Line Group in 1974, within months it would also take down its coach operations as well. With it a selection of near new Ford R1114 Duple Dominant 53 seat coaches became available for sale through the dealer Yeates. One example had a favourable price tag of £9,250 due to the changing economic situation around the country, proving a good deal for a six month old coach having covered just 9,000 miles, and prompting a rare purchase by Rambler of a full-size Ford coach.

The following year Bedford would be looking to launch their new YMT chassis, with an order placed by the company for a new 53 seat model with a Duple Dominant body, similar to previous orders. Registered as LJK 335P this new YMT would now cost some £18,588. It was also the first coach owned to be fitted with the then newly-introduced of a tachograph speedo. These fitments would become commonplace across the industry with changes on how drivers' hours could now be more accurately recorded. By inserting a bespoke medium grade paper disc to the back of the hinged opening speedometer unit, it recorded the trace on it of driving time, speeds and rest periods with accuracy and was an advance in technology. Until this time, the usual way of recording driver's duties, for a number of years previously, required the driver to use a small oblong book with sheets of graph paper marked out with a 24 hour clock, in which the driver would manually write their daily driving and rest periods as a record of their duties and requiring care and honesty to do this consistently.

The Ford R1114 Duple was part exchanged for this new Bedford YMT coach some seventeen months after its purchase and with inflation continually rising around this time, its allowance would be given as £12,250 (plus VAT @ 8%). The Ford had actually increased by £3,000 in value selling for more than Rambler had paid for it having now covered a further 5,000 miles.

On a bright day in January 1975 the former Court Line Ford R1114
Duple Dominant (YXD 470M) has just arrived at Western Road for a
repaint into fleet livery. It must be noted that the coach is already tightly
parked against the rear wall of the garage. The letters above the doors
'Rambler Luxury Coaches' were originally made up by Dick Rowland
years before, all individually cut from wood. (Colin Rowland)

Colin recalled one occasion he was driving the Ford himself on a
booking for tour operator SAGA in 1975, where the then entire fleet had
been chartered for a day trip to Le Touquet in France. The weather was
noted as turning poor later on in the day, so much so that in the evening
when returning home on board the passenger Ferry from Boulogne was
listing badly in the heavy seas, attempting its sailing back to the Port of
Dover. Not an enjoyable experience for the passengers on board.

Photographed on 24th May 1975 in Western Road opposite the
Prince of Wales Public House we find the Ford R1114 Duple
Dominant (YXD 470M) between hires. (Bob Cook)

Colin had already known John Goodwin for several years from where he worked at nearby Coombs Motors and through John's other motor trade interests, John having passed his PSV driving test ahead of Colin to be able to assist in parking coaches in the evenings in their compact garage, after his work was finished, also undertaking casual driving work when required. In 1974 things became more formal when John established himself alongside Rambler Coaches by going into business with Colin as partners to trade as 'Rambler Mini-Coaches'. The new partnership's first booking took place on 2nd September 1974 with a party from East Sussex Social Services travelling to Minster. Among the early regular customers were G H Brooker, ITT, Computor Devices and Balmer Priory Cricket Club. John was hired in by Tony Patten from Empress Coaches for transport to cover his regular commitments on occasions to Glyne Gap School in Bexhill and Robert Mitchell School in Ore, Hastings.

Notable vehicles as part of the mini-coaches business started with an 18 seat Bedford J2 Plaxton Embassy (AEX 45B) purchased in the August at a cost of £1,250, having previously operated with Bluebird Coaches in Weymouth. It proved to be a popular size coach straight away and just four months later it was replaced with younger 20 seat Bedford J2, again with Plaxton Embassy coachwork (NKJ 769F) from Kent based operator Streamline in Maidstone for some £2,375. This latter coach had the popular image of the time, the 'Keep on Truckin' man professionally sign-written on the boot lid by Wally Rainsford.

Rambler continental! John Goodwin (on left) and Colin Rowland are pictured in Le Touquet, France when on driving duties for a SAGA day trip in 1975 with Duple bodied Ford R1114 (YXD 470M) and Bedford YRT (TDY 494L). (Colin Rowland)

Taken on the same day, Messrs Goodwin and Rowland enjoy a moment
of relaxation at a local bar, with a coffee of course. (Colin Rowland)

The Rambler Coaches fleet line up taken in December 1974
at Rock a Nore in Hastings Old Town. (Colin Rowland)

This rare image captures both Bedford J2 Plaxton Embassy coaches owned.
The 1964 model (AEX 45B) has actually been sold in part exchange through the
dealer Yeates for the younger 1968 coach (NKJ 769F), the two vehicles enjoying
a brief moment in shared ownership. AEX 45B had been given the name 'Puppy
Love' after the popular song covered by Donny Osmond in 1972. (Colin Rowland)

In August 1975 a 1972 Ford Transit 12 seat minibus with Deansgate
conversion was purchased from Epsom Coaches in Surrey for a
respectable £1,725. Colin recalled in the cold and damp mornings of
the winter period that followed later in the year how perhaps the earlier
timing of its sale to them was apt. . . The 'York' diesel engine was not
renowned for always being an instant starting engine from cold, with
the minibus having to be towed around Warrior Square to coax it into
life on numerous occasions, from then on it ran well for the duration
of the day. A niggling issue started to develop when the engine would
just suddenly cut out when travelling up a hill in the local area just
after collecting passengers on a contract hire. After the vehicle became

stationary the driver would start it up again and it would then run. Colin would go out in the minibus with no passengers afterwards and couldn't replicate the problem. Eventually the issue was found. When the engine was running under load with passengers on-board, the air cleaner under the bonnet, which had an intake spout, would suck the air intake so hard it would draw the demister pipe down onto its intake mouth cutting the air flow and stop the engine. The problem was now easily rectified.

The year of 1976 was remembered for its hot summer season and sweltering heat with record breaking temperatures across the country, recorded further down the coast in Southampton to be 35.6 centigrade in the June. In Hastings the popularity of visiting student groups to the town remained popular, with young students staying with host families

RAMBLER MINI COACHES

12 - 20 Seaters for Private Hire

22 Western Road
St. Leonards-on-Sea
Sussex, TN37 6DG

Tel. Hastings 437266

Rambler Mini Coaches calling card c1974. Note the popular 'Keep on Truckin' figure of the time. (Colin Rowland)

This 12 seat Ford Transit Deansgate (FOU 216K) was the first
minibus to enter the Rambler fleet in August 1975 from Epsom
Coaches and is seen with the 20 seat Bedford J2 Plaxton Embassy
(NKJ 769F) at Breeds Place coach stand. (Colin Rowland)

locally. Coach hires for their excursions were undertaken to a wide range
of destinations such as Canterbury, Dungeness, Brighton and Bodiam.
Combined destinations of Oxford and Cambridge and of course to
London were operated for numerous language schools.

Colin recalled how well organised EF were as an organisation to
work with. Ahead of the season in earlier years paperwork would be
provided for all the scheduled excursions in advance for the entire
season. This paperwork was provided in no less than nine copies all
typed out in duplicate so that key personnel including tour leaders,
accounts departments, management and travel operators all had the
same information and nothing could go wrong. Finalised details would
come in at the end of May as initial groups were soon to arrive for their
studies in the UK. EF would also charter coaches for their student

John Goodwin enjoys an informal photograph on the seafront whilst potential customers study the excursions on offer to Canterbury, Dover and Folkestone for a reasonable £1.10 pence return fare. (Colin Rowland)

transfers via the incoming passenger ferries at Dover, Folkestone and Parkeston (Harwich) with more occasional transfers from Felixstowe and Newhaven. Continental coaches had already dropped the groups off at ports in Europe to board the ferries as foot passengers and luggage was now loaded up on large open trailers and towed on board by the ship's crew. On arrival at Dover Docks students would disembark, again on foot, with their loaded luggage trailers towed off from the car deck and landed on the dockside, then manoeuvred into place near to the waiting coaches for unloading. The regular sight of eager students jumping up onto the trailers themselves with large quantities of luggage stacked over four feet tall, to get their personal items onto the coach, was something that today would not be tolerated for health and safety reasons. In later years the popularity of port transfers would slow down with the growing market on organisations using low cost air travel, with a swing towards Gatwick, Heathrow, Stansted, and Luton for many of the coach transfers instead.

The summer of 1976 was also noted as being lucrative for the sales of cans of drink to the students onboard the coaches when travelling to and from destinations. At a reasonable 9 ½ pence a can, sales were going very well throughout this hazy year. In early August there was four days hire from the BBC for filming work in the local area, and other operators hiring for extra capacity included Monks Coaches of Staplecross, Campbell's Coaches in Sedlescombe, Pandora Holidays of St Leonards on Sea and Empress Coaches in Hastings.

In Colin and John's early years as business partners both men would often drive coaches on multiple private hire bookings. Of the many London sightseeing tours regularly booked by language organisations, one day both men had parked their coaches in a quiet street in London after dropping off passengers, deciding to go for a stroll in their free time before the return trip later in the day. Walking past a Police Station they were stopped by a constable outside and requested to take part in an identity parade. As this was not an optional request, they duly went inside with a number of other men already assembled there until asked to enter a room and stand in a line-up where a key witness would now enter the room to join all of them to see if they could identify the suspect for a crime that had been committed. What Colin and John didn't know was whether the actual person who had committed the offence was in the line-up with them.

Another second-hand acquisition under the banner of the mini-coaches fleet was a larger coach, a 1965 Bedford SB Duple Bella Vega 41 seater (CUF 490C) in the June. Arriving direct from Oakley Coaches John was aware before purchasing it that it was painted in a bright red and yellow livery, where John's expertise as a professional painter would be required for it to receive its new company colours. The preparation took longer than planned as Oakley had painted *everything* in red and yellow including the coachwork mouldings and trims, inside the locker doors, even the jack and wheel brace.

When John would order paint for respraying coaches into company colours, he would keep a close eye to ensure that the colour matches were always correct for what he had been previously using. Manufacturers paint schemes could change just slightly from time to time, so the correct

All three of the Bedford Duple Dominants in the then fleet are seen waiting to collect their passengers from the Adelphi Hotel in Warrior Square in St Leonards on Sea c1976. (Colin Rowland)

In these two fine studies Bedford YMT Duple Dominant (LJK 335P)
is seen when new in 1976. This coach would enjoy a long stay in the
fleet, eventually receiving the cherished registration number WUF
44. It was sold in February 1994 to Whites Coaches of Heathfield
at a respectable eighteen years of age. (Colin Rowland)

colour match was not always maintained over long periods of time. In
the early 1970's John would use Triumph Honeysuckle for the cream,
with the black being taxi black. (There are actually different shades of this
particular colour) In fact, the first Bedford VAL twin-steer acquired from
dealer Don Everall slightly surprised John and Colin, as they found that
this late second-hand purchase had, in fact, been coach painted by the
traditional method of brush painting instead of the more accepted process
of spray painting, by now the quicker accepted norm on commercial vehicle
finishes. Although the finish, as one would expect, was presentable, John
with an eye to perfection, did in time prepare and re-spray the coach in his
preferred choice of Glasurit paint products. The Bedford VAL should be
noted as becoming John's favourite type of coach to drive.

The clean lines of 1965 Bedford SB Duple Bella Vega (CUF 490C) are
well suited to the Rambler livery when seen on the Breeds Place coach
stand. Note the company Mini van in attendance. The coach was sold
in September 1977 to Plumridge in Horley. (Philip Cattermole)

New to Banstead Coaches in 1971, this 45 seat Bedford YRQ
Plaxton Elite (YOR 111J) was purchased direct from the operator
in September 1977. Seen parked in Terrace Road St Leonards on
Sea on 19th June 1978, it was sold at the end of the 1980 season to
Wise Coaches on the Upper Dicker in East Sussex. (Bob Cook)

Colin and John's business opportunities were not limited to operating just coaches. For two years in the late 1970's a venture of hire vans was offered with a Ford Transit and two Commer PB vans available for self-drive hire. The Ford and one of the Commers was painted by John in what would be described as a Rambler style livery with the second Commer painted in blue. A regular customer was Mr Trowl who would hire one for a pop group travelling with equipment to bookings. John also bought and sold vans, with a notable batch of fifty-four Minivans from a Power Station on the Hoo Peninsular in Kent acquired with John trading as 'The Van Specialist'. Colin had one of these Minivans himself taking pride in personally signwriting it.

A good maintenance regime was something both Colin and John prided themselves on knowing how to keep any issues to a minimum, with preventative work and keeping a good stock of parts, should unforeseen issues happen. An example of the hands on style of keeping coaches operational was demonstrated when a Bedford had an engine failure in London one late afternoon. With passengers swiftly taken care of with a replacement coach to return them home, the stricken coach would be recovered by tow truck for the slow journey back over sixty miles to Western Road. On its eventual return with assistance from

One of the self-drive Commer PB vans wearing a familiar livery. (Colin Rowland)

Seen outside the former Skinners Garage in Western Road
is Commer PB with 12 seat Rootes body (MPK 71L) bought
direct from Nelmes Travel in Hornchurch. (Bob Cook)

Alan Marchant of Coombs Motors and John Quinnell, the men worked
through the night, taking out the coaches mid-mounted engine and all
ancillaries from underneath in exchange for a complete replacement
engine. The coach duly departed the following morning at 07.00am for
a works contract.

On another occasion a water pump on the engine of Bedford SB (DME
998A) started to leak badly as the coach was travelling through Eltham in
London having set off from Northeye Prison in Bexhill on Sea, heading
for another prison transfer. By the time it had reached Eltham it could
travel no further. The driver had called through with the difficulties and
local coach operator Cliff's Coaches very kindly attended to make repairs.
In the meantime, the prison guards decided it would not be unreasonable
to allow the prisoners on-board to be taken to the local pub in order for

them to use the (toilet) facilities, being led off the coach and down the road, all handcuffed together! Colin always felt uneasy about the fact that the Prison Governor had stipulated the emergency door of the coach must be locked from the outside before it left the prison site for security reasons. It was also illegal from Ministry of Transport regulations to drive a coach without unlocking its doors and emergency exits first, so this type of booking had its own conflicts of interest.

One potential contract that a decision was made *not* to bid for in early 1977 was the invitation to tender for the concessionary bus services in Hastings, more commonly known as the pensioners bus services, funded by the local Borough Council, which had been operated by Maidstone & District Motor Services Ltd (M&D) since 1972. The council's development committee decided they wanted to tender the services, inviting Rambler, Empress and Pandora Holidays in St Leonards on Sea to submit their own prices for operating it for the period of one year, starting on 1st April 1977. Councillors had wanted to force the situation of what they termed as, 'M&D's monopoly in the area for running service routes, some councillors felt this was a way of breaking it. Both Colin and John felt that this type of stage operation was not for them, requiring seven services on Tuesdays, Thursdays and Fridays, so did not proceed to submit a price. Neither did Tony Patten at Empress Coaches. However, Mike Tilyard, the owner of Pandora Holidays decided to tender, also expanding his quotation to be a five day a week operation and a Sunday morning church run as well as part of the package. The Pandora tender came in at some £25,840 for the year compared to Maidstone & District's price of £23,745 for less operating days. Regretfully the demands of the service in actual operation proved to be a contributing factor of the eventual closure of Pandora Holidays. With the contract only being awarded for just one year, the only affordable vehicles that could be purchased to service the needs required were a number of second-hand Bedford VAL twin-steer coaches, proving not ideal to use for stage service for the hilly and demanding geographical landscape of the Hastings area. Issues including breakdowns made it difficult to keep the routes reliably maintained, compounded with roadworks around the town that started after Pandora's operations began. The following year the service reverted back to Maidstone & District when their next tender was submitted at a lower price than Pandora, albeit using more suitable heavyweight buses for the service.

The little known connection to the Rambler story now came about when due to shortages of fuel supplies to Maidstone & District, Colin and John would assist in supplying diesel for fuelling the Leyland Panther buses used specifically for the Pensioners service. When their service duties were completed on the days operated, the Leylands would

Est. 1924

RAMBLER COACHES

M. Rowland and Son

12 - 20 - 41 - 45 - 53 Seaters for Hire

22 Western Road
St. Leonards-on-Sea
Sussex, TN37 6DG

Tel. Hastings 437266

Calling card c1970's. (Colin Rowland)

travel down Western Road and reverse up onto the forecourt of the former Skinners premises now being rented by Rambler where they would be filled up directly from supply on site. John would be ordering maximum quantities of diesel, even filling up large 45 gallon drums for extra capacity to service both company's needs.

In March 1977 another Bedford VAL with 53 seat Plaxton coachwork (HJM 772H) dating from late 1969 joined the fleet, proving to be a favourite drive for John. From time to time its starter motor would jam and wouldn't work. As a temporary measure, until changing it could be done, John kept half a broomstick pole with him by the driver's seat. Should it stick, John would lift the small inspection flap located between the driver's seat and engine cover alongside and just gently drop the broomstick onto the starter below, which did the trick every time for the coach to then start. In fact, John ended up using the coach over the summer season, which amused his regular passengers on the contract bookings when the pole would sometimes need to be produced. The same month Colin would marry Miss Pauline Rummery, the two having first met back in 1970 at the 18+ Club in Hastings. Pauline was working for the local Gas Board but would eventually join Doreen Fisher, Marjorie Atherden, Jacqueline Sales and Muriel Rowland at the Rambler office in 1981 to assist in the ever growing administration for bookings. Doreen joked with Pauline on her first day in the office when she stated, just ahead of lunchtime, 'now this will be a revelation to you. . .. your husband Colin will soon be calling into the office and will have thought about a letter he wants written. He has already mentioned the first half of it which I have noted, now as he arrives, he will have thought about the second half!' Doreen was ready with a pen and note pad as Colin arrived and would quickly take the dictation in short hand to piece the two together as Colin soon departed back to his work at the depot again.

On the wedding day of Miss Pauline Rummery marrying Mr Colin Rowland,
this informal photograph taken at the Beauport Park Hotel in St Leonards
on Sea shows both Colin and his best man and business partner, John
Goodwin, on Pauline and Colin's special day. (Colin Rowland)

Diverse areas of business were keeping the coaches busy on regular
hires with a number of large local employers hiring Rambler's services to
provide transport for their staff to and from their workplaces. Customers
included Newtime Foods, Electro-Technical Services (ETA) and Thornes
Electrical in Bexhill. A school contract was operated bringing in pupils
from Eastbourne to the Convent of Our Lady in Filsham Road, St
Leonards on Sea, which fitted nicely with the Thornes contract too.
For a while Nuttall's engaged transport for their staff working on the
building of a new pipeline at what would become Bewl Water reservoir,
some twenty miles from Hastings.

School contracts would start to play a larger part in how the business expanded in the following years. As tenders from East Sussex County Council (ESCC) became available, routes on offer would always be costed with a return tender bid sent off in a sealed envelope to County Hall in Lewes. Initial success through obtaining routes from villages such as Peasmarsh, Northiam and Westfield to Thomas Peacocke School in Rye meant that two coaches, one of them doubling up on one route to collect pupils, would be followed by routes serving other local schools in time.

On 1st May 1978 a decision was made between Muriel, Colin and John, that the Rambler mini-coaches accounts would now be combined with Rambler Coaches, thus simplifying the trading arrangement and now making all three of them equal one third partners in the company as the business continued to move forward. One month later John and Colin made their biggest investment as yet, when John spotted two Bedford YMT Plaxton Supreme 53 seat coaches for sale that had been new to the coach operator Harry Shaw in Coventry just fifteen months before. Only one was to be purchased, but on inspection both Colin and John were undecided as both examples were in such good condition. The result being that both coaches were bought at a then eye-watering cost of £45,000 for the pair, a huge investment and a leap of faith. At the time these coaches were very much front-line vehicles and boosted the image of the company. Registered consecutively as VWK 7S and VWK 8S they proved to be good investments. John suggested that they part exchange the Bedford (TDY 494L) and Ford Transit minibus (FOU 216K) to assist in funding these newer coaches. A cheaper (and very tidy) Commer PB minibus (MPK 71L) was purchased from an owner driver and was collected on the way to pick up the new coaches and drop off the part exchanges.

Colin normally drove 7S and driver, Gordon Rowlands, in 8S. At the time a regular Sunday Church contract was operated with two vehicles for Chapel Park Road Baptist Church, near the Western Road base. The contract income paid for the hire purchase arrangement on the coaches as Colin would normally drive one route and John the other, to assist in saving costs.

A much rarer purchase was of a Bedford J2 to replace an earlier model in October 1978. This time though it would have Moseley Faro coachwork built by Salvador Caetano in Portugal. Like its older predecessor it was fitted with twenty seats, although visually it bore no resemblance to the Plaxton built product. Its design was square and angular in proportions with large windows, its modern European style design was certainly eye catching. Purchased from Yeates in Salisbury,

Inside the former Skinners Garage in Western Road, we find the 1975 Bedford J2 with 20 seat Caetano Faro coachwork (JFX 657N) previously operated by Mercury in Bournemouth. It joined the company in October 1978. (Philip Cattermole)

Parked tightly inside the Western Road garage is the 45 seat Bedford
VAM 14 Plaxton Panorama (JAA 507E). Purchased in November
1979 from dealer Yeates it was sold in March 1982, ending its days
as a caravan in the Bournemouth area. (Colin Rowland)

This 53 seat Bedford VAL Plaxton Elite (HJM 772H) had been new to Brown's
of Ambleside in January 1969, joining the fleet in March 1977. It enjoyed a
stay of nine years until sold to Cooks Coaches in Westfield. (Bob Cook)

Seen at Folkestone Harbour in 1979 are Bedford YMT Plaxton's (VWK 8S and VWK 7S) with Bedford YRQ Duple Dominant (VDY 626M). VWK 8S has yet to receive its new livery, still wearing the colours of its previous owner, Harry Shaw of Coventry. (Colin Rowland)

On a bright day Colin Rowland stands with his morning newspaper waiting for passengers with Bedford Plaxton Supreme (VWK 7S) on the Breeds Place coach stand for the MK Electric courtesy coach service to their local factory. (Colin Rowland)

the coach having been looked over by their representative first, the deal was done on this basis. When Colin went to collect it at their premises it had not yet arrived from its then owner Mercury in Bournemouth. After patiently waiting the coach eventually arrived at the dealer's yard having just completed its last booking and Colin was now able to set off home. On the journey back it soon became apparent that the braking system was to say the least, lacking, as Colin headed down a hill onto a roundabout in Southampton, the brakes failed completely. By luck no traffic was crossing over it at that moment, so the journey from there on became an even more careful run home. It was noted as a sweet running coach although the continental body being somewhat heavier in comparison to its British built counterparts, made the already slightly underpowered 3.75 litre 220ci four-cylinder Bedford engine work even harder.

The following May a four year old Bedford YRQ with 45 seat Plaxton Elite coachwork came into the fleet from Tappins of Didcot (HRD 12N). As the season was already underway it remained in its distinct black and orange livery for the next few months. When the time came to repaint the coach, its regular driver Gordon Rowlands was on holiday. On his return and much to his surprise John Goodwin had decided to repaint the coach not into livery, but a simple white with blue scheme complete with 'EF' signwriting for regular customer English First, not what Gordon was expecting to see. It would in time eventually receive the traditional fleet colours. However, it would be the first coach that John would modernise to give off the appearance of a newer vehicle. John took on the task of fitting the then brand new Plaxton Supreme IV front end from the windscreen downwards, carefully grafted to the earlier model Elite coachwork, giving the appearance of a brand new vehicle. Both John and Colin were so pleased with the results that when a late model 1973 Bedford VAL with Plaxton Elite III coachwork was purchased at just ten years old in March 1983 (RPB 222L) the same facelifted treatment was given to modernise its looks. It was then duly reregistered with a personalised registration as 1924 RH, the numbers and letters to mark uniquely the company's founding year and to 'Rambler Hastings' respectively. This was thought to be the only Bedford VAL model to have received such modernisation work. The vehicle was still in existence in 2023, having been re- registered as EUF 738L before its sale in 1992. The coach performed a broad range of bookings, although it was noted, when running on dockside transfers to Harwich, its Bedford 466 engine could be slow when fully loaded with passengers and luggage and the additional weight of having a Telma retarder brake, to bolster the modest braking performance of this model. Power was improved with the fitting of the larger Bedford 500 engine and a higher speed differential providing the coach with a comfortable cruising speed of 70 mph on the motorways.

In November 1979 an end of the decade purchase came in the form of a 1976 Bedford YMT with 53 seat Willowbrook 008 body. It was known as the Spacecar and had previously operated for National Travel London when new. This futuristic looking coach was advanced in its time for its style of coachwork when launched amidst a huge amount of interest at the Earls Court Commercial Motor Show in September 1974. Although a number of examples were built it had not sold in the great volumes hoped. Both Colin and John had originally travelled up country to a dealer to take a look at a selection which were being offered as lease deals. As both men arrived in the company service van in their dirty overalls, the representative didn't think that they fitted the bill to afford the finance package on offer. It was much to his surprise that they decided to purchase one coach outright instead.

Seen at the Willowbrook factory in Loughborough in November 1979, is the Bedford YMT with 53 seat Willowbrook 008 'Spacecar' coachwork (KUW 540P) soon to be collected by its new owner. Its design was considered quite futuristic in comparison with contemporary coach builders of the time. (Willowbrook – Colin Rowland collection)

HVD 588N was a 1975 Bedford YRT Plaxton Elite III that had been new to Premier Coaches of Watford. (Colin Rowland)

The Rambler Coaches booking office at 18 Western Road was in use from around 1978 replacing the family home as an office at number 22. It was photographed when closing for the final time on 29th December 1989, with the new office opening at West Ridge Manor at the start of January 1990. (Derek Jones)

As the new decade of the 1980's arrives the company will go from strength to strength in new areas of business, diversification and a new premises. Muriel Rowland and John Goodwin stand proudly with their Bedford YMT Plaxton Supreme (VWK 8S) at the company's new premises, West Ridge Manor. (Colin Rowland)

Chapter 5

Times of change 1980–1999

Towards the end of the 1970's the fleet had now grown to some fourteen vehicles, parked when not in use around Western Road, in garages, on forecourts and hard standing areas. Car ownership was slowly on the rise and once quiet side streets now had increasing numbers of parked vehicles in and around the local area. Thoughts would turn to the possibilities of a larger site with better access. Relocation to the main local trading estate Ponswood in St Leonards on Sea was not a possibility as the Borough Council did not want transport businesses being based there. However, Colin was asked by a member of the 18+ Group one day in 1979 who worked for the planning department on the council if he was still looking for another site, which of course the answer was yes. Mention was made of a potential plot of land on the outskirts of Hastings, near to the main A21 London Road in an area known traditionally as The Harrow. Further enquiries noted it was listed as

John Goodwin and Colin Rowland are photographed for a trade magazine feature on the company in August 1983, standing by Bedford YNT Plaxton Supreme V (GDY 500X). (G R Mills – Colin Rowland collection)

'Block D1 Westridge Estate' and would have the capacity to provide the much needed breathing space for the business and its fleet of coaches to all be on one site. After successful negotiations had taken place, designs were drawn up for a new purpose built Atcost built garage structure to take shape with other nearby neighbours eventually being Farrant's Haulage and Southern Water. There was an old abattoir nearby to the other side of them, and for a while there were several cows grazing in the fields immediately behind what would become the new depot site.

The new premises would be called West Ridge Manor, Colin's choice as he liked the idea of their new site being 'their Manor'. This was a slight take on the then popular TV series Minder starring George Cole as slightly shady businessman Arthur Daley who regularly made reference to the Manor, meaning the local area he operated his business from. The Borough Council had other ideas not long afterwards deciding they wanted the area named the West Ridge Employment Area. When Colin suggested that they may like to pay for the legal lettering carried on all the coaches to be individually re-sign written, the idea didn't go any further. . .

Rambler officially moved into the new depot premises on 1st May 1980 with a new garage telephone number of 0424 754881. Lombard Finance who had previously arranged finance for two coaches in the fleet kindly sent a bottle of champagne to congratulate Colin and John on the start of their next chapter.

The office remained in Western Road, which from the mid 1970's was now based at number 18. Skinners no longer needed to use the ground

The framework of what will become 'West Ridge Manor' is taking shape at 'Block D1' on the outskirts of Hastings in 1980. (Colin Rowland)

The newly completed Rambler Coaches depot c1980. Bedford NJM Duple (KDY 300H) is nearest the camera. (Colin Rowland)

Taken at the same time, this close up image of the depot shows of a trio of Bedford's that are; VWK 8S, HJM 772H and VWK 7S. Outside to the right a glimpse of Bedford SB Duple (DME 998A) can be seen. (Colin Rowland)

floor part of their office building, so was soon rented to become the Rambler Coaches booking office, in place of number 22. It would not be until 1990 that a new purpose built office was completed at West Ridge Manor, with both Colin and John usually popping back from their new base at lunchtimes on the weekdays to Western Road to catch up with looking at customer quotations and collecting post and correspondence to take away with them. One of the office team, Jacqueline, took her PSV test to drive a minibus and would drive on the Sunday church contracts on occasions. She recalled that at the time a large amount of their own

LVS 447P was a Bedford PJK Plaxton Supreme, new to Armchair, Brentford in 1976. Acquired in March 1980 it was fitted with 25 seats instead of the more standard 29 seat configuration, providing generous passenger leg room. At the end of the 1982 season it was purchased by Fuggles of Benenden. (Colin Rowland)

tours were operated to destinations such as Torquay, the Lake District and Scarborough. Doreen worked with Colin on all the itineraries needed for the tours themselves, with hotels booked, brochures were produced for marketing them. Colin had obtained a copying machine that could print off runs of brochures and quotation forms that had been designed by Pauline as well as individual drivers work tickets which would then be filled in by hand by Marjorie every day. The paper used was termed 'onion skin' sheet, fed around the very large drum as the handle was turned. Different coloured paper was used for each day of the week including pink, blue, white and orange to denote it, so all paperwork could be identified in day order. Eventually the time would come where a computer was purchased by Colin and some of the office team naturally took time to get used to the idea during their initial training day. The initial Apricot system had 10 megabytes of memory and could now produce drivers work tickets and details all backed up regularly onto a floppy disc to store the information.

Jacqueline also recalled the occasion when a fire had accidently broken out at Coombs Motors, over the road from their office, with thick black smoke bellowing out of the workshop and up into the sky. A member of the Coombs staff dashed over to ask if a 999 emergency call could be made to the Fire Brigade for assistance. Ironically a Fire Engine was itself trapped inside the workshops undergoing repairs. After the extent of the damage was realised, two of Coombs commercial mechanics, Alan Marchant and Gordon Green, spent some time working up at Rambler's West Ridge Manor premises under a special arrangement so repairs to their customers commercial vehicles could continue as the Coombs workshops were repaired. This was good news for John Goodwin, who now had two additional capable commercial mechanics based at the Rambler depot to lend a hand if needed.

In this interesting comparison of the then current fleet at the new West Ridge Manor depot we find Bedfords sporting British built coachwork represented by Duple, Willowbrook and Plaxton. (Colin Rowland)

Customers at this time included the Dunkirk Veterans, Post Office Social Club, St Pauls School, The Clevedon and Adelphi Hotel's, and the Welsh Club.

Inside the new depot a small office with a storeroom above was built for John by local carpenter Brian Giles, who also drove on regular occasions for Rambler. The building also boasted a forty five feet long inspection pit which greatly assisted in the ease of maintenance. An example of the new site making mechanical tasks easier, was demonstrated one evening when Colin and Pauline were just about to go out with John and a friend from the depot for a social night out, dressed in their finest clothes. A coach returning to base had its clutch slipping and Colin knew it needed changing as the vehicle was out again first thing the following morning. He quickly put his boiler suit on, the gearbox was taken out and clutch assembly changed, while his fellow guests chatted to each other and watched Colin's swift progress. Once the job was completed they then went for their evening out straight afterwards.

When the stock of company spares was transferred from the former Western Road premises, one of the Coombs Motors storemen, Graham Eaton, came up to the new site and spent two weeks carefully cataloguing and providing part numbers for all the Bedford parts. This meant that not only did Rambler now have their own full inventory, should Coombs not have a particular part in stock they could borrow it from Rambler's own store. The customer received that all important part quickly with the item used then replaced by Coombs. Coombs were eventually taken over by St Leonards Motors and its former premises in Western Road was demolished, the site was redeveloped by Southern Water. Graham moved on to Ditton Service Station in Kent, still working with his in-depth knowledge of the Bedford product before eventually setting up in business with his former work colleague Brian Morris, forming Vehicle Independent Parts (VIP), providing hundreds of customers in both the UK and abroad over the forthcoming years with Bedford parts to keep their vehicles operational. Graham is still in great demand for parts supply working alongside his daughter Holly in 2023.

In May 1980 a 1972 45 seat Bedford YRQ with Willowbrook 002 coachwork (VNU 75K) was acquired from representative Alan Smiles at the dealer Kirkby, the vehicle proving suitable for a number of different types of work. After four years of ownership Colin was loading suitcases in it one day and noticed that gaps had opened up in places on its body, one could even put one's finger in between parts of the body frame and glass. It now seemed the right time to sell the coach on to David Waterman at Yeates. Much later Colin was back at the same dealer looking at vehicles to buy and noted it was still in the yard, so Colin assumed that it had not found a buyer. On commenting to David about its presence there his reply was that it had indeed been a good coach for other operators having been sold by him three times since and well used by all the firms that had bought it, and he had made a profit on every subsequent sale. This particular coach had been involved in a bizarre accident when in Rambler ownership in which a car had collided with it when out on a local service contract, damaging the front panel on the offside of it underneath the driver's window. On the coach's return to the depot John immediately made repairs and painted the coach the same afternoon so it would be ready for use the following day. The next day when the coach was in exactly the same spot where the previous days accident had occurred the coach was hit by the same car in the same place at the same time! It was noted that after this second incident the car and its driver were never seen again.

Seen in Monaco when on tour is a Bedford YMT Plaxton Supreme IV (HVC 10V) new in September 1979 to Harry Shaw in Coventry and purchased in December 1980. (Colin Rowland)

Before the invention of the mobile phone, communication between drivers and the office or depot was something that required the driver to use a public telephone box, or find a willing person to ask for use of their home landline. When the business had first settled at West Ridge Manor a representative from Storno Radio Communication Systems made an appointment, providing a demonstration of its new Private System Wavelength two-way radio system for consideration. This used the channel licensed by the coach trade body, The Confederation of Passenger Transport (CPT). A demonstration set was temporarily fixed into a coach working on a rural route that was operating through to the village of Dallington, just over eleven miles away, with a rolling geographical landscape between both places. The trial was successful with communication between both the driver and base over the system. An order was placed for sets to be fitted to every vehicle in the fleet including Colin's own car. Local aerial installation engineer Ian Steel, who also drove for the company on occasions, erected a twenty-foot pole with aerial on top of the depot roof to provide reception, soon extended to forty feet to gain the best reception possible. The local area proved very useful for communication; in a time that the notion of having mobile phones was yet to exist, the Storno system assisted in lessening potential delays and speeding up communicating important messages to drivers away from base, the depot even making contact with a driver at Southend Pier in Essex. The City of London never proved particularly successful in getting direct communication, although this issue was helped by being able to radio through to Kentishman Coaches based in Swanley in Kent. Using their Storno system, they could then radio over from a much closer range to reach a driver in the Capital. Having said this Colin was surprised to hear a message coming through one day from a coach driver (not a Rambler employee) requesting 'anyone want a chat?', made more interesting by the fact he was on tour with a group in Rouen, France using the CIBS system.

Channel 1 was for the driver who could radio through an initial message using the coach's on-board handset, Channel 2 being the base set, where any verbal return dialogue could not be heard by other persons. The system became very useful for finding out driver's location, anticipated arrivals at pick-ups, destinations or for relaying delays as the driver could legally use the handheld microphone to communicate when driving and for general communication. When the advent of mobile phones finally started to become a new trend, John Goodwin was an early customer to embrace the future of this communication. Sadly, it was cut short one day when, on leaving the mobile phone handset inside his car overnight, he discovered a broken window the next morning and his new prized possession had gone. The Storno system finally became part of the company's history when Mr Paul Lea of Emsworth & District on the West Sussex and Hampshire borders bought the whole former Rambler package for his own fleet.

In September 1980 a call from David Waterman at Yeates in Salisbury came that they had taken in the company's former Bedford VAM Duple Viceroy (EDY 565E) and as it was still in their colours, as purchased new by them in 1967, would they like it back? Now at thirteen years old, it was considered worth bringing back into the fleet and a deal was done for £475 to re-purchase it. It had been sold in November 1973 to Plumridge Coaches in Horley and when the business was sold to nearby Crawley Luxury Coaches the coach came as part of the deal, but had not been operated by them. In Plumridge ownership it had been worked hard, the seats were by now thread bare and some new panels were required here and there. The chassis needed some welding as the flitch plates above the front springs, where it had been operated without the bump stops, the front axle had hit the chassis at times. With Johns signature panelling and painting complete, the seats were re-trimmed and the coach provided them with another nineteen years of good service, working at times alongside much newer Plaxton Supreme and Duple Dominant counterparts, and looking equally as good. When the new 'reversed' 'E' registration allocations were being issued by DVLA some twenty years on from when it had first been registered, one customer wrote to the company after their booking had taken place and thanked them for sending the new 'E' registration coach for their trip out. This coach now lays claim to being owned for the longest overall period of time by the company and also of being bought and sold into fleet the most occasions. In later years a decision was made to sell it to journalist and enthusiast Peter Simpson in December 1999, with its original registration retained by Colin Rowland and an age related registration as JUF 244E being issued. In April 2006 Peter decided to sell it and it would again re-join the fleet for the third time where it was reunited with its original registration mark. Its seats have now been re-trimmed once more in an attractive green and cream swirl moquette and it has been retained in preservation by Colin Rowland (2023) still wearing the colours of the only livery it has ever worn since new in 1967.

On occasions, Colin and John had sold coaches to Freemans of Uffington in Oxfordshire, the first being a Bedford YRT Duple (TDY 494L). In June 1978 another similar Bedford with Plaxton body (HVD 588N) joined them. They were delighted with the purchase and in January 1983 bought Bedford YMT Plaxton (VWK 8S) which John painted into their blue and white livery as part of the deal. They soon called again and asked if anything else in the fleet might be for sale, although nothing was. Warrens Coaches in Ticehurst however had mentioned they would be looking to market three coaches asking Colin and John if they wanted to sell them in a dealer capacity on their behalf which they were happy to do so. Freemans were duly contacted and soon arrived at Rambler's yard to look at a Warren's Plaxton Supreme, arriving in a second hand 1968 Bedford VAL Plaxton Panorama 1 52 seat twin steer (ATU 51F). Colin and John did not really think too much about the coach arriving at the depot only noting it was a VAL. However, once the deal was done Freemans left with their new purchase, but Colin noticed the VAL was still parked there. Wandering back across the yard he asked John why the coach was still on-site, he replied 'they just handed me the keys and the log book, so I guessed it must be ours'. . . The coach was operated for a few months in its former livery before being sold on to Kent based operator Farleigh Coaches. By coincidence Rambler had previously operated a near sister vehicle (ATU 53F) between 1970 and 1975.

Representing the smallest vehicle in the then fleet at the end of the 1981 season was a 16 seat Ford Transit with Strachan body (PPO 122M). New to Barnes at Runcton near Chichester, it was re-registered as 6881 R and sold in February 1986 to Hills of Hersham. (The Bus Gallery)

Regular bookings from the holiday specialist SAGA became a growing part of business in the early 1980's mainly for their customers holidaying in Eastbourne. Special trains were charted by them from areas such as Sellafield in Cumbria to Eastbourne Station where coaches would be waiting to transfer holidaymakers to a selection of SAGA's pre-booked hotels and guest houses in the town, just sixteen miles away from Hastings. With what could be up to ninety-six hotels and guest houses potentially available on the lists for accommodation, anything between three to seven coaches were needed to cover these regular weekly commitments. Passengers were collected from the rail station at 5pm and chauffeured around the various venues first, with the coaches then returning to the rail station to collect and sort out the luggage and drop the suitcases off at the same locations afterwards. Normally this part of the process would be completed within a reasonable timeframe although the luggage was in no particular order. On one occasion Colin recalled his disbelief when arriving back at the station to begin loading the luggage. He found a pile of suitcases that showed the appearance of 'being thrown up in the air by a JCB digger and landing in a pile again'. . . Station porters had not done their job properly unloading the cases from the train, and it took until 11pm that night to sort out all the luggage into the correct drop order and to then deliver the cases to the various locations around the town. For Colin however, the work did not stop on the Saturday evening, as the following day the SAGA representatives would visit guests to see how they had settled into their accommodation and to offer them coach excursions when holidaying over the week. It would normally be Sunday teatime before Colin received the final lists of passenger numbers travelling and to which destinations of the week's offerings, requiring coaches and drivers to be allocated to the pick-up points matching each of the destinations offered.

A demand for operating more continental work in the early 1980's, was confirmed when a customer asked if the company would be interested in a regular hire to travel through Italy to Brindisi on the Adriatic coast. At the time both Colin and John felt this would be too much of a big commitment for the lightweight type of coaches they operated, so declined the offer. This may well have left further thoughts for the type of new coaches they would purchase in the subsequent years. The relative simplicity of operating the Bedford marque however, ensured that this manufacturers product would travel to many further afield destinations outside of the UK with little trouble. On one particular tour of Paris in France, a Bedford YMT Plaxton Supreme (HVC 10V) had its engine water pump fail on the trip. A spare was carried and its driver Dave, who also happened to be a mechanic, changed it when parked near the Eiffel Tower. On his return home, Dave mentioned to Colin that there were no issues on the trip, but he couldn't produce the completed work ticket as it had been used by him to make into a gasket before fitting the new water pump to the engine.

The company's first 12 metre (just under 40 foot) long coach arrived in April 1982, being a new Bedford YNT with 500 turbo engine and 53 seat Plaxton Supreme V body. Many coach companies still found vehicles up to 11 metres (36 feet) the ideal length for a 53 seat coach, although from the early 1970's 12 metre long coachwork offering either additional leg room or a greater seating capacity of 57 seats became more popular. GDY 500X arrived just in time to be entered in the 1982 Brighton Coach Rally, bringing success for Colin to become runner up as 'Coach Driver of the Year'. More about the 1982 event can be sfound in the Appendix under Brighton Coach Rallies towards the end of this book.

In 1982 the smaller Bedford PJK model was proving a popular size of coach to hire, with both 25 and 29 seat variants already operated. With a growing demand for the midi-size coaches, an order was placed for a new 29 seat Plaxton Supreme IV model on the then current PJK chassis, with a host of optional extras and sporting the Bedford 330cu.in. turbo engine. Registered as JDY 888Y, the '888' sequence was chosen for a personal touch as Colin's fathers first new coach had been registered GDY 888 some twenty-eight years before. Other identical numeric registrations for new purchases did follow this trend in later years.

It wasn't long before Colin and John were already looking to make their next investment, finally taking the plunge into purchasing heavyweight chassis coaches, as mileages covered within the fleet were ever increasing. In late 1982, after being impressed with the assistance from John Dover at DAF, who had taken Colin and John to view a DAF MB200 DKTL being operated by Ron's of Ashington, an order was placed for a DAF MB200 DKFL with the newly launched high-floor Plaxton Paramount 3500 body. The coach entered the fleet as KDY 888Y

Bedford YNT Plaxton Supreme V (GDY 500X) is seen
in Folkestone in April 1984. (Derek Jones)

This 25 seat Bedford PJK Plaxton Supreme (CNY 338V) was new to
Thomas Coaches of Tonypandy in January 1980 and was acquired
via Yeates at just two years old in February 1982. (Derek Jones)

Seen on a fresh crisp morning at West Ridge Manor is the immaculately
turned out Bedford PJK Plaxton Supreme IV (JDY 888Y). (Terry Blackman)

costing a respectable £61,579. Initially an order had been placed for a new Bedford YNT chassis with an 11-metre Plaxton Paramount 3200 53 seat body, but with the introduction of the DAF product this order was cancelled and changed for the Dutch built chassis, the type of long distance and continental charters now being undertaken meant its choice would be an inspired one.

The DAF had a 53-seat specification with features including tinted and double glazed windows, as well as the rear window (an optional extra costing £1,332) and full draw curtains. An offside continental exit door for boarding and alighting on the correct side of the road when abroad, arm rests, footrests and ash trays to all seats and a radio / cassette player with Bosch public address (PA) system. An interesting request due to the coach's intended continental touring work, was a new sign made up on the inside of the continental door with labelling Emergency Exit not only written in English but French, German and Swedish. Plaxton requested the company sign off with them the correct spellings of the languages before the signage was produced. The subject of the correct shade of Rambler's colour green for the coach's livery came up again, as John Goodwin had, in advance, requested a sample of it be sent back to him from Plaxton ahead of the coach being sprayed with the paint codes they had been provided to ensure it was the correct match. Unsurprisingly to John the colour was not correct, so further samples were sent to ensure that the right colour match would be supplied for this impressive coach. Plaxton were said to be unhappy at the fact they had now become the owners of a large quantity of green paint, having taken the liberty in advance of producing the entire amount without sending a sample out first.

Initially there was no specific work for this coach, but with both Colin and John's keen business acumen and knowing the purchase was justified, a photograph of the new vehicle was sent to SAGA, showcasing it with an eye to obtaining some of their tour work. This move was a success as tours eventually took place to both Austria and Switzerland, normally headed up in early days with care and attention from drivers such as Peter Clark, Chris Tyler, Phil Bedford and Richard Walker.

In April 1983 the opportunity to buy what would now be termed as a heritage vehicle, came up when a Bedford OB with 29 seat Duple Vista body was purchased, identical to models operated many years ago by Colin's late father. Registered as LYC 731 it was originally new to the operator Blagdon Lioness in January 1950 and acquired from a Mr Jones in Orpington, Kent. It had latterly been stored in his own front garden, and the decision was made to tow it back although Colin felt it could well have been driven home under its own power. Restoration work was then carried out inside the Rambler depot mainly to woodwork with skills

A rare vehicle operated was Bedford JJL with Marshall body (HKX 553V). Seen at West Ridge Manor in 1982 with all over livery advertising 'Rambler Holiday Tours', the JJL's full story is told in the appendix 'Interesting Bedfords' later in this book. (Colin Rowland)

By now registered appropriately as 1924 RH, this Bedford VAL Plaxton Elite was new in 1973 as RPB 222L to Chivers of Wallington, joining the fleet at ten years old. It is thought to be the only such example of this model fitted with the later style Plaxton Supreme IV front. It is seen in Tonbridge on a private hire booking for the M & D and East Kent Bus Club on 14th May 1988. (Derek Jones)

provided by Peter Clark. Other drivers assisted in preparing the coach including Mick Cousins who became its regular driver and the coach was repainted into the fleet colours of the 1950's, making a fine addition to an already immaculate modern fleet. In its first season in use, a new idea to launch some vintage style excursions saw it taken down to the coach stand, now located at the Boating Lake in Hastings Old Town and trips were touted for customers with reasonable success. The launch of the trips was marked by John meeting the town's then Mayor, Cllr Sandie Barr, to mark its initial trip. In April 1989 it was entered in the UK Coach Rally, hosted at Southampton, carefully driven the long distance by Mick Cousins and Ivan Lusted, where it received much admiration and was duly awarded an array of prizes at the event. The Bedford OB remained

The Bedford OB Duple Vista (LYC 731) passes the historic Brighton
Pavilion on the same day as the Historic Commercial Vehicle Society
London to Brighton run is taking place on 7th May 1989. (Derek Jones)

with the company for twelve years until one day when a gentleman called
in unannounced and enquired if the OB was for sale as he heard it might
be. Although it was a surprise for Colin and John to hear, a price was
suggested and agreed. Some months later once arrangements had been
made, the coach made the long journey to Mr Hugh Ryan's home in
Ireland to become part of his Connemara Bus fleet.

Later in the 1983 season the fleet now stood at 18 vehicles, 14 of them
Bedford models. Colin's wife Pauline left her position in the Rambler
office in the September, and on 4 October 1983, their first child was
born who they named Hannah. Fortunately, the out of hours calls from
the business were still being taken by Muriel who switched the phones
over from the office to her home in case of any queries or potential
problems that needed to be dealt with as a point of contact.

The following year another identical new DAF MB200 DKFL Plaxton Paramount 3500 (A888 MDY) was purchased. Regular tours for SAGA were now operated from London Victoria to destinations such as Austria and Switzerland. Both coaches were very reliable vehicles and excellent in use on these longer tours, averaging more than fourteen miles per gallon with the six speed splitter manual gearboxes. The manufacturers back up was tested on one occasion when one DAF driven by Phil Bedford had picked up road debris causing a bad radiator leak when in Poland on a Bank Holiday. DAF themselves dispatched their DKV agent who rectified the problem within a short space of time with more than satisfactory repairs, the mechanic even followed the coach in his van for twenty miles in case of any issues, such was their commitment. The coach completed its lengthy round trip with no further issues. The representatives from DAF Aid once stated that they were happy to do

The bold signwriting carried by the DAF MB200 DKFL Plaxton Paramount 3500 (KDY 888Y) seems appropriate in this classic continental scene with the backdrop of the Eiffel Tower in Paris. (Colin Rowland)

Arriving at Thorpe Park on 15th April 1989 for a South Eastern
Coach Operators 'SECOA' children's fun day we find DAF MB200
DKFL Plaxton Paramount 3500 (A888 MDY) about to drop off its
excited passengers. Fred Pilbeam is driving. (Derek Jones)

anything should any problems arise, this was put to the ultimate test
on one trip. A passenger developed terrible toothache on a continental
tour, the driver personally calling them up to ask if they could help; they
duly arranged an appointment for the passenger to see a dentist.

The Rambler tradition of buying the Bedford product was far from
over as Colin and John kept to a policy of buying vehicles most suited
to the type of business that they wanted it for. In May 1984, when a
Bedford YMT, with Unicar coachwork (another make, as with Caetano
some years earlier, marketed in the UK by Moseley of Loughborough)
joined the fleet (JJF 881V). This coach signalled a new era in how
vehicles would have their company name applied when painted into
fleet livery. This time it would not be traditionally sign written but have
vinyl lettering applied to its coachwork instead. Local sign writer Walter

'Wally' Rainsford arrived at the Rambler depot, not with his paint and brushes, but with a sheet of vinyl which was cut into large sections and applied onto the large side feature windows and key panels of the Unicar. Then with a sharp knife the letters would all be individually cut to shape and the excess vinyl carefully removed to reveal the words 'Rambler' in perfect hand cut style. Wally's services were used for many years and his work was always excellent. One of Wally's many varied jobs over his long career was the application of a mural relief of leaves using gold leaf around a main arch inside Christ Church in Ore, Hastings.

The company was by now purchasing more examples of the newer Plaxton Paramount coachwork. The vinyl industry was fast developing, a new local company named Pendragon was used to apply the vinyl lettering to future purchases with computerised machines that could

Passing St Matthews Church in Hastings is 1980 Bedford YMT with Unicar coachwork (JJF 881V), new to Wainfleet in Nuneaton and purchased at four years old. After two years in service it passed to Maybury in London. (The Bus Gallery)

now pre-cut the lettering more quickly for final application in a shorter space of time, the days of the traditional method of signwriting would now be coming to an end.

In February 1985 the first Volvo joined the fleet on the purchase of a second-hand 1973 Volvo B58 with Duple Dominant body. Colin had received a call from a representative of the finance company Allied-Irish, who asked if they may be interested in placing a bid on the coach which was parked in the former Taylors Coach yard in Rottingdean near Brighton. Colin was told that they needed two bids and already had one for £15,000 so with Colin not interested in it he obliged with an offer of £12,000 knowing it would not be accepted and that their other transaction could take its course. Sometime afterwards someone at a higher level within the company called and said that they would accept

In the summer of 1986, 1973 Volvo B58 Duple Dominant (RHX190L) is seen at Longport Coach Park in Canterbury in the colours of EF language school. Previously operated by Brooks in London, after three years of ownership it was sold to Southern Land Tours in Eastbourne. (Derek Jones)

Waiting in Rye in the late Spring of 1985 for the return of its last passengers, is Bedford YRT Duple Dominant (NBW 704L) with driver Les Morris at the wheel. It later received the registration 405 UPJ. In 1990 it was sold to Cooks Coaches in nearby Westfield as EUF 783L and would eventually end its days as a static caravan. (Derek Jones)

Seen near to the company's Bedford TK breakdown truck is the 17 seat Bedford CF Reebur (YUJ 926T). (Derek Jones)

the £12,000 as the other deal had fallen through. Colin now mentioned that he wasn't that interested and £1,200 would be nearer the mark. To his astonishment the offer was accepted but it would have to be plus the VAT! A quick decision was made to view the coach before arriving at the company's finance office, taking a look at it in its separate location. It was noted that not only was the vehicle in good condition, it had 53 re-trimmed seats and six new tyres fitted as well. Having taken a cheque with them for the payment, Colin in his haste twisted his ankle getting up the stairs of the firm's office to hand over the payment! Once back, the engine did suffer from oil leaks, but with a strip down by a mechanic at Farrant's extensive workshop next door to the Rambler premises it was soon rectified and wore the white and blue livery of EF language School, proving to be a very worthwhile purchase.

After operating the first Volvo B58 in the fleet, the opportunity arose through contact with the dealer Yeates to have a new example of the then current Volvo B10M-61. An example was purchased with a 49 seat Plaxton Paramount 3500 body with toilet, paving the way for many further examples to be operated in the years ahead. Transfer bookings were now being undertaken for tour operator travelsphere for coaches to collect their clients from the Ramsgate, Margate and Canterbury areas in Kent, along with other coastal pick-ups on the way back around the south coast. At Hastings, a comfort stop would be made at the conveniently placed Fishmarket Coach Park with a change of drivers before continuing on to Weymouth to meet the Channel Island Ferry. Here, the groups would transfer as foot passengers to the attractive Island of Jersey. The coaches themselves could not continue the tours in the Channel Islands as there was a seven feet six inch width restriction on all vehicles in use around the island, with local coaches taking up the tours as groups arrived.

RAMBLER

Coaches

Contracts
Private Hire
Holiday Tours
Continental Charter

8 Western Road
St. Leonards-on-Sea
East Sussex TN37 6DG
Office: (0424) 437266/439200

Garage: (0424) 754881

Company calling card c 1983. (Colin Rowland)

It would not be uncommon for the Bedford VAL twin-steer coaches to be used on such transfers, and although no longer considered front line vehicles at the time, their standard of presentation was such they were perfectly acceptable for use on travelsphere bookings. Tour work for this company followed later with the first coach to be painted into the dedicated travelsphere livery of dark blue with white stripes being a two year old Volvo B10M Plaxton Paramount (H612 UWR) acquired from Wallace Arnold in 1994. In the years ahead further coaches would also receive this travel company's colours. In the off-season tours to German Christmas Markets were popular with thirty six tours normally staged from the last week in November until the second week in December.

A popular trend in the 1980's and 1990's by a number of operators in the UK, was the fitting of newer style lower front panels to coaches dating from mainly the 1970's era. This provided a more modern look of the latest style of coach, so that customers would feel they were travelling in a younger vehicle. Plaxton, the long-established Scarborough based coach builder could see this was a potentially lucrative emerging market. In early 1981 they were writing to operators around the country to promote their service in not only refurbishment packages for older coaches with options from resprays into new modern livery designs, re-trimming interiors, headlining's and laying new interior floor linos. With the then economic climate having slowed in the UK, this alternative option to facelift older Plaxton Elite and early Supreme models with the latest Supreme Mk IV fronts would provide operators with a more up to date look on their ageing vehicles for smaller outlay.

Driven with great care by Mick Cousens down the historic and particularly narrow All Saints Street in the Old Town of Hastings, is the Bedford OB Duple Vista (LYC 731). (Colin Rowland)

The combination of Bedford YRT and YMT models with Duple Dominant coachwork was a popular choice for Rambler, with both new and second hand examples entering the fleet from 1973 until the last example was sold in 2001. PAM 516M was acquired in 1986 from Barnes Coaches (then at Aldbourne in Wiltshire, moving later to nearby Swindon) and seen at West Ridge Manor in the spring of 1987. (Derek Jones)

This practice had already been previously performed twice in house by John on two of their own fleet, although when Bedford YMT Plaxton Supreme (VWK 7S) was returning on a day trip from London with students on board from Hamburg in Germany, it was involved in a serious accident at Green Street Green near Orpington when driven by Dave Freeman. A man driving a Ford Transit van had already hit four cars before deliberately swerving and driving head on into the coach causing severe front-end damage. Fortunately, no one was seriously injured but the coach had to be dispatched to the dealer Yeates for major repairs to take place. Colin asked if it would be possible to fit a newer front end when repairs were underway although not with a slightly younger

Parked alongside the Bathing Pool Holiday Camp on the St Leonards on Sea seafront we find the 1985 Bedford YNV Venturer with Plaxton Paramount 3200 coachwork (B888 PDY) at the 1986 SECOA Coach Rally staged nearby. (Derek Jones)

Mk IV Supreme front panel for the coach but with the then very latest Paramount style in line with Plaxton's newly launched current range, the reply was easily a yes. Once work had been completed, a request from Bill Hind at Yeates was that although the insurance company had taken care of the expenditure there would be a slight outstanding bill of £12 to pay. Colin didn't really think too much about it and settled this relatively small balance. Much to Colin and Johns surprise when they viewed the rebuilt coach for the first time it had actually received a completely new front from top to bottom including the new one- piece Paramount windscreen, the latest style dashboard and with a new passenger door and side glass that was redesigned with a sloping bottom curve the same as the new Paramount model. This rejuvenated coach gave much further service and was eventually sold to nearby operator Cooks Coaches in Westfield, now under the ownership of Brian Gain.

Bedford YMT Plaxton Supreme (VWK 7S) is seen after receiving substantial damage through an accident. Major repairs were required in order to return this coach to operational duties. (Colin Rowland)

A call was received one day from a representative of National Express to see if the company would be interested in supplying a coach for their service operation, something that had never been considered up until this time. It would be specifically for the 067 route to London which was a seven day a week commitment. The rates on offer were considered reasonable with an enhanced rate for the coach to be operated in full white National Express livery, meaning of course a dedicated coach for the contract which was accepted. Regular drivers would normally be Don Pelling, Phil Bedford and Mick Cousens using the 1983 DAF Plaxton Paramount (KDY 888Y) with this coach now re-painted by John into the simple white livery for its new role. With John's imagination for something personalised it would be re-registered with a specifically chosen registration number NIJ 8067. With a slight spacing of the 8 before the 067, this imaginative choice of number incorporated the

Seen after return from repairs at the dealer Yeates, the same coach is now unrecognisable in comparison to its original coachwork, receiving a new Paramount facelift from coachbuilder Plaxton. It is seen at the SECOA Rally in Palm Bay, Margate on 11th April 1987. (Derek Jones)

vehicles fleet number 8 (also seen above the front number plate) and the service number 067 whilst the 'N' hinted at 'National'. The coach was always fully valeted and washed down before departing every day. Both customers and coach controllers at London's Victoria Coach Station would regularly comment on the high standard of presentation of the coach on arrival in the capital. Independent operators who contracted to operate National Express services would be given penalties for non-compliant operation to ensure a good quality level of service. Unliveried coaches, poor standards of operation, cleanliness of the coach etc; would certainly incur financial penalties. In the year that Rambler operated the service, there was just one issue with a piece of glass being smashed on the coach and John called National Express immediately to let them know they would have to use a liveried coach. Due to their otherwise

The DAF MB200 Plaxton Paramount 3500 (NIJ 8067) formerly KDY 888Y, is seen in the summer of 1990 in National Express livery. As per the usual high standard of presentation it was immaculately turned out at all times for service. Its driver was Mick Cousens. (Derek Jones)

100% compliance no penalties were awarded. Both Colin and John were slightly bemused after the successful year in operation had been completed when the service reverted to a formal National Bus operator, the by now privatised Hastings and District, using mainly older vehicles and not always in the correct livery.

The company's largest ever order for new coaches came about for the 1987 season with the arrival in April of three Plaxton bodied coaches that year. A 53 seat Volvo B10M and two Bedford YMPS models with shorter 33 seat coachwork, made an impressive sight in joining the fleet. Sadly, they would also turn out to be the last *new* Bedfords ordered as the manufacturer would soon be ceasing production. Both Colin and John were aware of this and felt it important to be able to add new models from their favourite manufacturer, for what would be the last

Arriving at West Ridge Manor after a private hire booking in August 1991, is the Volvo B10M-61 Plaxton Paramount 3500 GLE (C588 SJK). This was the first Volvo purchased new by the company. Ray Howard is behind the wheel. (Stephen Dine)

time. Although smaller size coaches had been purchased at different times over the years to fill a requirement for smaller groups, they did not make up a large percentage of the fleet. Colin's wife Pauline had made note of a number of regular occasions even in the early 1980's that there was more demand for the smaller vehicle and suggested obtaining further examples in the 29 seat range to meet demand. The two new 33 seat Bedfords would underline the company's commitment for operating smaller vehicles, as the 29 seat Bedford PJK (JDY 888Y) had been averaging some 100,000 kilometres a year in use. When it was part exchanged at Yeates for one of the new 33 seat coaches, it had

New to the company in August 1986 we find the 16 seat Freight Rover (D941 UDY), seen passing through the village of Guestling on its way back to Hastings on 16th July 1991. (Paul Gainsbury)

by then covered some 390,000 kilometres. Colin had hoped to buy all three new vehicles from Yeates although David Waterman there could only supply one of the Bedford chassis. Alan Marchant from Coombs Motors contacted John Maguire at Bedford direct, who through various calls found that there was another chassis available at the dealer Kirkby. In turn all three vehicles, a Volvo B10M and the two Bedford YMPS chassis arrived at Plaxton's Scarborough works to have their coach-built bodies constructed.

The two Bedford's became D133 VJK (Yeates) and D134 VJK (Kirkby), with the Volvo being registered as D137 VJK as Colin felt should customers notice the Volvo and a Bedford together on a two coach booking, it would give the impression to a customer of them having a larger fleet with a sequence gap in the number plates. Records show that twenty-four of the YMPS model with the Mark III version of Plaxton

A smartly attired Colin Rowland is seen with one of the three new purchases he will be collecting from Plaxton in Scarborough. The Bedford YMPS (D133 VJK) is due to be started with a hose connected to its exhaust pipe, so that fumes do not enter the building as it is moved. Kent based operator Scotland and Bates is also soon to take delivery of its new Volvo B10M Plaxton Paramount 3500 that is yet to be registered as D481 OKP. (Colin Rowland)

Paramount coachwork upon them were built, most obtaining 'D' registrations and just a few of the very last on the new 'E' registration as the last new Bedford products were finally being delivered to operators.

One of the coaches undertook a Norwegian Tour to Scandinavia for a Travel Agent based in Kings Road, St Leonards on Sea, via the Dover ferry on two occasions driven in the steady hands of regular driver Dave Whiting. Colin eventually retained D133 VJK for preservation when it was withdrawn from service in 2005, by which time it had covered some 1.4 million kilometres.

Both Bedford YMPS Plaxton Paramount coaches (D133 VJK
and D134 VJK) are captured together on camera at West
Ridge Manor when new in 1987. (Derek Jones)

Colin was certainly having a busy start to the 1987 season both in business and in his own personal life, ahead of the three new coaches arriving his wife Pauline gave birth to their second daughter, Laura on 20 March, who would later go on to join her father in both an office and driving position for the company.

Undertaking stage service work was also expanding as further contracts were tendered for and successfully won. The company was not shy in purchasing what might be considered more unusual types of bus for this work. An interesting example for the local number 2 service route in July 1987, was of a 1973 Seddon 25 seat bus with Pennine body (TDT 624L). Just the right size for the route being perhaps more of a midi bus than the traditionally accepted full-size bus that might only operate at half its capacity.

With Colin and John's usual business acumen, it was purchased for a good price, but the process of collecting it from the dealer proved to be a troublesome challenge. As it was being driven from the dealer's yards between Loughborough and Salisbury for collection its small 4-cylinder Perkins engine blew up en route. It was now offered at an even more attractive price by the dealer should Rambler want to recover it themselves. The Coombs Motors Bedford TM recovery truck was duly dispatched to hunt out the stricken bus and then winched up ready for the long journey back to East Sussex. As the tow truck left the M1 to join the M25 motorway, when both bus and tow truck somehow parted company with not only damage to the bus but the tow truck now breaking down due to the incident causing a lump of wood to go through its engine oil sump.

Despite all this, the bus did eventually enter service with a rebuilt engine, repaired bodywork and smart livery, being well suited to the task it had been bought for, but presented further challenges during the two years it was operated. The local geography of St Leonards on Sea is made up of many inclines and hills, and a new driver was taken by surprise one day when descending Church Road towards the junction with St Margarets Road, where a right turn would be made. The hill becomes steeper close to the bottom of the hill, and on braking to stop at the junction, the front-engined Seddon bus would nosedive forwards, digging its front end into the road and lifting the single rear wheels off the ground in the process. In time seasoned drivers would take a left turn ahead of the junction and go off route around the parallel side street into St Margaret's Road via Magdalen Road to avoid this scenario being repeated.

In most respects the bus behaved well in operation but with one notable exception when the gear lever broke off when in service in the West St Leonards area of the town. The driver radioed through with

In this more unusual study taken in 1987 at West Ridge Manor we find three
Plaxton Paramount bodied coaches all new to the company in the years
1983 (KDY 888Y), 1987 (D137 VJK) and 1984 (A888 MDY). Note the earlier
style of signwriting and the original telephone number for the booking office
in Western Road on the two earlier DAF coaches either side of the Volvo
which has the newer style of lettering by now in use. (Derek Jones)

the problem John Goodwin knowing both the issue and solution said
'there's a spanner inside the cab, undo the floor cover, take it off and
take off the bolt on the top of the gearbox, then walk around with it to
Hastings Motor Sheet Metal (about half a mile away in Caves Road) and
ask them to weld it back together'. The driver duly did this and with the
gear lever swiftly repaired, the driver then re-fitted it to the bus and was
able to carry on to finish his shift. The passengers that had been waiting
patiently on-board in the meantime were happy with the end result too.

In the early hours of the morning of the 16th October 1987 the South
of England was taken by surprise by storm force winds which became
known as 'The Great Storm' and devastated a wide area including
much of East Sussex. Although high winds had been forecast by the
Meteorological Office the changing weather pattern was unforeseen and

caused considerable damage over numerous counties. In the borough of Hastings alone an estimated 5,000 trees were felled by hurricane force winds said to be up to 103 miles per hour with a further 5,000 damaged. Many roads and routes in and out of the local area became blocked and buildings severely damaged, some collapsing. Electricity supplies were cut off in some areas and telephone lines brought down. Tragically in Hastings itself two people died, a number that may well have been higher if the storm had not struck in the early hours of the morning.

As daylight dawned and the winds had eased the devastation to the West Ridge Manor depot became apparent. Driver Dave Whiting was already at work early in the morning as he was scheduled to take a coach away on a tour of the Lake District. The situation was worsening for him as a concrete fence from the adjoining property had ripped loose and hurtled through the main building doors, with it the full force of the wind took hold of the depot structure with parts of the lower brick wall of the depot collapsing one side and further damage to the roof and upper corrugated sides. Dave made a dash inside the building for the internal storeroom upstairs to try and escape to safety and to call John Goodwin. Although Dave said afterwards it was a frightening experience, he commented that it was the deafening and relentless noise of the storm itself that was unbearable. Unknown to Dave, inside the building a water pipe had burst and the inspection pit was filling up with water. When daylight broke other members of staff had by now managed to get in to work. The slow process of a team effort began clearing debris and bailing out the inspection pit as well as assessing damage to vehicles and the site. Farrant's Haulage who were based next door helped out by supplying huge tarpaulin covers from their lorries to act as temporary covers to help keep the worst of the weather out of the building before repairs and rebuilding could eventually take place.

The aftermath of the great storm that swept across Southern England in the early hours of the 16th October 1987. With no power on site, staff including Richard Joseph, Roy Curtis, Chris Tyler and Dave Wilson, have formed a chain in order to empty the inspection pit of water between the smashed doors of the depot, with coaches strategically parked around them for protection as the high winds have not yet died down. (Colin Rowland)

Towards the end of the year yet another new coach was ordered from dealer Arlington Motor Company for the 1988 season, a Volvo B10M-61 (E184 EJK). This time it was the company's first Van Hool Alizee H bodied coach, as Plaxton could not supply a vehicle until the season was underway. The classic but stylishly modern lines of this Belgium coach builder's product suited Rambler's livery well. At the same time the deal was being concluded, John had spotted a nice Bedford YMT Plaxton Supreme (JJF 880V) in the yard with an asking price of £14,000. John in his usual style of enjoying some negotiation informed Colin that they

The full force of the damage caused to the West Ridge Manor
premises can be seen in this photograph. (Colin Rowland)

Well remembered staff in this group photo taken in 1988 are (left to
right) Richard Walker, Richard Joseph, Phil Bedford, Mick Cousens,
Fred Pilbeam, Roy Curtis and Chris Tyler. (Colin Rowland)

This Volvo B10M-61 Van Hool Alizee was new to the company in March 1988 as E184 XJK. When photographed on the St Leonards seafront on a warm late spring evening for a calendar photo shoot, it was by now re-registered as LDY 173. Sold in late 2005 it would find a new home with Suffolk based Whincop Coaches of Peasenhall. (Stephen Dine)

might make an offer for this coach as it was a very tidy vehicle. As John wandered over to the office Colin said to him, I'm not coming in' and watched John disappear inside. He came out later on informing Colin he got a deal done for £7,000.

Drivers have a vital role in keeping their passengers and other road users safe, and this is most evident on rare occasions of accidents, whether major or minor. One particular incident took place during a motorway journey in the early 1990's before the general ban on use of the outside lane by buses and coaches was introduced in 1996. Dennis Javelin G168 ODH was being driven in the outside lane at its then permitted maximum speed of 70 mph, with a full complement of passengers on board, and up until then the journey had been uneventful. A car that had started

The first Dennis to be purchased by the company was a 1989 Javelin model with Plaxton Paramount 3200 body (G168 ODH) from Elizabethan Travel at just one year old. Seen outside Hillcrest School in Rye Road, Hastings in March 1992 its driver was Roy Curtis. (Stephen Dine)

to overtake the coach in the centre lane began to pull across in front but clipped the corner of the coach and suddenly lost control, veering into the central reservation. The coach driver had to take immediate action, and attempted and emergency stop at speed, but this forced the coach into a skid resulting in the vehicle spinning 180 degrees across all three lanes of the motorway and ending up on the hard shoulder. Fortunately, not only were no passengers hurt, but the coach itself had no damage to it, although all four of the rear tyres required changing due to flat spots in the tyre tread caused by the skid. The driver Mick Lovatt, was praised by passengers for his efforts in avoiding the accident that had unfolded in front of him. When Police arrived the motorway had to remain shut down completely in order to turn the coach around as of course it was now facing in the opposite direction.

In the early 1990's further school contracts were taken on, this time as privately booked routes that were organised and paid for through parents subsidising the travel for pupils to attend Claverham Community College in Battle from Hastings, Bexhill and Sidley areas. The routes were given the straightforward route designations of A, B, C & D, that had previously been operated by Cooks Coaches who had decided to cease operating them. A collection of diverse coaches were purchased for these new commitments and between April and September of 1990 four second hand Bedford YMT vehicles arrived. Two with the then popular Duple Dominant coachwork and two further examples that were firsts

A much rarer purchase was of this Volvo B10M-56 with 11 metre Plaxton Paramount 3500 high floor body (NDY 820), seen in Robertsbridge in East Sussex. It had been new in 1985 to Glenton Tours in London as B191 XJD. It was later exported to Malta in May 1991. See chapter 'Coaches for Export' when it was photographed in 2020. (Colin Rowland)

into the Rambler fleet, one with a Caetano Estoril body (AAL 521A) and the other with a Van Hool 300 line body (NDC 284W). Three of them were painted in a livery of cream with no green or black. A number of school contracts were operated in rural areas which was unforgiving on the coaches' paintwork, especially one route in the village of Dallington. The simple livery of cream was less inclined to show up the fine scratches from overgrown hedges that could not be avoided and was easier for John to repaint or repair than the much darker green and black livery, should the need arise.

In August 1991 the purchase of a second hand 1983 Bedford YNT with Plaxton Paramount 3200 coachwork (KUR 585Y) started a trend of Rambler actively looking to find more of this type of coach to gradually phase out the earlier style of Duple Dominant and Plaxton Supreme YMT models. Sourcing vehicles needing some work and using their own facilities to refurbish them, a number of more modern looking Paramount models were put to work during 1993 and 1994. Stocks of reconditioned Bedford 8.2 litre 500 turbo units were kept ready to replace tired engines if needed and seats deemed tired were sent off to be re-trimmed in up to date and attractive moquette, along with new lino on the floors and any other remedial repairs. John's expertise in body repairs and painting ensured that these coaches, at around eight or nine years old, looked up to date and could perform a wide range of duties from local school contracts to day trips for students and private hire bookings. The YNT and Paramount 3200 coaches were 11 metres long and most had 53 seats. No less than twelve second-hand examples came into the fleet over an eight-year period from the dealers Kirkby and from Julian Brown at Kent based Wealden PSV, with other examples purchased direct from their previous owners. On one trip that Colin took with Julian Brown, an operator had a Bedford YNT that he was looking to sell, but he also had two more vehicles that he would only sell as the three together. Julian did make the purchase with Colin having the YNT model, but one of the others was a Volvo B57 bus, thought to be one of only two that had ever graced the shores of the UK and was indeed a rare vehicle which Julian did manage to sell on.

One sole Bedford YNT purchased was a 12 metre long example, sourced when Colin went along to an auction in Manchester and spotted a 55 seat example (C345 RSG) that had previously operated for Wilsons of Bonnyrigg, Midlothian. This coach was fitted with a rare conversion of air suspension in place of traditional leaf springs to the rear with the air bags located behind the axle. There was a single large air bag on each side which as Colin noted could make the coach roll depending on road conditions. It was an American designed set up that was a professional

Seen near the top of Battery Hill in Fairlight with wonderful far reaching views of Camber and the East Sussex coast in the background, is Bedford YLQ with Alexander Y type 45 seat body (MGS 437V) working on the service 44 back to Hastings. The date is 3rd July 1992. (Terry Blackman)

aftermarket conversion, with parts for it available direct through Bedford themselves, much to Colin's surprise. After being re-registered as NDY 962 it served the company for over four years before being sold on to Port Erin Hotels on the Isle of Man.

An unusual Bedford that was not quite what it appeared, entered the fleet in August 1991 being a Bedford YLQ with a 45 seat Alexander Y Type body, purchased from The King's Ferry in Gillingham, Kent. Although bearing a 1980 registration (MGS 437V) its chassis actually dated from 1976. Its Alexander body had also first been built in 1973 on a YRQ chassis as a demonstrator (WXE 264M) which was later taken off and fitted to the YLQ chassis and used as a test bed with a 'blue series' 500 engine fitted, for what would become the new YMP model.

Seen one evening in May 1992 at the Boating Lake on Hastings seafront is Volvo B10M-60 Plaxton Paramount 3500 (UDY 512), new to Parks of Hamilton as F27 HGG. (Stephen Dine)

On a bright afternoon on 14th October 1992, driver Phil Bedford pauses for the camera on arriving at Claverham Community College in Battle, in Volvo B10M-61 Van Hool Alizee (SDY 788) new to tour operator Shearings as D558 MVR in 1987. (Stephen Dine)

On hire to Embassy language school, four of the fleet are seen on 3rd June 1993 waiting to head off on a half day afternoon excursion, headed up by the 1967 Bedford VAM Duple Viceroy (EDY 565E) still in regular use at an impressive twenty-six years of age. (Stephen Dine)

In this more unusual photograph taken in Parliament Square in London on 5th August 1994 we find Bedford YMT Duple Dominant (910 OCV) captured on camera as it navigates its way through the city's traffic. It was new to Coliseum in Southampton as OTR 412S. (Derek Jones)

A further expansion of the fleet was needed in 1993 when an approach was made by a representative from Hastings College for transport on a new contract around the south east on weekdays. Students from the United Arab Emirates (UAE) would be based at the former Northeye Prison complex that had, after closure as a Prison, been taken over by them as a training centre. Travel for eight dedicated vehicles was required to colleges including Hastings, Eastbourne, Brighton, Tonbridge, Crawley, Worthing and Ashford in Kent, on training for a technical future within the UAE Armed Forces, operating until the project finished at the end of 2010. As the students studies finished two weeks ahead of local schools and colleges every summer term, by fortunate coincidence the coaches would gain another regular annual booking for the East Sussex Music Summer School. Children of a range of ages were collected from local areas including Heathfield, Crowborough, Battle, Rye and Hastings to take part in courses at St Andrews School in Eastbourne.

In February 1994 one of the then current fleet, a Bedford YMT Duple Dominant (WUF 44), originally registered LJK 335P was sold along with two other members of the fleet to the operator Whites of Heathfield. Although the sale in itself was unremarkable, the coach had been purchased new in the June of the hot summer of 1976 and had now completed nearly eighteen years of service to the company. At the time it was by far the longest time a coach had been operated.

In the winter seasons between 1994 and 1996 a regular charter took place requiring a number of coaches, initially sub-contracted through Fuggles Coaches in Benenden, for a large hire known as Ski-Train. A selection of the fleet travelled down empty to Dover Docks, where groups of holidaymakers were converging at the Port to meet the waiting coaches, with both luggage and skis, for travel by ferry from Dover to the French Port of Calais. The coaches then took them to Calais Station for their onward journey by train to busy ski resorts, such as Val d' lsere in the French Alps. Rambler were chartered to supply eight to ten coaches alongside the Kent based operators Kingsman International of Faversham for the French Sealink ferry customers, with Scotland & Bates of Appledore and Crosskeys in Folkestone using the Townsend Thoresen ferries. Eventually coaches were booked directly from the client, valued business at a quiet time of the season. Some coaches would be left at the rail station in Calais over the weekend after dropping off the Friday passengers to save running costs of taking all the empty coaches back to Hastings. On the Sunday journeys returning back, a spare battery jump start pack was always taken from the depot just in case a coach did not start. The temperatures were normally cold, even in Northern France. On one journey the weather was noted so icy and conditions poor, that as the coaches made the slow but careful journey from the Port to the local station in Calais, vehicles were sliding on sheet ice and touching the kerbs. It was an effort to get passengers dropped off for their onward journeys and not to miss the train connection. After a period of time of the coaches being left in France between the runs, the Port of Dover made an invitation to bring the coaches back to the UK and park them in the Port instead, as the authority was paid per vehicle movement in and out of the country. . . Colin recalled that on one particular early Sunday crossing when setting off from Dover for France in two empty coaches with a selection of drivers (the other vehicles having been left in France) as the Freight ferry cast off Colin was surprised to see they were in fact the *only* two vehicles travelling on the ferry itself. A rare occurrence.

Parked in German Street in the quiet town of Winchelsea on 15th March 1993, is Bedford YMT Plaxton Supreme IV (405 UPJ). Driver Phil Bedford is enjoying a moment of rest oblivious to having his photograph taken. (Paul Gainsbury)

Industrial action at the Port was at times not uncommon, causing disruption and stopping service over the channel. On one occasion Colin asked a representative from Ski-Train 'why not take the new Eurotunnel service by train instead?' This was duly arranged and without fuss the coaches travelled inside their bespoke carriages by train through the Channel Tunnel to the continent instead. In the early days of operation coach drivers would be normally given vouchers when travelling to entice them to switch from the traditional ferry crossing. Colin was surprised on how quickly his vouchers grew when running the service twice a week. When the time would end for operating the service, they had made hundreds of trips by both Ferry and Eurotunnel for the Ski-Train service.

Further continental work was taken on over the winter of 1997 into 1998 to take a coach on the long trip to Val d' Isere in the French

Bedford YNT Plaxton Paramount 3200 (1924 RH) makes its way through Guestling on a school hire in 1992 driven by Mick Cousens. It was new in May 1983 to Reliance in Hitchin as KUR 585Y. (Andrew Gainsbury)

Driver Paul Green photographs Volvo B10M-60 Plaxton Paramount 3500
(UDY 512) at the Italian and Swiss border near Como on 3rd October
1994 when working on a continental travelsphere tour. (Paul Green)

Alps for a London based owner-driver operator, who had been doing
the journey without issue in a slightly older Leyland Tiger coach. As this
kind of hire was featuring more regularly in the company's portfolio,
using a new Volvo B10M coach did not seem too much of an issue.
Colin recalled that the regular booking felt like a nightmare in the end.
Over the course of the winter season the coach broke down three times
although the issues were swiftly dealt with. On one occasion the regular
driver Ray Boakes, blocked a peage toll on the motorway as the coach
had lost air pressure on stopping at the barrier and its brakes would not
release to move off. Such are the hazards of sending coaches over onto
the continent in severe frosty conditions in the wintertime.

On another travelsphere tour we find Volvo B10M-60 Plaxton Paramount 3500 (VDY 468) in heavy snow. Purchased in 1994, it had been new in 1991 to Wallace Arnold as H612 UWR. It was sold to Barnes Coaches in Aldbourne, Wiltshire in 1996. (Colin Rowland)

Seen on a late afternoon on 6th August 1994, Bedford YNT Plaxton Paramount 3200 (ODY 395) departs Brighton's Madeira Drive for its journey home. New to Sheffield United Transport as A627 YWF in February 1984, it joined the fleet in March 1993 and was sold to Mervyns Coaches in Micheldever, Hampshire in January 1997. (Derek Jones)

A slight departure in the trend of new purchases was the acquisition
of two Scania K113CRB Van Hool Alizee T8 coaches in January 1995,
registered as M222 CDY and M222 DDY. Both vehicles gave excellent
service to the company, only ever wearing travelsphere livery. M222
CDY is seen at Dover Docks on 20th July 1997. (Paul Green)

The Theatregoers Club of Great Britain was a regular customer for a number
of years and on 13th June 1996 Volvo B10M-61 Jonckheere Jubilee P599
(TDY 388) is seen in Chichester on a booking. New in 1988 as E697 NNH
with sister vehicle E696 NNH, both coaches joined the fleet at the end of
the 1995 season and were sold together just one year later. (T Donnachie)

Having disembarked its passengers at Robertsbridge Community
College, Bedford YMT Duple 320 Express (MDY 397) makes its
way over the railway crossing back to the depot on 13th March
1998. Its previous owner was well-known operator OK Motor
Services of Bishops Auckland as C538 OTY. (Paul Gainsbury)

The Toyota Coaster with stylish Caetano Optimo coachwork found favour with
numerous UK coach operators for its comfortable small coach credentials,
proving a popular choice from the mid 1980's with production of updated
versions continuing into the 2010's. H170 EJF (seen as H917 DFG) was
a 1991 21 seat example and is seen at the National Exhibition Centre in
Birmingham on 8th October 1998. (Unknown – Colin Rowland collection)

Parked together at the premises of Cooks Coaches in nearby Westfield, an excellent comparison of the use of personalised registrations reserved to three new Berkhof Axial 50 bodied coaches are seen. R222 XDY was a 53 seat Dennis Javelin new in September 1997, with R222 VDY and R222 WDY both 49 seat Volvo B10M-62 models, new in March 1998 and August 1997 respectively. (Colin Rowland)

Aside of Colin and John operating a large fleet of coaches the chance to indulge in more unusual purchases from time to time was not unknown. A large project was purchased in May 1996 when a Bedford WLB with 20 seat Economy bus body, first registered as NG 2414 in April 1932, was purchased with a view to a long-term restoration to take place. Gradual conservation of this rare survivor as time allowed in the far rear section of the main depot would begin. In time it was joined by other vintage and classic era coaches into the 2000's for the continued preservation and enjoyment of their ownership.

In 1998 Muriel Rowland sadly passed away at the age of eighty years. It brought to an end not only the company's link with its pre-war years, but to a partnership of both a mother and son in business since the passing of her husband Dick Rowland some thirty two years before. A decision would be made between Colin and John to finally make the company a Limited status for the first time in its history, which was completed on the 23 March 1999. The first actual new purchase of a coach by Rambler Coaches Ltd would not take place until 2001 when a Volvo B10M-62 with Berkhof Axial 50 coachwork (Y222 PDY) was delivered.

Chapter 6

21st Century Travel – 2000 and beyond

The new millennium saw a number of changes for the company over the forthcoming years. Colin was already turning fifty years of age in 1999 when he was considering the notion of his long term plans of wanting to retire. It was difficult to imagine but both he, and from the 1970's, John Goodwin, had worked endless long hours with loyal and dedicated staff to build up a reputation of offering a first-class service with an immaculately presented fleet of coaches, so discussion on how the business would continue in the long term would be a much considered subject.

Working with new tour operators as the new decade progressed had grown to become a larger part of the Rambler portfolio of business. A number of well-established names in this sector would have their brand and livery displayed on the company's vehicles, including SAGA, Trafalgar, Insight, travelsphere, Tracoin, Just Go, Grand UK, Alpha.

Arriving at the picturesque Bodiam Castle in East Sussex on 5th
July 2017 is 2002 Volvo B10M-62 Plaxton Paragon (GDY 500X)
purchased in 2009 as YR52 MEU. (Philip Cattermole)

Private hire bookings for individual groups, clubs, societies and schools and for student organisations remained popular over the summer seasons, long standing customers such as EF, STS and Embassy and private organisations such as Senlac Tours, Mr Fuller, Discovery Tours, Mr Putland and Eastbourne based SFA among them. Many popular destinations for these visiting overseas groups remained the same over the previous decades to attractions such as Leeds Castle and Canterbury, Cambridge, Oxford and of course London Sightseeing tours.

Two new coaches were already on order for delivery in readiness for the first season of the new millennium with a Scania K114 Van Hool T9 (W222 KDY) arriving in time to be entered in the Brighton Coach Rally in the April of 2000. It initially wore the attractive blue livery of tour specialist travelsphere and would soon be operating on continental tours.

Promotional flyer c 1999–2000

Photographed at the Van Hool factory in Belgium in early 2000 is the unregistered Scania K124 with 49 seat Van Hool T9 body to become W222 KDY. This would be the first new purchase by the company of the 21st century. (Colin Rowland)

The second coach however did not arrive as planned, finally delivered in September and missing much of that season. Its presence though, was a complete departure from previous purchases, in the shape of a Mercedes Benz 0404 built by Hispano in Spain. Its delay didn't create any issues as a demonstrator model (T110 SOA) had been loaned for the interim. The coach that was to be sold, in part exchange, remained in use until the new Mercedes Benz finally arrived. The factory was initially running to time in the early stages of its build until a very large order for the construction of buses was received, so existing coach production was put to one side in order to clear this much larger order first. The Mercedes Benz had already been allocated the registration mark W222 HDY in readiness but by the time it was delivered the next series of UK number plate issues had moved on to the new 'X' registration. With a change of plan the opportunity came up to register it as X500 GDY, no coincidence as it was a reversal of the registration of the Bedford YNT bought new in 1982 (GDY 500X). This coach had been sold in 1988 but had been repurchased again in 1998. Both coaches when seen together made for an interesting comparison with their mirror image number plates and contrasting designs. The upside of the late arrival of the new coach brought an array of optional extras at no cost that had been given as part of the order. This 49-seat coach with a centre sunken toilet and an electrically powered offside continental door, also had three-point seat belts to all seats, much rarer on full size coaches in the UK at the time, with many coaches still fitted with lap belts only. It was powered by a 12.5 litre V6 engine with automatic gearbox which was noted for good fuel economy. The Mercedes Benz enjoyed a long stay of nearly fifteen years, touring in the UK and Europe extensively. Initially painted in the blue livery of travelsphere in time it would receive traditional fleet colours, becoming a popular coach of choice for regular customers and long-established local guide Clive Richardson on his coach holiday tour programme. It was said that just one hundred and one of these coaches were built for the UK market, although records suggest that this figure probably included 33 examples delivered to Bus Eireann in the Republic of Ireland in 1999.

When near to having covered some 1,000,000 kilometres, it was taken at the end of the 2015 season to the dealer Bob Vale for sale. Evesham Growers (EVG), who on occasions would purchase a coach to transport workers from Evesham to the company's sites as staff transport, were looking to replace a vehicle with their normal requirement for a 57 seat capacity vehicle. On arriving in Bob Vale's premises, the owner immediately spotted the still immaculate 49 seater with toilet and said 'I want it'. On being told of its seating capacity he said, 'it doesn't matter

Seen on 13th March 2002 in Brighton is the Mercedes Benz 0404 (X500 GDY) sporting the first of its travelsphere liveries. (Paul Green)

Captured in Eastbourne on 14th July 2005 is Mercedes Benz 0404 (X500 GDY) on hire to travelsphere and now wearing a revised livery. (Paul Green)

In Terminus Road in Eastbourne we find Bedford YNT Plaxton
Supreme (GDY 500X) driven by Ian Steel. (Alan Snatt)

I've never had a coach with a toilet before!' The coach served them
well remaining in use up until 2020 when at twenty years old it was
withdrawn due to gearbox issues and parked up on site now out of use.
As a footnote, the unused number plate that should have been allocated
to this coach (W222 HDY) remained on retention and was eventually
allocated to one of John's much enjoyed Vauxhall Omega cars. In 2023
it was still to be seen around the Hastings area after John's ownership,
still bearing the same registration number.

The diversity of second hand purchases continued with two notable
coaches a little more unique than the normal combinations to grace the
fleet. In the February Colin had visited a coach dealers' premises and
noticed two identical vehicles in the livery of Geoff Amos Coaches of
Northampton parked on site. Further inspection revealed that these two
Caetano bodied coaches were in fact built on the Dennis Dorchester

Seen in Cornfield Road, Eastbourne on 27th March 2002 on hire to
SAGA is Volvo B10M-62 Plaxton Premiere 350 (NDY 962) driven by
Mick Lovatt. New as P427 LJH it joined the fleet with sister coach
P428 LJH in May 2001. Enjoying a long career it was sold for scrap
in May 2017 at some twenty-one years of age. (Paul Gainsbury)

chassis with Gardner turbo engines. The model although having sold in
small numbers was not a common type in comparison with its eventual
replacement the Dennis Javelin with Cummins engine. This would
become a popular product for UK coach operators especially as Bedford
had pulled out of the market of producing commercial chassis at the
time of the launch of the Javelin model. Both Dorchesters were 51 seat
vehicles with manual ZF gearboxes, one with a toilet and thought to
be the only two coaches built as such in this combination. Both were
purchased by Rambler, although only SJI 3929 actually entered the
active fleet. It was not long after they were back in Hastings, they were
admired by Brian Gain of Cooks Coaches in nearby Westfield on one of
his many social visits. He liked them so much that within five months

he had bought the example without the toilet. In turn it would now be painted into Cooks distinctive pale yellow livery with the addition of green stripes looking quite attractive. The remaining coach enjoyed a stay for just under two years giving good service, remaining in white with the stripes of its former owner on the sides painted into green and black. Its only slight downside in operation was that its turning circle when turning on a left-hand lock was unusually poor. It was noticeable at a local college in Robertsbridge that when leaving the site at the end of the road the coach just couldn't make the tight left-hand turn in one manoeuvre. Unlike other members of the fleet such as Volvos and Bedfords the Dennis always had to be reversed back in two manoeuvres in order to leave the site, just the nature of the build of the product. It was eventually sold to Hills Driving School in Plumpton to start a new and successful career as a training vehicle.

Dennis Dorchester Caetano Algarve (formerly SJI 3929) has now received the cherished registration FDY 383. When photographed on 8th July 2001, within months it would be sold to Hills Driving School in Plumpton. (Paul Green)

In 2000 further diverse business was obtained through the tour company SMS who organised coach transfers for clients holidaying on cruise ships visiting the Western Docks at the Port of Dover for Cruise Line Costa. Both Gatwick and Heathrow airport transfers were also operated with excursions soon added to the portfolio of business, and it required up to six coaches taking passengers from Dover to London for sightseeing tours. The days would be a challenge for driver's hours, as coaches were expected to be in Dover for 07.30 but would not leave until around 09.00, having already used valuable driving hours on the journey along the coast from Hastings first. In the late afternoons the drivers had to ease their way out of the central London traffic and back to Dover, in order to drop passengers back for the waiting cruise ship, then making the final fifty mile journey home empty to Hastings. On occasions trips were operated to Canterbury, Rye and Deal with Kentish tours, fitting much better with the driver's legal day.

Calling Card c 2000's (Colin Rowland)

There was a tight time schedule for coach transfers between airports and the waiting cruise ship at Dover, and cruise line operators would use experienced staff to keep unforeseen issues to a minimum, so this normally worked well.

On occasions Colin would personally drive a coach himself for these transfers and was normally the last driver to leave in case of any delays on the last incoming flights. On one occasion at Heathrow flight and luggage collection delays meant time was minimal for the onward journey by coach to Dover. Cruise liners cannot normally wait beyond their designated departure times without incurring costs and disruption to the sailing schedule. Fortunately, the journey was free of delays and on arrival at the quayside at Dover's Western Docks Colin could see a crowd of ship's crew by the boarding area. As he pulled up alongside, he had barely applied the handbrake before the crew had all the coach's side and rear luggage doors swung open and suitcases were quickly emptied with passengers swiftly led to the ship's embarkation boarding area. Eventually the SMS operation moved to Southampton and although Rambler were offered the option to continue by providing coaches for the passenger excursions and transfers, the business had to be regretfully declined due to the extra mileage involved. Other operators employed on the cruise liner contracts were Kent based operators Scotland and Bates, Crosskeys Coaches, Bayliss Travel and DJ Coaches.

In a surprise visit to the booking office one day, an elderly gentleman came in with a photograph for Colin of one of his 'old' coaches. Colin had no idea what it may be, assuming it would be a nice image from perhaps the 1960's era. He was astounded when the man produced a photograph he had taken of Dick Rowland's first coach from the early post war years, the 1929 built B.A.T Cruiser (GE 7766) operated between 1946 until 1949. Colin was bowled over as he had never seen an image

On the St Leonards seafront two Volvo B10M-62 Jonckheere Deauville coaches (ODY 607 and ODY 395) are to be found. Both were new to Shearings in 1995 as M613 ORJ and M605 ORJ respectively. (Stephen Dine)

of the actual coach before. The only picture he had previously seen of this type of vehicle was from a period sales brochure.

Probably the lowest point in business for both Colin and John happened in early 2002 when they received a visit from three representatives of VOSA, (Vehicle Operator Services Agency) requesting to check drivers' hours and tachographs as part of the agency visiting operators around the UK. Colin noted, at an early stage, that one of them had a particularly negative attitude towards the company, cemented by a comment made that they were 'number two on their hit list'. One of the other men attending, apologised to Colin for his colleague's manner. . . Tours operated to Lake Garda seemed to be of interest to them, it transpired that two other coach operators had been prosecuted in connection with how the tours could be operated in compliance with the driver's hours rules. When requested Colin duly handed over their driver's completed tachograph charts filed from previous tours, and he did not feel there were any issues at this time. The drivers' hours regulations (which had evolved in the UK and across Europe due to EU requirements since the 1970's) require careful management because of the complex system of breaks, rest periods and weekly rest for drivers, and these must fit with the hire patterns of both day trips and tours (Other work such as school contracts and stage carriage work does not fall into the same regulations) and can create a challenge for businesses that operate a mixture of different types of work.

To compound these problems at the start of the traditional busy summer period, John, after being discharged from his local hospital for tests through illness, had been given some devastating news that he was seriously ill and, with the tight scheduling to maintain the company's commitments it had in turn left the company vulnerable. Of fifty-two drivers employed VOSA wanted to prosecute seventeen of them although a number of cases were eventually dismissed. Recent cases brought against other coach operators by VOSA were raised to use as weight against the company in an eventual hearing by the Traffic Commissioner fines were imposed on both the company and drivers, Colin and John paid the drivers fines. The Traffic Commissioner decided that he would take no further action, drawing a line on what was now the end of an unhappy chapter for the company.

Aside of Colin working in the main office at West Ridge Manor, the office team over the years has included Linda Longley, Pamela Armstrong, Linda Hughes with Brian McGuire and John Tanner. They were joined in January 2006 by Colin's daughter Laura, who would take her PSV driving test in May 2009. Whilst training for it, discussion came up about the test route both John and Colin had taken themselves locally decades before on their own PSV tests. There was a noted tight road junction in Hastings that was very difficult to make a turn without

Father and daughter. Colin Rowland with daughter Laura at the
Rambler Coaches 90th anniversary event in 2014. (Stephen Dine)

running over a kerb, something that would be a driving test fail. John
laid down the gauntlet that if Laura could drive their old test route she
would be a 'proper coach driver'. One evening Laura decided to take up
the challenge and drove the test route herself in a 12 metre long coach
accompanied by colleague Jacqueline who already possessed a PSV
licence. On the trickiest section at the road junction of Newgate Road
(at the west end of Amherst Road in Hastings, the tight right hand turn
into Bohemia Road (where a pedestrian crossing is situated) followed by
an immediate tight left hand turn into the proceeding Tower Road, the
place where a likely 'fail' could happen. Laura had turned out of the first

road junction indicating right perfectly then immediately indicated left and turned into Tower Road, not running over the kerb as expected. She was well on her way to following in her father's footsteps.

The company's first double deck buses came into the fleet with a successful tender award from the local council for a regular service to St Richards Catholic College in Bexhill-on-Sea, starting in September 2006 with one of its first dedicated drivers Mick Kelly. Two 1991 Leyland Olympians (H649 PVW and J706 CEV) both with 71 seat Alexander Belfast RH bodies had previously operated for Dublin Bus in Ireland and came via Ensign in Purfleet. In time two more double deck vehicles would be operated. These buses proved good in service with the only downside that they were too tall to fit inside the depot for maintenance. The use of four post lifts outside was required to access them underneath

Awaiting collection in February 2004 at the Plaxton Transbus coachworks in Scarborough are two new Volvo B7R Profile models. Registered as CR04 RAM and JG04 RAM both would stay in the fleet until September 2015 before moving on together to Fowler's Travel in Holbeach Drove near Spalding. (Colin Rowland)

A new purchase for the 2006 season was of a Volvo B12B with Berkhof Axial 50 coachwork seating 53. CR06 EDY is seen after heavy snowfall when on a continental tour. (Colin Rowland)

for repairs and inspections which made an impressive sight when seen towering high above the front of the depot building. The last double deck vehicle to be operated was a Volvo B7TL29, with Plaxton President body (X661 LLX) and was a regular sight on a weekday service operated from Hastings to Claverham Community College in Battle, normally driven by Peter Birch for a number of years until its withdrawal.

In May 2007 a new Volvo B12B coach was purchased (JG07 RAM) with Volvo's own 9700 Prestige model coachwork, a high specification model for the UK coach market. The price for this new model just the year before had been described by Colin as astronomical in comparison with other new coaches available on the market. The following year the price had been reduced to that of a similar chassis on Plaxton coachwork, making it a much more appealing prospect. Colin had enjoyed the experience of being flown

Seen at Hastings Station is the 1991 Leyland Olympian with
Alexander RH body (FDY 83) purchased via dealer Ensign as H649
PVW, for the September 2006 school term, working the 304 service
to Claverham Community College in Battle. (Terry Blackman)

out with his new partner Jacqueline and friend Alan Marchant, for a tour of
the Volvo factory in Wroclaw in Poland, to see vehicles already in different
stages of build. What impressed Colin was the sight of coaches that were
at the advanced stage of completion at the end of the production line. He
noted that the 9700 models would then be plugged in by technicians for
the first time to diagnostics equipment and with all the checks completed
the Volvo factory in Gothenburg, Sweden was called up and the coach's
engine would now be started up remotely from Scandinavia to share data
some 1,000 kilometres away, such were advances in vehicle technology. The
Rambler 9700 model was duly delivered to the UK based Volvo dealership
Yeates, to the desired specification as a 49 seat tourer with on-board toilet
and in full Rambler livery. The following March another similar 9700 new

Seen in the former Stade Coach Park in Hastings when new in May 2007, is Volvo B12B with Volvo 9700 Prestige coachwork (JG07 RAM). (Colin Rowland)

model, this time registered CR08 RAM was again added into the fleet along with yet another new Volvo B12B JG08 RAM carrying a traditional Scarborough built Plaxton Panther body that had also been purchased just one month before.

The fleet would finally reach its largest peak in 2010 on the acquisition of two 53 seat Volvo B10M Plaxton Paragon's (YN51 WGY and YN51 WGZ) purchased in the January. They were up seated as versatile 57 seat coaches and would become fleet numbers 40 and 41. Their arrivals also gave YN51 WGZ (later registered as UDY 512) the honour of becoming the 200th coach purchased since business had resumed post war operation in 1946.

On a travelsphere continental tour Volvo B12B 9700 (JG07 RAM) looks very much at home in its picturesque location. (Unknown – Colin Rowland)

With driver John Rooney behind the wheel, Volvo B10M -62 Plaxton Panther (DDY 557) is seen on an MSC Cruises day tour in London. New to the company as GX02 AED with sister coach GX02 AEE in March 2002, It would enjoy twenty years of ownership by the company. (Alan Snatt)

Drivers Darren Stewart and Jamie Dunham pose for the camera after dropping their passengers off at Thorpe Park in Surrey on 29th June 2010. (Stephen Dine)

Both coaches initially remained in an all-white livery and were well used with John prioritising them on a range of bookings, both averaging 100,000 kilometres a year, in their first two years of ownership alone. Early in 2012 a call came through to the Rambler office from a travel operator Tracoin who were agents for tour companies such as Insight and Trafalgar, they wanted to arrange a meeting to discuss hiring coaches for tour work that, if agreeable, would start that same season. On the back of this successful conversation two brand-new coaches were purchased for the new business. The first coach used would be a Volvo B9R with a Plaxton Panther body (JG12 RAM), with 53 seats, to touring specification and ordered from Volvo Bus. The second however, was something perhaps a little more special.

Wearing full Grand UK Holidays livery is Volvo B12B Plaxton Panther (JG08 RAM) seen in Eastbourne on 23rd November 2011 when operating a Turkey and Tinsel tour. The driver is Dave 'Stella' Davies. (Terry Blackman)

On 17th August 2011 Volvo B7R Plaxton Profile (CR04 RAM) can be found parked in the peaceful town of Sandwich in Kent. (Philip Cattermole)

Colin had visited the November 2011 Coach Show staged annually at the Birmingham National Exhibition Centre and was particularly taken with the attractive Mercedes Benz Tourismo on display with West Midlands based dealership Evobus in Coventry. This 49 seat demonstrator model was in a special 125th anniversary livery, with only one exclusive example built for delivery to each country that Mercedes-Benz supplied products to their dealerships. This was in fact the only right hand drive model thought to have been built, sporting an eight speed power shift gearbox and more powerful Mercedes-Benz engine. When Colin viewed it at the show, sadly it was already sold to another operator, although it later transpired they could not raise the finance to complete the purchase so Colin was delighted when he latterly discovered it still available. As one would expect it came with a host of extras with a very nicely appointed interior. On the sides of the metallic sliver coachwork Mercedes-Benz had applied all five of the variations of its three-pointed star motif, charting their eras of commercial vehicle production, the designs of which were reputed to have cost £4,000 alone to be produced. Registered as CR12 RAM this coach would remain in its anniversary livery complete with its specially created Tourismo 125 badge on the front, but an issue immediately arose when the tour operator it was to be allocated to insisted the coach had to be painted white for their customer. After careful consideration, the problem was resolved by having the entire coach professionally wrapped in white vinyl at a reasonable cost of £2,000 to receive its Trafalgar tour company livery. This was the first time this process had been undertaken, but the loss of the coaches gleaming livery was not an option. After the coach eventually finished on its tour duties, the white livery the vinyl wrap was carefully taken off again, revealing the original paintwork in perfectly preserved order.

On a bright afternoon on 7th April 2017 Mercedes Benz
Tourismo (CR12 RAM) glistens in the sunshine whilst parked
on Sandown seafront on the Isle of Wight. (Paul Green)

By April 2013 John was now in declining health and deciding not to renew his PSV licence, would step back from his full time role in the traffic office for what had been years of working long hours, seven days a week, but had been such a big part of his life. For a number of years Doug Davies and Mark Birch had worked alongside him due to the amount of on-going workload in order to run the traffic office, which itself was separate from the main booking office and the staff there. Over the years such was John's commitment to the quality of the fleet's presentation he had once even fallen asleep through exhaustion while completing a job and fell off the top of a set of high steps with a tin of black paint!

Colin would keep John informed of developments within the business and John did return to West Ridge Manor for the very special occasion

Seen at Duxford on the 11th July 2015 is the Volvo B9R
with 53 seat Plaxton Panther coachwork (JG12 RAM), new
to the company in March 2012. (Paul Green)

of the Rambler Coaches 90th celebration day on 18th April 2014 to enjoy meeting with customers and staff both past and present. The date of the event was timed to coincide with what would have been the start of Dick Rowland's operation in the Easter of 1924 and with West Ridge Manor open to the public and enthusiasts alike, much of the then current fleet was available to not only see but enjoy organised trips on around the town, supported by an AEC Routemaster from Julian Brown at Wealden PSV and a Bedford OB Duple Vista identical to three examples operated in the 1950's, owned by the editor of Bus & Coach Buyer Magazine Stuart Jones. The then Mayor of Hastings, Councillor Alan Roberts attended the event and cut a specially made cake as part of the day's proceedings. Towards the end of the day a number of the fleet then took part in a procession around the town to finish what had been a successful day celebrating a milestone for the company.

Wearing the livery of tour operator Trafalgar, Mercedes Benz Tourismo
(CR12 RAM) conceals when photographed on 30th April 2015
its special metallic silver 125th Mercedes Benz anniversary livery
that remains intact underneath its vinyl wrap. (Paul Green)

Staff old and new gather for a group photograph with the
backdrop of the company's longest serving coach, the 1967
Bedford VAM Duple Viceroy (EDY 565E). (Terry Blackman)

Photographed by its driver on 4th September 2014 just after acquisition when on a UK based Just Go tour, is Volvo B11R with 53 seat Jonckheere JHV coachwork (BG14 OOE). Previously a Volvo demonstrator model, it was purchased in the July of the same year, just three months after being registered. (Paul Green)

Seen when just one month old in May 2015, we find Mercedes Benz Tourismo (UK15 RAM) built to full touring specification with 49 seats, in Rye Road, Hastings, between hires. (Terry Blackman)

Sadly, just two years later on the 29th April 2016, John passed away following a long illness at the age of seventy-one years. For Colin the loss of both his business partner and friend meant the dynamics of what had become their success was now finally at an end. With his death it left a large hole in the morale of the staff that lamented his passing.

At John's funeral service held at Hastings Crematorium on 20th May within his order of service the words chosen poetically said.

'O Lord please grant that I may see

The day when petrol tax is free

When traffic lights are always green

And traffic jams are never seen

And wardens do not wait afar

To stick a ticket on my car'

John Goodwin (19th January 1945 – 29th April 2016)

On a winter's morning at the VOSA test station in Ivy House Lane, Hastings we find Volvo B12B Prestige 9700 (CR08 RAM) presented in readiness for its annual MOT inspection. (Colin Rowland)

In March 2017 the company's first Mercedes-Benz Tourismo tri-axle coach was delivered new into the fleet (CR17 RAM). The company was no stranger to three axle coaches over the years having numerous examples of the iconic Bedford VAL twin-steer models in the past. This time though, the Mercedes-Benz configuration had two rear axles as was becoming more commonplace for coaches to accommodate the weight requirements not only from quantities of heavy luggage, but also from specifications such as air-conditioning and double glazing as standard, increasing the unladen weight of the vehicle itself. The tandem axle featured rear steer to aid manoeuvrability when turning in tighter places. Delivered in the traditional green, black and cream livery, its

Seen outside The Smuggler Public House at Pett Level working the morning service to Rye College is the 1996 Volvo B10M-62 Plaxton Premiere (GDY 493), previously with Bus Eireann. A favourite coach of Colin Rowland who can be seen behind the wheel, it was still giving sterling service to the company in 2023 at twenty-seven years of age. (Terry Blackman)

Volvo B12B (LR07 RAM) with 49 seat Van Hool Alizee coachwork was new as SK07 FUW in 2007 and acquired at just two years old. It would later receive the cherished registration VDY 468. (Alan Snatt)

With the stunning backdrop of Chatsworth House in the Derbyshire Dales providing the perfect picture for driver Paul Green, we find Mercedes Benz Tourismo tri-axle (CR17 RAM) on 22nd June 2017 when just three months old. This would be the last new purchase by Colin Rowland before retirement. (Paul Green)

On 6th April 2016, the Irizar i6 (CR13 RAM) can be found travelling along Brighton's Madeira Drive. New to Clarkes of London in June 2013 as YN13 EHD, it joined the fleet in November 2015. (Paul Green)

regular driver was Darren Stewart. It had been Colin's intention to look towards retirement for some time, in fact enquires about the possibilities of selling the business had first been made back in 2001. Years on and with John Goodwin having sadly passed away, being able to continue in business felt totally different from what Colin called 'the good old days' that he had shared with John. The UK coach industry itself in the 21st Century bore hardly any resemblance to the time that Colin had first started out in the family business full time on the death of his father in early 1966 when he was just a young teenager.

In 2017 Colin had now made the hard decision that by the January of 2018 he would bring the business to a close, although with an approach from another coach operator already established in the North of England looking for a more southerly base, an agreement was eventually reached

Representing the smaller vehicles in the fleet is this attractive
Yutong TC9 with 35 seat coachwork (CR65 RAM), new in January
2016 and photographed at the South East Bus Festival at
Detling Showground in Kent the same year. (Alan Snatt)

for the sale of the business to take place on 25th September 2018 at
a meeting in Lewes in East Sussex. Colin and his partner Jacqueline
had a celebratory cup of tea and cake in a local tearoom afterwards,
reflecting on the fact that after some ninety four years Rambler Coaches
would now start its next chapter with new owners and for the first time
no longer in the ownership of the Rowland family. Perhaps fittingly for
Colin, his last purchase before retirement was of a 1976 Bedford J2 with
Caetano Faro 20 seat body, acquired in a personal capacity in June 2017,
as it took his fancy as a running project. Colin had started out in the
business by purchasing a Bedford product half a century earlier, and had
the good fortune to be able to make his last purchase from the very same
manufacturer, this product undoubtedly helping to build the Rambler
Coaches business over the decades.

Colin hopes that you have enjoyed both his father's story and of his and John Goodwin's too. For Colin, his time in business reached a conclusion in 2018, some *fifty-two years* after the death of his father and reflected on the words of his late mother Muriel, who back in 1966, suggested that perhaps it was time they 'called it a day'.

This book has been dedicated by Colin to the memory of his late mother, father and business partner John Goodwin who between them created the legacy of Rambler Coaches – The Rowland years.

The Rowland family c 1953. Dick and Muriel Rowland are pictured with their young son Colin beside the 1949 Bedford OB Duple Vista (JUF 637). (Colin Rowland collection)

Appendices

Memoirs of John Goodwin
Memoirs of Gordon Rowlands
Memoirs of Clive Richardson
Brighton Coach Rally's
Personalised number plates
Bus services
Service vans and breakdown trucks
Interesting Bedford's
Coaches for export
Fleet list
The Skinners AEC
The Gallery

A youthful John Goodwin attends the 1968 Brighton Coach
Rally as a visitor to meet the Rambler entrants taking part with
Bedford VAM Duple Viceroy (EDY 565E). (Colin Rowland)

Appendix 1

Memoirs of John Goodwin

I was born in 1945 and schooled at Mercatoria School, then at St Mary in the Castle before going to the technical school at Priory Road in Hastings. When finishing there I joined Coombs Motors in Western Road in the Whitsun. At the time I was living in Ore and had been helping out in my father's body shop opposite the Shah Pub in Mount Pleasant Road, so already had an idea of the knowledge of high quality painting. My interview at Coombs was with Joe Brown, he could be known as an 'in your face' kind of person, but I got on well with him. Our team was Bill Sweetman and Ken Bailey, we were all errand and tea boys as starters in the trade. I was in the workshop to start with doing mechanical repairs and changing clutches. Tom Allen and Bill Smith were the older hands that I worked with, so I had advanced knowledge of the trade even at fifteen years old. I recall working on Bedford CA's, PC vans, the Vauxhall twelve and fourteen models and Wyverns. The Bedford TK truck was a new model at the time and I recall the HA van, new at £396, or £412 with chrome bumpers when it came out in 1964.

When an opportunity came up in the paint shop, I took it. Dennis Laybourne was the man in charge working with Len Thomas and Ray Sargent. Ray owned an Austin A35 van that he ran on recycled thinners. There was a Bedford TK drop side truck in that had been a demonstrator at Coombs and was then sold on to Walbertons in Bexhill, it was Wedgewood blue in colour but was changed to a cream livery for them. Damage repairs and painting CAJ's was a regular thing and we used to sell a number of vehicles to M P Harris with Bedford TJ tipper trucks in part exchange. In order to smarten them up for sale I would mix up batches of paint we had around to get them looking nice. I did a nice one in blue and Hailsham Roadway bought this particular TJ, they liked it so much they asked for three more. I had to try and re-formulate the colour again. . . There was a firm called Tenco paints at the bottom end of Western Road so I went down to them with some of the mixed colours and said I need more can you help.

One of the Directors at Coombs, John Lorton, asked if I liked preparing cars for re-sale which would require a full body make over, paintwork T Cut and minor repairs if needed, to bring a vehicle back into almost showroom condition. A Ford Zodiac came in from a farmer at Loose Farm in Battle, it was two-tone in colours, turquoise and old English white but it was so filthy you couldn't tell. The white wall tyres were black. With a major T cut and wax I got it back into excellent order and it did look nice. Several customers would change vehicles every two years, I would get Volkswagen campers in and once had a Pontiac Parisian in silver that came from Callar Radios in Ore Village. On at least two occasions the local Council would bring in their mobile library van which was a Bedford S model, blue and charcoal grey in colour, in the summer months for a rub down underneath and underseal all done by hand, in advance of the winter months. We used to do a lot of undersealing and when the Ziebart treatment came in we would use it to try and keep the rust at bay as vehicles used to rust more then, until technology improved in later years. Every summer we would also have the Bedford S type BICC gritting Lorries in. They would be fully de-rusted as they would get bad due to the nature of the work they did. After de-rusting I would brush on a deoxidine, a clear solution that dried like a gel then the whole vehicle would be painted in maroon.

A local coach operator, George Hirst who traded as Hastings Coachways, but also used other names including Pandora Holidays and Hirst Travel, had an office in London Road with the coaches mainly based in St Margaret's Road, which is the site now owned by Empress Coaches. He had bought a Bedford OB from Cliff's Coaches in Eltham and wanted it painted. I did it in a very in-vogue scheme of Mountain Rose and Royal Glow, Vauxhall colours from their paint scheme of the time. It was nice but George thought the price too dear so did future jobs himself afterwards. I remember George also buying some Duple Viceroy coaches all in the blue and red livery of Whittle and as space in the St Margaret's Road site was limited, they were parked around the local streets near to Coombs.

I would always work late at Coombs and one day Joe Brown asked if I could drive a coach as Mrs Rowland of Rambler Coaches was asking for someone to put a coach away one evening as a driver had parked it up outside after finishing his job in the one-way street. They had a small compact depot with some waste ground to put them away on. Colin watched me back in parking it across the road for the night. Eventually Colin asked me why not have a drive out, so I took their Bedford EDY 565E out for a run through Ore Village, Fairlight and Pett and back up the steep Chick Hill for a feel on driving, Colin as my instructor was only seventeen. I grazed the passenger door handle on the wall in the narrow High Street in Hastings but after that I was away with the experience. I did take my Public Service Vehicle driving test (PSV) in 1969 driving EDY 565E, incidentally it was the first day in the job for the local examiner for the Ministry of Transport Mr Tony Hoxley who said 'you are my first customer' I passed first time.

The same year I had a row at Coombs Motors and left the job on the spot. I now wondered what I should be doing so decided to buy and sell vans. I did deals with both the local Ford dealers Hollingsworth's and Coombs Motors for vehicles such as Ford Transits and Bedford CA's. In the early 1970's vehicles were so easy to sell on. I traded from Highland Mews with five garages owned by Charlie Mills from Hillcrest Garage who also owned a showroom in Bohemia which I took on, although it was noted as never a good location for selling cars. I would buy and sell for Charlie too. Charlie later sold the showroom on to Dick Whittington who had Eversfield Garage.

I would paint coaches for Colin and Mrs Rowland with assistance in preparation coming on occasions from Richard Joseph and Brian Giles who drove part time for Rambler. They would join in for the preparation and masking up and I would spray in one colour first, then as paint was drying it was all up to the local Kentucky by borrowing the firm's minibus, have something to eat, then back and put more paint on, then back up to Kentucky and back to paint the roof last. The job was usually finished by the following day. One day I was painting a particular coach that stuck out over the pavement from the garage and onto the road in Western Road, I think it was a Bedford VAL (HJM 772H) and was so engrossed when painting the roof that as I sprayed with the paint gun over the end I blew paint over a policeman who was walking past below me at the same moment. . . he just said 'I'm going to walk around the block now and when I come back I hope you have finished'.

I did not have any interest in coaches as such although I enjoyed painting them and would still be parking them up in the evenings until Colin turned twenty-one years of age. Between us we had the idea of Rambler Mini Coaches although Mrs Rowland was less than happy as she felt three vehicles was more than enough. In 1974 we bought an 18 seat Bedford J2 Plaxton Embassy (AEX 45B) that was then traded for another similar later model 20 seat Bedford J2 (NKJ 769F) and a former Epsom Coaches Ford Transit 12-seater (FOU 216K). The latter J2 was eventually replaced for a Caetano bodied example. I would drive it on mainly evening jobs. Parking was so tight for the vehicles when in Western Road. We acquired a garage next door to the existing one that Colin's Dad had already rented which Colin had had to cut pieces out of the insides of the doors so that the wiper and washer arms of the coaches cleared as the doors were closed it was that tight inside.

When another long-established coach operator Empress Coaches came up for sale in 1970 on the death of its founder Harry Phillips, I suggested the proposition of a partnership to his son Harry junior, but sadly nothing came of it. The business was later bought by another Coombs Motors employee, Anthony 'Tony' Patten the following year.

The partnership between Colin and I gradually became more permanent as we were both sharing drivers on occasions traditionally employed by Mrs Rowland so things in time became more integrated, it was not really planned but just happened. We were buying coaches at good prices when deals were available, doing them up and running for a while then selling on to build up the fleet. In the days of Bedford coaches, you could do quite a bit yourself especially with having Coombs Motors up the road for parts. At times late night repairs at the Western Road garages could be inconvenient for residents so we contacted the local Council about finding a larger site in a less residential area. The council would not allow service industries onto the trading estates but with Southern Water having taken a new site just off the Ridge on the outskirts of the town it was not long before we were able to find something suitable in the same location.

I remember when the dealer Yeates had taken in two late example Bedford YMT Plaxton Supreme 53 seaters new to Harry Shaw in Coventry. Registered consecutively as VWK 7S and VWK 8S they were nice coaches. It was difficult to choose at £22,500 each which one would have made an ideal addition to the fleet, so I said to Colin, let's have both then. The two together would have set us back a cool £45,000 for the pair. I was mates with Graham Griggs at Lombard in Battle Road, St Leonards on Sea and on hire purchase we could get the deal done with a one-third deposit down. I had done the maths and on selling a Bedford YRT Duple (TDY 494L) and Ford Transit (FOU 216K) as the deposit a further cheeky offer was put forward to salesman David Waterman for £30,000 for the pair the deal was done. Mrs Rowland went mad! She insisted we were not having hire purchase on vehicles, but it was too late. Colin didn't sleep for a week, I think. They were good specification coaches in their time, Colin drove 7S, and Gordon Rowlands drove 8S. Thinking of drivers, in the early days I remember Gordon Wansell, also Dave Martin and of course Dave Whiting joining us part time when we were in still in Western Road, later going full time. If a winter job came in, we would call the bookmakers in Kings Road (where Dave normally was) to check he could drive it.

When we first had Storno radios fitted in the coaches in 1980 I was the first person in at work when they would go into use. I arrived early around 05.30- 06.00am to prepare the coach for the Thornes contract with Bedford VAL Plaxton (HJM 772H) and after checking the oil and water I remember then using the Storno handset when the words came through from the driver as 'Rambler base to Rambler Elite, I'm in' was the first call on the radio.

In those days the checking of the oil and water was vital on a daily basis compared to later years. Other regular contracts were for Newtime Foods when in Battle then latterly at Ivy House Lane in Hastings, Thornes, Convent of Our lady (Filsham Road) and ETA in Sea Road.

When Maidstone Borough Council's 'Boro'line' transport operation ran into financial difficulties I made an offer on two Bedford buses that were available although the lady that was responsible for selling them declined the offer. Undeterred I got a nice bouquet of flowers organised which I had sent up care of Boro'line for her attention. She was so impressed with the gesture she came back and said, 'I'll let you have them'. The opportunity came up again at a later stage when some Plaxton Verde buses came up in West Sussex as finance repossessions and for the lady there the gesture worked again. . .

Talking about our fleet colours, the original green we used I had re-named in the 1970's for purposes of re-ordering as Rambler Green. For the black I used Valentines Super Black, good stuff but latterly unobtainable. The cream at times could also differ but I managed to settle on Triumph honeysuckle. In later years I would mix the paint scheme myself to ensure it was what I wanted then to have it matched for accuracy. Vehicles would be painted in cellulose and then machined to polish afterwards giving us the famous Rambler shine. In the days of having a sign writer before the advent of vinyls we used Wally (Walter) Rainsford also Harry Bailey who lived in Upper Church Road.

(Company records from 1949 note a sign writer by the name of Mr Pain who lived on the West Hill in Hastings, who also painted all of the company advertising boards).

Author's notes: the company's highly polished livery was admired by many other coach operators across the UK. A testament to John's work was of a coach that was re-purchased by them in 1980, the 1967 Bedford VAM (EDY 565E).

John is seen at the Rambler Coaches 90th celebrations at West Ridge Manor in April 2014 where he enjoys the day's events. (Stephen Dine)

John re-painted it after repairs at the time and in 2023 it was still in cosmetically immaculate condition some forty three years later. Incidentally EDY 565E had never worn any other livery than that of Rambler Coaches.

John also shared his memoirs of how early number personalised registrations were acquired over the years and these notes are part of a separate chapter under personalised number plates.

Is that you John?

A light hearted poem of the trials and tribulations of what could feel like John Goodwin's normal working day in the life of a coach operator. Written by a member of staff in the early 1980's – by Anon.

Is that you, John? It's Peter here – I've stalled outside the school.
The engine just won't start again, it's as stubborn as a mule
It did the same yesterday, but then I got it going,
I meant to tell you late last night, but you were busy towing.
I'll have to have it on the road within an hour or so;
That airport trip is on today; It's urgent as you know.

Is that you, John? It's Chris here – I'm in a blooming mess.
My coach is blowing thick black smoke, (Injector gone I guess)
I can't drive on to Stoke like this; It's forty miles or more,
So need to send the Turbo up with Dave, I'm on the A24.
I'm Late already-what a day. Are you still there? Hello!
The pips have gone-I've no more change, so do your best please John.

Is that you, John? It's Graham here – my split-rims flown to bits.
It's hit some fella's brand-new car (He's having seven fits)
The tyre on the offside front is hanging off the wheel.
I've run into a roundabout (the one by British Steel)
The traffic's piling up behind and causing quite a jam.
We're going to need the breakdown truck as quickly as you can.

Is that you, John? The office here – Colin would like a word.
Now listen, John – the garage now is quiet, so I've heard.
You've no more work this afternoon, when Spacecar's off the pit.
So, get the two Bedford's in and grease them up a bit.
And if you've time around four o'clock the bus is coming in—
Her silencer needs welding she's making quite a din.
And buy the way-about your phone – It's been engaged for ages
If you've been phoning up your girl ill knock it from your wages.
Not much goes on around this place without I get to know.
So don't forget – (are you still there?) Hello-Hello-Hello!

Appendix 2

Memoirs of Gordon Rowlands

Rambler Coaches first full time driver, 1969–1981

I had been working for coach tour operator Wallace Arnold, based at their Paignton depot for the Torquay holiday trade and my duties would include driving their AEC's with 7 feet 6-inch wide bodies specifically used for navigating the narrow bridges on the Dartmoor tours.

On moving to Hastings, I first worked briefly for the local furniture removal company Bryant's but then came to Rambler Coaches. On interview for the job Mrs Rowland picked up on that I had worked for Wallace Arnold previously and with this experience she snapped my arm off to start with them, so I was in, becoming the firms first full-time regular driver.

I recall the garage where the coaches were kept in Western Road, it was so tight on space that when putting one inside I had to reverse the

Gordon Rowlands with Bedford VAM Duple (EDY 565E). (Colin Rowland)

coach very carefully in and very slowly as I was right at the rear just let the rear of the coach touch the back wall then ease off. This meant that the front doors would close. Colin had even cut notches out the frame of the doors so the wiper arms of the vehicle would fit against it when closed, it was that tight. I remember there was a part time driver, Doug Sutch, and recall mentioning why didn't they make more of doing winter work, darts teams, pubs etc, as they hadn't been doing so much of this before, which they gradually did.

In the summer the seafront coach stand trade was busy and customers would be booking regularly when on their weeks stay. There was an old guy who had been coming to Hastings for over forty years. He wore a suit and tie with a waistcoat and would come along every evening for the mystery drives. His seat was always behind the driver and he was never charged for his coach fare. The reason was that he had a mouth organ. Once the coach was underway, he played all the old tunes on the trip, he would only have a couple of drinks at the pub and really getting the atmosphere going on the coach and passengers would sing along. I loved the job. I would say to passengers before setting off on trips 'now take a look at the passengers opposite you, say hello and get to know them!'. People would get talking, sometimes finding out that they might live

With the advent of heavy snowfall, the excursion on Boxing Day 26th December 1970 that Gordon Rowlands would have been driving is now cancelled. Bedford VAL (ATU 53F) will remain out of use until the weather improves. (Gordon Rowlands)

not too far away from each other from where they had come and really enjoy the trip. The Bedford (EDY 565E) was my regular coach to drive up until it was sold in 1973, I then had the brand new Bedford YRQ (VDY 626M). I remember taking the Bedford VAL (ATU 53F) on a hire booking to Windsor, on this particular trip it was so hot that when I got there, I was completely dripping wet with sweat through my shirt.

When I drove on The Goodies film shoot, I recall picking up at a hotel on Hastings seafront and taking the cast and crew to both Bodiam Castle and to a quarry in the Pett Level area. The shoot there was depicting 'Landing on the moon' at Fairlight which was very realistic. In Bodiam for the scenes there which the coach was used in I never drove more than 2 mph for the filming although on the finished footage the cameras

Gordon (on the left) and Colin are captured in a moment of amusement together later the same day at 22 Western Road, the Rowland family home. Both men were scheduled to drive, but with duties cancelled due to snowfall both went to the local pub instead where Gordon got unexpectedly and merrily drunk! (Gordon Rowlands)

speeded it up. . . The medieval hats the girls wore with their costumes were funny, it amused me how on earth they could walk around with such tall hats on! Nice people, no trouble or demands from them, much time was spent waiting in the coach for the next call.

In the hot summer of 1976, I was on the coach stand on Hastings seafront selling the excursions. Standing by the coach one day dressed smartly in collar and tie, it was so bright and hot that suddenly I must have passed out and fell over by the coach. I had to be picked up and put on the coach to come round!

Memoirs of
Clive Richardson
'Blue Badge Guide'

Working over a number of years for local language schools in Hastings, in January 1988, I become a qualified Blue Badge Guide and set up my own business as Clive Richardson's Coach Tours. Having already booked coaches in my previous work I was no stranger to working with local coach companies. These included Cooks in Westfield, Empress in Hastings, Monks of Staplecross, Vicarys in Battle, 1066 in Hastings and of course, Rambler Coaches.

Since 1988 and up until the pandemic in 2020 I had probably operated anything between 2,500-to-3,000-day trips and tours. The sights and situations that sometimes happen are of no surprise to both myself as a tour guide or to the professional driver working alongside me. With over twenty years of booking with Rambler Coaches, I recall on a trip to Groombridge Place in Kent, it was a pleasant surprise for the day to have been allocated a brand-new coach for this particular trip. On arrival at our destination, the driver, after initially standing and admiring the new coach decided to start giving it a polish although it was already shining. A peacock nearby must have caught sight of itself in the reflection of the coach's paintwork and running at the coach threw itself at it, thinking it was another peacock! The driver, after trying unsuccessfully to shoo it away, had to get the broom out of the side locker to fend it off, not before paintwork damage had been done to the side panels of the vehicle.

A number of my excursions took in a stop at a Garden Centre for our first break of the day. At one of them I saw a bamboo plant that I particularly liked so I purchased it to take home. Unfortunately, I had miscalculated the height of the plant so it would not fit in the coach's underfloor luggage space. After a discussion with the driver, an ideal solution was reached to put the plant in the coach's toilet cubicle inside the interior saloon, problem solved. On the way home a customer needed

Seen in Chatham when on a Clive Richardson day excursion in 2004 is a Volvo B10M-62 Jonckheere Deauville (ODY395) new to Shearings as M605 ORJ. Driven by Kevin Roberts, Clive Richardson can be seen in the courier seat. (Alan Snatt)

to use the toilet and after coming out she said, 'this is unbelievable, they think of everything! its tropical in there, its lovely'!

On one particular tour to North Devon, we had collected a couple from Warrior Square with their *one* suitcase. After arrival at the Hotel and with passengers disembarked, all luggage was taken off the coach and collected by porters and dropped at guests' individual rooms. At the hotel the man from the Warrior Square pick-up said to me 'where's my 2nd suitcase? it has my wife's medication in'. First the coach was checked, then I checked with all the other guests at their rooms for it, nothing. The next day the coach would be setting off for the Eden Project, so after briefing the driver he took the group solo for the day. I called the man's Doctor to ask for his wife's medication details to be faxed over to the Hotel so I could then arrange to go to a local pharmacy and collect the new medication. All the time the man blamed me for losing the case and made sure to complain to the other passengers about it. After the tour had returned I heard no more, until another passenger, who travelled with me regularly and happened to know the person, mentioned that when the man got back home he opened his front door and the second suitcase was still sitting on the doormat, just where he had left it.

A number of Rambler drivers would know specific areas around the country really well, for example any Yorkshire or Lincolnshire areas I would ask for Brian 'Yorkie' Wood to drive as he knew the counties so well and had family there. Barry Cannelle was great with Derbyshire, Darren Stewart for anything in the South of England, Ivan Lusted for the continent and for London trips I would ask for Peter Pope, he was so knowledgeable about London. On a particular day trip, we had not even turned onto the A2 for the City when we spotted a massive queue of stationary traffic ahead stretching off into the distance. All of a sudden Peter turned off saying 'I know how to get around this'. We went down a narrow lane and past a Golf Course, where surprised players watched us as we went past, eventually coming out at Eltham. It took just fifteen minutes more than the planned arrival time at our destination on what would have been the clear route. We had saved a huge amount of time compared to being stuck in the stationary traffic. Peter was a steady driver and brilliant with London.

Due to the amount of trips I operate we would often get stopped by the Ministry of Transport (*authors note: currently known as DVSA*) sometimes in virtually new coaches. They were always a presence in different parts of the country at various places, although nothing was ever found wrong with our coach, on being inspected they were a disruptive delay. Once we were stuck at Thurrock Services for over two hours, nothing wrong with the coach, just the men taking their time. Coming home on a tour from Torquay we had stopped at Exeter Services in a new coach. The Ministry men were making an issue with a seal on the coach's emergency door but no-one could actually see what 'the issue' was. I noticed a number of older rust bucket coaches that came and went from the services in the lengthy delay whilst our passengers waited. Complete bureaucracy. Rambler's record in providing safe reliable coaches in over twenty years was impeccable. I recall just two breakdown situations which were swiftly dealt with.

On a funnier note, it was not unknown for the business partner in Rambler, John Goodwin, to actually stay at the depot all night, catching just a little sleep in the height of a busy season with coach movements happening all the time. One driver early one morning arrived at work tight on time to leave. After opening up his coach he left the depot promptly to ensure he would not be late. The only thing was he hadn't realised John was having a nap on the back seat of the coach, John only woke and appeared inside as the driver was already on his way up the road!

Appendix 4

British Coach Rallies

Rambler Coaches have taken part in a number of British/UK Coach Rally events over the years, an event that showcases the best of the coach industry's products to the trade, enthusiasts and the public alike. In its peak years, when the event was staged on Brighton's Madeira Drive on its seafront, it drew huge crowds eager to see the rows of nearly all brand-new coaches. The trade and public could also watch the skills of professional drivers manoeuvring their coaches around set driving courses, to vie for the chance to win the title of 'Coach Driver of the Year' as part of the weekend's itinerary.

The first British Coach Rally was staged at Clacton-on-Sea over a weekend in April 1955. An event first inspired by two earlier rallies staged on the Continent for both coach operators and drivers to meet and showcase their coaches, taking part in a timed road run. The new British event would set off from four set locations at staged intervals, each at around eighty miles away from the finish at Clacton-on-Sea. A Concours d 'Elegance and various driving skills tests would take place

The final destination is in sight for coaches arriving at Brighton's Madeira Drive that have set off at different starting points, miles away in a road run, navigating a planned route with maps to arrive for the weekend's event, the British Coach Rally. There is no mistaking on the signage where the finish line is. (Colin Rowland collection)

in Clacton over the weekend culminating in prizes being awarded for various classes of winners. The event sponsored by the journal Passenger Transport, was a success, with a larger venue needed the following year. Some eighty coaches were expected to attend the 1956 event which now moved to Brighton in Sussex. The elevated promenade provided an excellent viewing platform for spectators to enjoy seeing not only the many coaches on show on the lower level of the promenade, but also to watch the driver test course in action from a bird's eye view. In 1957 the event moved temporarily to Battersea Park in London due to the Suez crisis restricting the supply of fuel, although the following year Brighton

241

was back on the map running continuously until 1988. Between 1989 and 1991 the rally moved to Southampton, before returning to Brighton in 1992. In 2010 it moved to Peterborough Show Ground and in 2013 to Alton Towers.

The Rambler connection first came about when Colin entered a coach for the 1966 event, although just for the second day of the weekend's activities to show off their brand-new Bedford VAM Plaxton Panorama (DDY 250D) driven by Tony Patten, as Colin was still too young to be able to obtain his PSV driving licence. The coach did not win any prizes due to the vast array of similar British built Duple and Plaxton bodied coaches vying for the trophies on offer. Colin felt their coach was the best in the show as its powerful green and black livery stood out amongst the rows of other fine exhibits in mainly lighter liveries. The day out was enjoyable, so the following year the brand-new Bedford VAM Duple Viceroy (EDY 565E) was entered for both days of the event and again in 1968, driven by Tony on both occasions. EDY 565E was sold in 1973 but re-joined the fleet in 1980 where it would take part in the 1982 rally to great acclaim.

For the 1982 event, Colin and John had also entered their then brand-new Bedford YNT Plaxton Supreme V (GDY 500X). It was a tight schedule for collection at the Plaxton coachworks in Scarborough to be ready to take part. On the coach's build sheet Colin noted the wording 'Plaxton Rally Entrant' which meant quality control was to an even higher attention to detail, as it would be carefully scrutinised at the Concours de Elegance part of the event by industry professionals. On Colin's arrival at the Plaxton works to collect it, much to his amazement the coach was not yet ready and had not been sign written, the vehicle standing inside the factory in plain livery. With urgency now on the matter, no less than six sign writers were summoned and were immediately signwriting the entire coach. When completed the coach had to be pushed out of the factory by a small team of people. If it had been started up, the workforce building other coaches parked around it would down tools inside for at least 20 minutes due to exhaust fumes being generated inside the building.

The long journey back from Scarborough of three hundred miles was nearly over, with just over twenty miles left, when at Pembury on the A21 the low water warning light suddenly shone up on the dashboard. The coach was quickly brought to a halt with a leaking radiator soon confirmed. This brand-new vehicle was now carefully towed in by Coombs Motors where it was discovered that when the body had been constructed on the chassis, loose rivets had been discarded onto the chassis rails, which in turn eventually loosened with vibration becoming sucked up by the fan of the engine and blown into the radiator, puncturing it. The radiator was repaired late on the Friday and the coach travelled off early the next day for the weekend's event. The weekend itself went much better and on the finals of the driving skill tests on Madeira Drive in Brighton on the Sunday, Colin was by now in the finals himself and had only slightly touched one cone in the tight manoeuvres, although way ahead in time of what would be the next best placed person. The only other driver now vying with Colin for the Coach Driver of the Year title was slower around the course itself, but crucially hadn't touched a cone for which points were awarded, there were hundreds tightly placed around the course. Colin was pipped to win the Coach Driver of the Year title in 1982 but was awarded the runner up prize for his respectable first time of driving a 12 metre long coach without any previous familiarisation.

Subsequent years have seen Rambler Coaches take part on numerous occasions at the UK Coach Rally, with both brand-new and longer serving members of the fleet, such has been the high standard of vehicle presentation when in regular use. As a footnote, sadly in 2020 and 2021 as was the case with so many events being staged, the National UK British Coach Rally was cancelled due to the Covid-19 virus that had gripped the world. Up until this planned year a very well-known attendee was Mr Cyril Kenzie, proprietor of Kenzie's Coaches of Shepreth in Cambridgeshire, who had entered every single event since the very first rally in 1955. Cyril had also the privilege to have been Coach Driver of the year in 1957 and 1969. Cyril sadly passed away in 2021 at the age of ninety-three.

A selection of photographs of participating coaches from the Rambler fleet have been included, all taken when the event was staged in Brighton except the 35th event in 1989 held in Southampton.

1966. 12th Coach Rally. Bedford VAM Plaxton Panorama (DDY 250D) entry number 24 driven by Tony Patten. (Keith Page – Southdown Enthusiasts Club)

1967. 13th Coach Rally. Bedford VAM Duple Viceroy (EDY 565E)
entry number 28 driven by Tony Patten. (Colin Rowland)

1968. 14th Coach Rally. Bedford VAM Duple Viceroy (EDY 565E)
entry number 12 driven by Tony Patten. (Colin Rowland)

1982. 28th Coach Rally. Bedford YNT Plaxton Supreme V (GDY 500X)
entry number 47 driven by Colin Rowland. (Colin Rowland)

Also Bedford VAM Duple Viceroy (EDY 565E) entry number
40 driven by Peter Clark. (Colin Rowland)

1983. 29th Coach Rally. Bedford PJK Plaxton Supreme IV (JDY 888Y)
entry number 16 driven by Peter Clark. (Colin Rowland)

Also Bedford YNT Plaxton Supreme V (GDY 500X) entry
number 62 driven by Colin Rowland. (Colin Rowland)

1988. 34th Coach Rally. Volvo B10M-61 Van Hool Alizee (E184 XJK)
entry number 37 driven by Colin Rowland. (Derek Jones)

Also in trade display area: Bedford YMT Plaxton Supreme IV (SDY 788) 'entry
display 192' to promote Cummins engine conversion. (Colin Rowland)

1989. 35th Coach Rally. Bedford YMT Plaxton Supreme IV (YEB 105T) entry number 53 driven by Colin Rowland. (Derek Jones)

Also Bedford OB Duple Vista (LYC 731) entry number 46 driven by Mick Cousens and Ivan Lusted. (Derek Jones)

1990. 36th Coach Rally. Volvo B10M-60 Plaxton Paramount 3500 (G135 UWV) entry number 22 driven by Colin Rowland. (Derek Jones)

1999. 45th Coach Rally. Volvo B10M-62 Berkhof Axial 50 (R222 VDY) entry number 22 driven by Nigel Glover. (Alan Snatt)

2000. 46th Coach Rally. Scania K124 Van Hool AlizeeT9 (W222 KDY) entry number 39 driven by Ivan Lusted. (Colin Rowland)

Also Mercedes Benz 1020 Optare Solera (V222 JDY) entry number 36 driven by Darren Stewart. (Alan Snatt)

2001. 47th Coach Rally. Volvo B10M-62 Berkhof Axial 50 (Y222 PDY)
entry number 26 driven by Colin Rowland. (Alan Snatt)

2004. 50th Coach Rally. Volvo B7R Plaxton Profile (CR04 RAM)
entry number 25 driven by Colin Rowland. (Stephen Dine)

Also Bedford PJK Plaxton Supreme IV (JDY 888Y) entry
number 27 driven by Darren Stewart. (Alan Snatt)

2005. 51st Coach Rally. Volvo B12M Berkhof Axial 50 (DDY 557, previously
CA52 LAO) entry number 56 driven by Ian Jupp. (Alan Snatt)

Also, Volvo B10M Plaxton Paramount (1924 RH, previously H631 UWR)
entry number 58 driven by Russell Ward. (Alan Snatt)

2007. 53rd Coach Rally. Mercedes Benz 0404 Hispano Vita
(X500 GDY) entry number 26 driven by Ian Jupp. (Alan Snatt)

2008. 54th Coach Rally. Volvo B12B Volvo 9700 Prestige (CR08 RAM)
entry number 25 driven by Colin Rowland. (Colin Rowland)

SECOA Coaching Weekends

Rambler Coaches were members of the South East Coach Operators Association (S.E.C.O.A) attending its monthly meetings and taking part in the associations own annual get-together which became known as a 'Coaching Weekend'. First held in April 1978 in Margate, it visited that town for several years before moving to Folkestone, and usually returned to a venue in any one of those two towns. It was an internal social event for the association, rather than a publicly-advertised rally, but each year attracted up to thirty or so coaches from operators around Kent, South East London and East Sussex. Unlike the Brighton rallies where entries were usually brand new vehicles, at the SECOA events these were the exception rather than the rule, and instead a range of vehicles often several years old and usually in active service until the day before the event were brought along, some of them of unusual types or

1960's models such as the Bedford VAM. Rambler soon joined in and often won one or more of various categories of awards for either vehicles or drivers.

The 1985 event had been a particularly good weekend for the company, winning The Sealink Cup (for best 1973-75 vehicle) The Olau Line Cup (for Mr G Phillips – driver with the best Continental knowledge) and The Plaxton Trophy (for the Plaxton coach gaining the highest points in classes 2–6).

In a subsequent SECOA meeting, the subject came up to see who would be willing to host the following year's annual rally and, much to Colin's surprise, this was followed by his business partner John Goodwin stating he would be happy to oblige in doing so. What followed in 1986 was the staging of Hastings's very own Coach Rally. As expected, John would plan and execute every exact detail personally. Easter 1986 was rather earlier than usual, being over the last weekend of March, so the SECOA event was brought forward to the weekend of 8th and 9th March. The first day consisted of vehicle judging and drivers' knowledge questions, followed by a tour of Hastings later in the day for visiting guests and cocktail party, hosted by the Mayor of Hastings followed by dinner dance at The Royal Victoria Hotel in St Leonards on Sea, which turned out to be the last group booking before its closure and subsequent takeover to reopen as a Best Western Hotel.

The following day consisted of driving skills tests where coaches were located at the large car parking area on the St Leonards on Sea seafront in Sea Road near to the Bathing Pool Holiday Camp, the road specially closed for the event to take place, with lunch at the Royal Victoria Hotel and presentations later in the afternoon. Dudley Haynes from Banstead Coaches was a guest Judge, as an experienced coach operator himself, with the weekend event being an enjoyable and successful one.

The early morning sea mist will eventually lift as the day's events are soon to start for Bedford OB Duple Vista (LYC 731) and Volvo B10M-61 Plaxton Paramount 3500 (C588 SJK) taking part in the 1986 event. (Colin Rowland)

Dudley Haynes of Banstead Coaches is seen behind the wheel of the Bedford OB Duple Vista (LYC 731) on the St Leonards on Sea seafront. (Derek Jones)

In glorious sunshine for the 1989 SECOA Coaching Weekend, staged Palm Bay in Margate, we find the Bedford YMT Plaxton Supreme IV (SDY 788) immaculately turned out. (Derek Jones)

Colin's long term friend Alan Marchant (on the left) has not only worked with Colin on numerous projects through Coombs Motors, but has also driven for the company and attended a number of British Coach Rally events over the years. Alan and Colin are seen with Traffic Commissioner Chris Heaps (on the right) at the presentations ceremony for the 2001 event. (Bus and Coach Buyer Magazine)

Appendix 5

Personalised number plates

The trend in recent years of motorists purchasing a personalised or 'cherished' registration number started to become more popular in the 1970's, when pre-1963 dateless registrations became of wider interest. Newer registration issues from 1963 onwards were easily identifiable by having an additional letter to denote its year of issue, changing annually, thus easily dating the age. Transferring interesting earlier registrations onto a newer vehicle for personal or financial reasons is far from a modern practice and has been possible since vehicle registrations were first introduced in 1904, but in earlier years it was confined to a smaller minority of motorists keen enough to negotiate their way through the sometimes complex regulation, procedures and fees involved. Commercial operators of buses, coaches and other commercial vehicles have found it worthwhile to allocate dateless numbers to their vehicles making it harder for a potential customer to guess at the correct age of a

Photographed in 1964 we find the former Rambler Coaches Bedford SB Duple Vega (GDY 888) now with its new owner, the contractor Croad in Portsmouth. It would return to dealer Bakers in late 1965 to be broken up at the end of its commercial use. Also in Croad's ownership alongside is Bedford OB Duple Vista (GDL 618) previously with West Wight of Totland Bay on the Isle of Wight. (unknown – Bob Cook collection)

coach they may be hiring, especially if the vehicle has been maintained in excellent condition. Coaches are expensive assets when purchased new and remain high value items in the first half of their long working lives, but their original registration allocation gives away their actual age.

Rambler Coaches began to use personalised registration numbers on a number of vehicles in their fleet, in later years for reasons of local interest, transferred from vehicle to vehicle as the fleet is updated, with a number of registrations having their own story to tell along the way. Before the advent of more widespread popularity of the use of reallocating older number plates onto newer vehicles, interesting ones owned by the company have sadly disappeared when the coach they were on was sold. Colin recalled seeing one of his father's former coaches parked at the dealer Bakers in Farnham in November 1965 when they visited the trade show being held there and where an eventual order for a new Bedford VAM would be placed. The 1954 Bedford SB had by now finished its subsequent commercial use with its last owner Croad, a Portsmouth based contractor, having been taken back in part exchange for a newer coach. It was now awaiting its final fate, being slowly broken up at the rear of the dealer's yard as its working life was at an end. The coach still proudly displaying its Hastings issued registration number GDY 888. On reflection Colin wished he had removed the number plate as a memento. He did take the seat number from seat 36 as a souvenir, which was the single seat at the front of the coach that he had sat on many times as a young child when out with his father, but the idea of actually trying to negotiate to buy the registration number to transfer onto another vehicle was something that had not been considered at the time.

Years later John and Colin would begin to look for cherished registration plates themselves with an early example still on its original vehicle, a 1959 Brighton registered Morris Minor bearing WUF 44. Its owner John Fowle who was a sales representative for the local Watling Tyres branch was approached and the registration was purchased for £75 and transferred onto Bedford YMT Duple Dominant LJK 335P. John received an age related registration from DVLA for the old Morris which continued in use until chassis corrosion would finally cause the vehicles demise. After a number of years of WUF 44 gracing this particular coach and then a later model, the registration was eventually sold to the owner of a dog kennels, having an obvious connection to their business.

In September 1983 a Bedford NJM Duple Vega 31 (KDY 300H) was sold to nearby Bexhill Swimming Club, replacing an earlier coach owned

Seen together when the transfer of registration WUF 44 has been completed from a 1959 Morris Minor, onto the 1976 Bedford Duple Dominant LJK 335P, this image makes for an interesting comparison. (Colin Rowland)

by them. It was offered to Colin and John for disposal but declined as they were not really interested in having a part exchange coach to dispose of. After the club had sign written the former Rambler vehicle, albeit still in its original livery, Colin decided to pop over to Bexhill to take a look at it. He then noticed the clubs outgoing coach parked alongside, a 1960 Bedford J4LZ1 Plaxton Consort 29-seater, bearing the Southampton registration 5421 CR. On realising it bore his own initials, Colin now asked if they wanted the coach disposed of and the reply was yes, take it please. Colin duly transferred the number onto his Vauxhall Cavalier car with the old coach being re-registered by DVLA as XUF 34A. The elderly Bedford was sold to a new owner in Rye who in

Seen in Beeching Road in Bexhill on Sea on 19th March 1983 with Bexhill
Swimming Club, is the 1960 Bedford J4LZ1 Plaxton Consort (5421 CR). Its
Southampton registration would be transferred to Colin Rowland. (Derek Jones)

turn converted it into a camper. It was a surprise sometime later when
a letter was received from its new owner who had indeed completed the
conversion and gone on his holidays in it, the photo enclosed showing
the coach surrounded by Camels in Morocco!

In October 1984 a Bedford YRQ Plaxton Elite (HRD 12N) was
sold to J2T Video, a manufacturing company based on Denton Island,
Newhaven as staff transport and the following year a Bedford YMT,
Willowbrook (6751 KP, originally KUW 540P) would join the same
company on sale. On one of these occasions an elderly (and now rare)
1963 Bedford SB with Yeates Pegasus body was taken in part exchange.
The Pegasus body was slightly different on the SB chassis in that the
front axle of the vehicle was moved back to enable the coach to have
a passenger door at the immediate front, rather than behind the front

Bedford OB Duple Vista (LYC 731) is waiting for its next passengers on a 'round the town' tour. Alongside is Colin Rowland in his Vauxhall Cavalier car now bearing the registration 5421 CR. (Colin Rowland)

axle as all Bedford SB models did, enabling a capacity of 44 seats instead of the maximum of 41 seats in its original configuration. The coach's registration, 6881 R, was subsequently transferred onto a 1975 16 seat Ford Transit minibus although when the Ford was sold the registration remained on the vehicle as part of the sale.

When vehicle registration transfer applications would be submitted, occasionally the local DVLA office would ask to view a vehicle to verify it was the actual model carrying the registration and matching chassis number, to ensure the transfer was not fraudulent, the donor vehicle then driven to Brighton for presentation. On one occasion, John Goodwin took a Hillman Minx with the registration number 405 UPJ for intended transfer onto a coach to the Brighton office. On carrying out the inspection the team were not particularly interested in the car as such, just that the identification numbers on the vehicle matched with the logbook and their records in case of fraud. John, after completing his successful trip home noted that he had to take care driving as only one brake appeared to be working on trying to stop the car.

Only once did the purchase of a number plate turn out to be part of fraudulent activity. The registration number DDY 222, originally a Hastings issue dating from around 1948, had been purchased from an advertisement in the Exchange & Mart newspaper. Once the transfer had taken place, a call from the Police latterly came through requesting how the registration was obtained. Conversation revealed that two men had been travelling around scrapyards in the country searching for old vehicles, with one of them working at DVLA, 'the inside man', re-issuing the vehicle logbooks and selling the registration numbers on. Fortunately, DDY 222 could be retained as the Police said so many numbers had been taken it would be impossible to find the extent of the duo's activities. Having this registration would inspire both Colin and John to secure further local current registration issues in the 1990's. When two new Scania Van Hool coaches were purchased in January 1995 they were allocated specially reserved registrations M222 CDY and M222 DDY. Over the forthcoming years eleven registrations bearing the numbers '222' joined the fleet and one of these (M222 CDY) was later transferred to a different vehicle.

The style of number plates carried would slowly switch to an interest in gaining various allocations of the local DY Hastings County Borough issues due to the firm's obvious local connection with the town. Colin and John never purchased any early DY issues covering the period of licencing from 1904 until 1937 although John's idea of finding a local registration meant different issues dating from the late 1930's onwards would grace the fleet. An early example was BDY 430 that had once been registered to a 1938 Vauxhall car. FDY 83 and FDY 383, due to their glancing similarity tended to be placed on similar model coaches, at times allocated on double bookings for fun to see if an eagle eye customer noticed the similarity. In a time before the advent of the internet, John would regularly scan newspapers and magazine advertisements in order to find another registration. Despite efforts to get a full allocation of every year of Hastings issued numbers dating from 1937 until 1964 a few registrations slipped through their hands. ADY was found on an old Austin in a yard in Bohemia in the Town but despite offers the owner would not sell and over the years the car stood slowly deteriorating until it was finally scrapped some years later. EDY 818 was nearly acquired but sadly the sale did not proceed.

BDY 389 was found advertised under 'boats' in a newspaper for sale. It turned out that this number plate was actually on a Francis Barnett 'boat tail' motorcycle not in running condition. A mutual deal was struck with local cycle shop proprietor Ken Turner, based in Western Road who restored the motorcycle, with him retaining the bike and Colin and John the number plate. The registration VDY 468 when acquired was first allocated to a coach in 1964, a Bedford VAS1 Duple Vista, new to Reeves of Faversham and latterly with Donsway in Dunkirk, both Kent based operators. After withdrawal the coach became a mobile home and was noted by enthusiasts in Brighton as LKE 158B with its registration number transferred off in January 1994, finding its way onto a newer coach in the Rambler fleet. On one occasion a registration dealer called through as a client of theirs had spotted the registration TYW 50 on one of the Rambler fleet and enquired if it might be for sale. John with his powers of negotiation concluded a deal that would be a straight swap for two DY-multiple registrations in exchange.

In 2001 the DVLA registration issuing system went through its biggest change since the introduction of the suffix number plate in 1963 when the system was again changed, with a new configuration to cope with the thousands of new vehicles being registered every year. This now meant UK number plates displaying two letters (for the area of issue) followed by two numbers which would change every six months, in March and September. Colin was worried that it would now not be possible to place their own personal reserved allocations onto new purchases after the last of the old style registrations was issued in 2001 to a brand-new Volvo B10M-62 as Y222 PDY. At the time Stephen Dine (author of this book) pointed out a logical choice would be to use the last three letters to spell RAM. Colin quickly replied with, 'what about the two letters on the left of the number plate?' for which Stephen said, 'use the old Hastings DY issue, or if you are buying more than one new coach why not use yours and John Goodwin's initials.' This did indeed happen as in February 2004 two new Volvo B7R Plaxton's became JG04 RAM and CR04 RAM. In September of the same year a new Mercedes-Benz 0814 Plaxton became JG54 RAM with further such issues following. In 2009 a two year old Volvo B12B Van Hool (SK07 FUW) received the registration LR07 RAM, using the initials of Colin's daughter Laura. The last new coach purchased by Colin, a Mercedes-Benz Tourismo in March 2017, was given the allocation CR17 RAM. With new purchases now usually receiving a registration containing the letters RAM, the choice of CR06 EDY for the Volvo B12B Berkhof Axial 50 in 2006 provided some interesting variation from the usual pattern.

As can be seen from the fleet list, a number of pre-suffix registrations arrived with the vehicles they were already attached to, including a few that were on coaches including 5421 CR, 6881 R, 710 VCV, 910 OCV. Those purchased directly from dealers or non-passenger vehicles included TYW 50, 1924 RH, 950 KPE, 6751 KP, NCF 715, 405 UPJ, WUF 44, 8876 FN, 419 CLB, NIJ 8067.

Local pre-suffix Hastings issues included BDY 389, DDY 222, DDY 557, FDY 83, FDY 383, GDY 493, HDY 405, HDY 565, JDY 673, KDY 814, LDY 173, MDY 397, NDY 820, NDY 962, ODY 395, ODY 607, PDY 42, PDY 272, RDY 155, SDY 788, TDY 388, TDY 946, UDY 512, UDY 910, VDY 468 as well as BDY 430 which has never been used on a PSV.

More recent local registrations containing 'DY' and special numbers 222, 500 or 888 obtained between 1982 and 2001 included GDY 500X, JDY 888Y, KDY 888Y, A888 MDY, B888 PDY, M222 CDY, M222DDY, N222 EDY, R222 WDY, R222 XDY, R222 VDY, T222 ADY, T222 GDY, V222 JDY, W222 KDY, X500 GDY, Y222 PDY.

Under the new registration system, plates using RAM letter combination have been CR04 RAM, JG04 RAM, JG54 RAM, CR06 EDY, JG07 RAM, LR07 RAM, CR08 RAM, JG08 RAM, CR12 RAM, JG12 RAM, CR13 RAM, CR14 RAM, UK15 RAM, CR65 RAM, CR17 RAM. LR07 RAM and CR13 RAM were added later and applied to acquired vehicles SK07 FUW and YN13 EHD respectively.

Appendix 6

Bus services

In 1980 the National Bus Company (NBC) was seeking to reduce a number of unprofitable rural routes by its subsidiaries such as Maidstone & District Motor Service Ltd (M&D) around the country. In East Sussex, Rambler Coaches were successful in securing one of these NBC routes, an eight mile service from Bexhill to Hooe via Sidley with a subsidy from East Sussex County Council. Operating on Monday to Fridays it fitted in with a works, schools, and swimming baths contract. A 1975 Bedford YRT / Plaxton Panorama Elite coach (HVD 588N) was initially used being replaced by a Bedford YRQ / Willowbrook Expressway (VNU 75K), but just two years later policies changed, the service reverting back to National Bus Ltd. However, the venture into tendered service work was not over and a number of local routes have been operated since, mainly as part of East Sussex County Council tendered contracts, normally fitting in with a local school contract and occasionally registered as a commercial service if this was able to provide additional income.

Bedford YRQ Willowbrook 002 (VNU 75K) is seen on Bexhill seafront with driver Dave Freeman when working on the Hooe service. A Bexhill Bus Company Leyland National is seen passing to its left. (Derek Jones)

An early commercial stage service to be operated was the 88 which came about when regular driver Alf Gadd asked if additional hours were available between his part time schools duties. This local town service was set up independently by the company, gaining a loyal following and over time contributed a small return. In January 2002 the company was approached by Tesco to see if they would be interested in operating their own free bus service in the local area as Stagecoach was ceasing to provide this. Initially three vehicles would be required, two working from the Bexhill area and one from the Hastings area, to its flagship store at Hollington in St Leonards on Sea. A route from Rye (latterly extending into Camber) was also operated and at times ran with a full complement of passengers and standing ones too. The 88 service was now discontinued, the emphasis now being on operating the Tesco

```
Hooe to Bexhill bus service on Tuesdays and Thursdays


TIMES outward                              TIMES return

HOOE   Red Lion      09.50                 Bexhill Marina     12.15
Ellerslie Lane       09.59                 Bexhill Town Hall  12.19
Bexhill Town Hall    10.12                 Ellerslie Lane     12.31
Bexhill Marina       10.15                 Hooe Red Lion      12.40
```

Timetable detailing the service times for the Hooe service. (Colin Rowland)

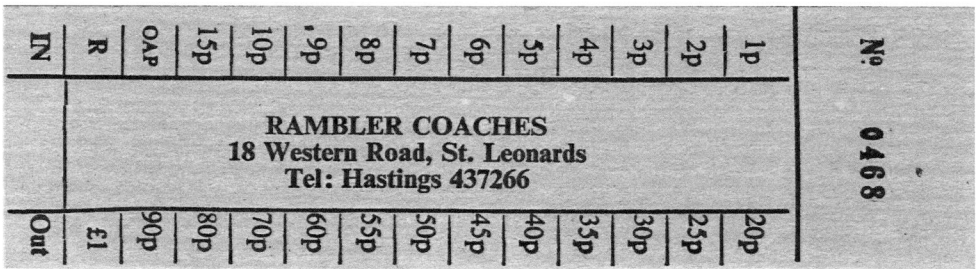

Ticket for the Hooe – Bexhill service. (Bob Cook)

routes which were not registered as stage services as chartered direct by Tesco, with no fares being exchanged. It operated successfully until ceasing in September 2021 due to a decision by Tesco to scale back the bus services.

A number of service routes have been operated over the years since with an array of buses. A selection of photographs of these are included to illustrate the varied duties.

PGR 620N was a Bedford YRT with Willowbrook body and dated from October 1974, joining the fleet from Yeomans of Hereford in April 1986. It was up seated to a sixty seat capacity and is seen at the Tesco Hollington store in St Leonards on Sea in 1987 working the service 2. (Derek Jones)

On a wet day in Milward Road, Hastings again on the service 2 we find the 1973 Seddon Midi with 25 seat Pennine coachwork (TDT 624L) purchased in July 1987, having previously operated for Maun in Mansfield. It seen working on the service 2. (Terry Blackman)

Looking particularly smart in Ramblerbus livery is the 1981 Bedford
YMPS (WNH 52W) with 33 seat Maxeta body working on the
service 32 as it pulls out of Winchelsea Road in Hastings on its
way to nearby Hollington in April 1995. (Terry Blackman)

In this wonderful winter scene from early 1991 in Queens Road,
Hastings, we find the Bristol RESL6L (TCD 481J) with 45 seat Marshall
body on the 88 service. New to Southdown Motor Services in 1970 it
joined the fleet from Kent Coach Tours in November 1990. Note the
company service van following close behind. (Terry Blackman)

Bedford YNT Plaxton Paramount 3 200 (ODY 395) formerly A627 YWF, is photographed by its driver Paul Green on 20th October 1994 when operating a regular Thursday service 47 from New Romney, Kent into neighbouring East Sussex to Rye Market. The coach's express doors made it ideal for this role. (Paul Green)

Passing through the village of Pett on 15th May 2003 is a 1995 Dennis Dart Marshall (UDY 512) purchased from Fleetmaster in Horsham in 2002 as M513 VJO. It enjoyed a stay of four years in the fleet before sale to Autocar in Five Oak Green. (Paul Green)

On a late summers day in 1991 we find the 1980 registered Bedford YMQ with Alexander Y type body (MGS 437V) at Winchelsea Beach, working the service 44 to Hastings with driver Don Pelling. Details of this vehicle's history can be found in the appendix Interesting Bedford's. (Paul Gainsbury)

Three of the then working bus fleet are seen together for a staged photograph at West Ridge Manor. From left to right; Maxeta bodied 8m Bedford YMQ (WNH 52W) in its first livery of red, Bedford YLQ (MGS 437V) and Bristol RESL6L (TCD 481J) now wearing its green Ramblerbus livery. (Stephen Dine)

Coaches would also be used to cover stage carriage duties if required. In October 1990 Bedford YMT Duple Dominant (DMT 904V) is picking up passengers at Hastings Station on the service 88. Its driver was Mick Cousens. (Terry Blackman)

Identical Bedford YMT Wright TT bodied buses consecutively registered as CKN 142Y and CKN 143Y were new to Maidstone Borough Council in October 1982. Purchased together in June 1992 they are seen at Hastings Station in August of the same year. (Stephen Dine)

Seen in June 1992 at Station Approach in Rye, we find the 1980 45 seat
Bedford YLQ Duple Dominant (ECB 791W). Its driver Sue Kemsley is taking a
break before returning to Hastings on service 44 to Hastings. (Stephen Dine)

At West Ridge Manor after their day's duties have been completed
are Leyland Olympians, FDY 83 (H649 PVW) and FDY 383 (J706
CEV) both with Alexander RH bodies. Both vehicles were purchased
from Ensign after operating for Dublin Bus. (Alan Snatt)

In the company of two Stagecoach Bristol VR's in May 1994, is Bedford YMT Duple Dominant (KWB 695W) seen at Station Approach in Rye, when on the service 312. New in January 1981 to Wigmore, Dinnington, it was purchased from Rider York in March 1994. Its stay was brief at just one year before moving on to Coach Services of Thetford. (Terry Blackman)

Driven by the immaculately dressed Michael Brown, is Dennis Dart Alexander Dash (J505 GCD), seen near to Bodiam Castle on 15th May 2014. New to Stagecoach in Hastings in March 1992, it was one of three similar buses purchased in 2004, the other two examples being J507 GCD and J534 GCD. (Philip Cattermole)

Passing over the railway crossing in Station Road, Robertsbridge
on 13th March 1998 is the 1986 Bedford YMT Wadham Stringer
(NDY 820) formerly registered C302 RRX operating the service 380.
Previously in operation with the Ministry of Defence at Aldermaston
it would eventually be exported to Malta. (Paul Gainsbury)

With the vehicle's driver not wanting to reveal his identity to the
photographer, 1979 Leyland National (UDY 512 – formerly BPL 459T),
is seen on 10th December 1998 at Ravenside Retail Park, Glyne Gap,
Bexhill on Sea. Arriving via Wealden PSV from London & Country with
its original engine by now replaced with a Volvo unit. It was later sold
on for further service to Eastonways in Ramsgate. (Paul Gainsbury)

Parked between duties in Priory Road, Hastings in April 2007 is Volvo B10M-56 (F709 WCS) with 53 seat Duple 300 body, later receiving the registration UDY 910. It was new to Hutchison of Overtown in 1989. (Terry Blackman)

Seen passing the Plough Public House in the village of Crowhurst on the Tesco Free Bus service on 24th May 2011 is one of a pair of Volvo B10B-58 with Plaxton Verde body and became the third Rambler vehicle to use the registration UDY 910. New in 1995 to Nottingham City Transport as M607 UTV it would join the fleet in November 2007 with sister bus M606 UTV from Gemini Travel in Neath, Glamorgan. (Terry Blackman)

Seen operating service 44 in Hastings Town Centre is C203 GKR, a 1986 Bedford YMT with Wright TT body. It arrived in March 1995 via Wealden PSV, having operated for the Glossopdale Bus Company and then Evans, Tregaron. Its driver was Tony Aylett. (Alan Snatt)

Passing through Tenterden High Street in Kent on a private hire booking on 17th June 2015, we find Volvo Olympian (S136 RLE) with 62 seat Alexander RV body. New to Metroline in 1998 it came from Ensign at the end of 2009, being withdrawn in February 2016 after accident damage. (Philip Cattermole)

Heading through the picturesque East Sussex countryside having
just passed through Fairlight on its way to Rye when on service
44, we find Bedford YMQ with Wright TT bodywork (MUY 41X)
purchased at ten years old from Martin Perry. (Terry Blackman)

M525 WHF was a 1994 Volvo B10B with 53 seat Wright Endurance body,
previously with Beestons in Hadleigh, Suffolk. Seen on Bexhill seafront
when operating the Tesco free bus service it would later return to the east of
England to see service with Dews Coaches in Somersham. (Alan Snatt)

Travelling through the small town of Winchelsea in July 2015 when operating
on the Tesco free bus service, is 2004 Dennis Dart SLF with 37 seat Plaxton
Pointer body (MW54 BLU). It was acquired with sister vehicle MV54
BLU from Stagecoach in Manchester in April 2015. (Terry Blackman)

This smart looking Mercedes Citaro (BU04 EXS) enjoyed a period
of time on loan to the company and was captured on film at
West Ridge Manor on 20th February 2016. (Alan Snatt)

Finding its way into Hastings via Junction Road on the 304 service from Claverham Community College in Battle on 10th October 2018, is 2001 Volvo B7TL with 80 seat Plaxton President body (X661 LLX). Having served with Metroline in London, it came via Ensign in March 2013 and would see another seven years service before being sold for scrap. (Paul Green)

Seen on a wet day at West Ridge Manor is a 1988 Volvo B10M-61 with 51 seat Northern Counties body (NDY 820). Purchased in May 2004 it had previously operated for Birmingham Omnibus Company in Tividale as JIL 5279. Withdrawn in November 2011 it was sold to Wealden PSV, now bearing the registration E364 NEG. (Paul Green)

RAMBLERBUS SERVICE 2

Timetable from 3 October 1988

HOLLINGTON - ST. HELENS via West St. Leonards, St Leonards, Hastings, Mount Pleasant & Broomgrove

MONDAYS to SATURDAYS only   Sc.Da.

HOLLINGTON, Tesco		9.23	11.09	1.10	2.56	3.19	4.45
Stonehouse Drive, Flats		9.27	11.13	1.14	:CR	3.23	4.49
Wishing Tree Roundabout		9.31	11.17	1.18	3.00	3.26	4.52
HARLEY SHUTE, Edinburgh Road	7.50				3.05		
Fernside Avenue, Shops	7.54	9.33	11.19	1.20		3.28	4.54
West St. Leonards, Rail Station	7.59	9.39	11.25	1.26		3.32	4.58
St. Leonards, Warrior Square	8.05	9.47	11.33	1.34		3.37	5.03
Bohemia Road/Church Road	8.08	9.52	11.38	1.39		3.40	5.06
HASTINGS, Wellington Place	8.14	9.58	11.44	1.45		3.45	5.11
Milward Road, Manor Hotel	8.18	10.03	11.49	1.50		3.49	5.15
Langham Hotel	8.20	10.05	11.51	1.52		3.51	5.17
Hoadswood Road/Elphinstone Road	8.22	10.07	11.53	1.54		3.53	5.19
ST. HELENS, The Ridge, Cemetery	8.26	10.11	11.57	1.58		3.57	5.23

ST. HELENS - HOLLINGTON via Broomgrove, Mount Pleasant, Hastings, St. Leonards & West St. Leonards

MONDAYS to SATURDAYS only   Sc.Da.

ST. HELENS, The Ridge, Cemetery		8.30	10.16	12.02	2.03		4.02	5.28
Ochiltree Road		8.32	10.18	12.04	2.05		4.04	5.30
Elphinstone Road/Hoadswood Road		8.34	10.20	12.06	2.07		4.06	5.32
Langham Hotel		8.36	10.22	12.08	2.09		4.08	5.34
Milward Road, Manor Hotel		8.38	10.24	12.10	2.11		4.10	5.36
HASTINGS, Cambridge Road	7.29	8.44	10.31	12.17	2.18		4.15	5.41
Bohemia Road/Church Road	7.33	8.49	10.38	12.24	2.25		4.20	5.46
St. Leonards, Warrior Square	7.36	8.53	10.44	12.30	2.31		4.23	5.49
West St. Leonards, Rail Station	7.42	8.59	10.51	12.37	2.38		4.28	5.54
Fernside Avenue, Shops	7.47	9.04	10.56	12.42	2.43		4.32	5.58
HARLEY SHUTE, Edinburgh Road	7.49	9.06		12.44		3.06		
Wishing Tree Roundabout		9.11	10.58	12.50	2.45	3.11	4.34	6.00
Stonehouse Drive, Flats		9.13	11.00	12.52	2.47	3.13	4.36	6.02
HOLLINGTON, Tesco		9.18	11.04	12.56	2.51	3.18	4.40	6.06

Sc.Da. - School Days only

CR.   via Crowhurst Road

18 WESTERN ROAD, ST. LEONARDS-ON-SEA

RAMBLERBUS 44 - 344 - 345 RYE - HASTINGS
VIA. WINCHELSEA BEACH - PETT LEVEL - FAIRLIGHT - OLD TOWN

Effective from 31.10.94

	44 NSa	44	44	44	344 NSa	44 Sch	44 Sch	345 NSa	344 NSa	345
Rye (Rail Station)						1515FG		1630		1750
Rye (Harbour)						1525		1638		1758
Rye (Rail Station)		0850	1040	1240	1440		1610	1646	1650	
Winchelsea (Bridge End)		0855	1047	1247	1447		1617		1657	1808
Winchelsea Beach		0858	1050	1250	1450		1620		1700	1811
Smugglers End		0900	1052	1252	1452		1622		1702	1813
Pett Level		0903	1056	1256	1456		1626		1706	1817
Fairlight Cove (Hotel)	0730	0909	1103	1303	1503		1633		1713	1824
Fairlight Glen	0736	0915	1113	1313	1513		1643		1723	1834
Ore (Christchurch)	0738	0917	1116	1316	1516		1646		1726	1837
Old Town (Boating Lake)	0742	0922	1122	1322	1522		1652		1732	1843
Hastings (Cambridge Rd)	0746	0924	1124	1324	1524		1654		1734	1845
Hastings (Rail Station)	0748	0926	1126	1326	1526		1656		1736	1847

	44	44	44	44	344 NSa	344			344 NSa
Hastings (Rail Station)	0748	0936	1136	1336	1536	1636			1740
Hastings (Cambridge Rd)	0751	0940	1140	1340	1540	1640			1744
Old Town (Boating Lake)	0753	0942	1142	1342	1542	1642			1746
Ore (Christchurch)	0758	0949	1149	1349	1549	1649			1753
Fairlight Glen	0802	0953	1153	1353	1553	1653			1757
Fairlight Cove (Hotel)	0812	1003	1203	1403	1603	1703			1807
Pett Level	0819	1010	1210	1410	1610	1710			1814
Smugglers End	0823	1014	1214	1414	1614	1714			1818
Winchelsea Beach	0825	1016	1216	1416	1616	1716			1820
Winchelsea (Bridge End)	0828	1019	1219	1419	1619	1719			1823
Rye (Harbour) ■	0832								
Rye (Rail Station)	0840*	1026	1226	1426	1626	1726			1830

Rambler Coaches Hastings 754881

■	School days only
*	Continues to Freda Gardham School on school days
FG	Freda Gardham School
NSa	Not operated Saturdays
Sch	School days only

Services 344 & 345 provided as part of East Sussex County Local Rider Network

Mondays to Saturdays (Not Bank Holidays)

E.S.C.C. County Card accepted on all journeys

Designed & Printed by IMPACT 01424 855558

RAMBLERBUS   SERVICE 47

RYE - NEW ROMNEY

VIA STATION APPROACH - CINQUE PORTS STREET - TOWER STREET - LANDGATE (RETURN VIA SOUTH UNDERCLIFF- THE QUAY - WISH STREET - FERRY ROAD) - FISHMARKET ROAD - NEW ROAD - EAST GULDEFORD ROAD - BROOKLAND - BRENZETT - IVYCHURCH - OLD ROMNEY - NEW ROMNEY.

THURSDAYS ONLY

RYE, Railway Station	0900	1345
Brookland, Church	0918	1403
Brenzett, School	0921	1406
Ivychurch, Bell	0926	1411
Old Romney, Cross Roads	0931	1416
NEW ROMNEY, Ship Hotel	0936	1421
NEW ROMNEY, Ship Hotel	1035	1425
Old Romney, Cross Roads	1040	1430
Ivychurch, Bell	1045	1435
Brenzett, School	1050	1440
Brookland, Church	1053	1443
RYE, Railway Station	1111	1501

Operated by: Rambler Coaches,
Whitworth Road,
St. Leonards-on-Sea, East Sussex
Tel 0424 754881

This local bus service is provided on behalf of Kent County Council. If you have any comments or suggestions please write to The Director of Highways and Transportation, Springfield, Maidstone, Kent. ME14 2LQ

Kent County Council HIGHWAYS & TRANSPORTATION

Printed by IMPACT 0424 855558

RAMBLERBUS   SERVICE 66

HASTINGS TOWN CENTRE - WARRIOR SQUARE - LONDON ROAD - PEVENSEY ROAD - THE GREEN - SEDLESCOMBE ROAD SOUTH - SILVERHILL - THE BRIERS - NEW SAINSBURYS - THE RIDGE - CONQUEST HOSPITAL

							NSc		
Town Centre	0915	1015	1115	1215	1315	1415	1515	1615	1715
Pier	0918	1018	1118	1218	1318	1418	1518	1618	1718
Warrior Sq.	0920	1020	1120	1220	1320	1420	1520	1620	1720
Christchurch	0922	1022	1122	1222	1322	1422	1522	1622	1722
Top Pevensey Rd.	0924	1024	1124	1224	1324	1424	1524	1624	1724
Top Springfield Rd.	0926	1026	1126	1226	1326	1426	1526	1626	1726
Silverhill	0928	1028	1128	1228	1328	1428	1528	1628	1728
Briers	0930	1030	1130	1230	1330	1430	1530	1630	1730
Sainsburys	0934	1034	1134	1234	1334	1434	1534	1634	1734
Hospital	0940	1040	1140	1240	1340	1440	1540	1640	1740

							NSc	
Hospital	0945	1045	1145	1245	1345	1445	1545	1645
Sainsburys	0951	1051	1151	1251	1351	1451	1551	1651
Briers	0955	1055	1155	1255	1355	1455	1555	1655
Silverhill	0957	1057	1157	1257	1357	1457	1557	1657
Top Springfield Rd.	0959	1059	1159	1259	1359	1459	1559	1659
Top Pevensey Rd.	1001	1101	1201	1301	1401	1501	1601	1701
Christchurch	1003	1103	1203	1303	1403	1503	1603	1703
Warrior Square	1005	1105	1205	1305	1405	1505	1605	1705
Pier	1007	1107	1207	1307	1407	1507	1607	1707
Town Centre	1010	1110	1210	1310	1410	1510	1610	1710

NSc Not School Days

Hastings Borough Council Concessionary Passes accepted.

Rambler Coaches, Whitworth Road, St. Leonards-on-Sea. Tel 754881

Mondays to Fridays (not Bank Holidays)

Printed by IMPACT 0424 722779

RAMBLERBUS SERVICE 88.

**START DATE
29 OCTOBER 1990**

ORE — HALTON — TOWN CENTRE — BOHEMIA — SILVERHILL — TESCOS.

						NS		NS		NS
Tesco	09.15	10.00	10.45	11.30	12.15	13.00	13.45	14.30	15.15	16.45
Lancaster Rd	09.17	10.02	10.47	11.32	12.17	13.02	13.47	14.32	15.17	16.47
Hollington P.O	09.21	10.06	10.51	11.36	12.21	13.06	13.51	14.36	15.21	16.51
Silverhill	09.25	10.10	10.55	11.40	12.25	13.10	13.55	14.40	15.25	16.55
Wheatsheaf	09.29	10.14	10.59	11.44	12.29	13.14	13.59	14.44	15.29	16.59
Sainsburys	09.33	10.18	11.03	11.48	12.33	13.18	14.03	14.48	15.33	17.03
Hastings Station	09.35	10.20	11.05	11.50	12.35	13.20	14.05	14.50	15.35	17.05
Queens Parade	09.38	10.23	11.08	11.53	12.38	13.23	14.08	14.53	15.38	17.08
Safeways	09.41	10.26	11.11	11.56	12.41	13.26	14.11	14.56	15.41	17.11
Park Gates	09.43	10.28	11.13	11.58	12.43	13.28	14.13	14.58	15.43	17.13
Langham	09.45	10.30	11.15	12.00	12.45	13.30	14.15	15.00	15.45	17.15
Halton Flats	09.47	10.32	11.17	12.02	12.47	13.32	14.17	15.02	15.47	17.17
Ore Village	09.49	10.34	11.19	12.04	12.49	13.34	14.19	15.04	15.49	17.19
Ore Kings Head	09.52	10.37	11.22	12.07	12.52	13.37	14.22	15.07	15.52	17.23

							NS				NS
Ore Kings Head	09.15	10.00	10.45	11.30	12.15	13.00	13.45	14.30	16.00		17.30
Ore Village	09.18	10.03	10.48	11.33	12.18	13.03	13.48	14.33	16.03		17.33
Halton Flats	09.20	10.05	10.50	11.35	12.20	13.05	13.50	14.35	16.05		17.35
Langham	09.22	10.07	10.52	11.37	12.22	13.07	13.52	14.37	16.07		17.37
Park Gates	09.24	10.09	10.54	11.39	12.24	13.09	13.54	14.39	16.09		17.39
Safeways	09.26	10.11	10.56	11.41	12.26	13.11	13.56	14.41	16.11		17.41
South Terrace	09.28	10.13	10.58	11.43	12.28	13.13	13.58	14.43	16.13		17.43
Hastings Station	09.30	10.15	11.00	11.45	12.30	13.15	14.00	14.45	16.15		17.45
Cambridge Rd PO	09.34	10.19	11.04	11.49	12.34	13.19	14.04	14.49	16.19	17.15	17.49
Wheatsheaf	09.38	10.23	11.08	11.53	12.38	13.23	14.08	14.53	16.23	17.19	17.53
Silverhill	09.42	10.27	11.12	11.57	12.42	13.27	14.12	14.57	16.27	17.23	17.57
Hollington PO	09.46	10.31	11.16	12.01	12.46	13.31	14.16	15.01	16.31	17.27	18.01
Lancaster Rd	09.50	10.35	11.20	12.05	12.50	13.35	14.20	15.05	16.35	17.31	18.05
Tesco	09.52	10.37	11.22	12.07	12.52	13.37	14.22	15.07	16.37	17.33	18.07

NS NOT SATURDAY

SERVICE 88 MONDAYS TO SATURDAYS

NO SERVICE SUNDAYS AND BANK HOLIDAYS.

RAMBLER COACHES, WESTRIDGE MANOR, WHITWORTH ROAD, ST. LEONARDS
TEL. 754881

Hastings Borough Council Concessionary Passes accepted.

BURWASH-SIDLEY   360
via Hurst Green-Sedlescombe-Westfield

Schooldays only

Service no.	360	360	360
Operator	RC	RC	RC
	am	am	pm
BURWASH High Street	.	7.33	.
Etchingham Post Office	.	7.38	.
Hurst Green Royal George	.	7.42	.
Robertsbridge George	.	7.48	.
Mountfield School	.	7.52	.
Whatlington Royal Oak	.	7.56	.
Sedlescombe Coach & Horses	.	8.02	.
Kent Street Nortons Farm	.	8.06	.
The Harrow Junction	.	8.10	.
Westfield Church	7.55	8.15	.
The Harrow Junction	8.00	8.20	.
Hollington Blackman Ave Shops	8.05	8.25	.
Harley Shute Rd Bexhill Rd	8.09	8.29	.
Bexhill St.Mary Magdalene Sch	8.19	8.39	3.40
Sidley Sussex Hotel	8.22	8.42	3.43
SIDLEY Bexhill Sixth Form Coll	8.25	8.45A	3.46

Operated by Rambler Coaches

Explanation of codes:

A: Continues to St. Mary Magdalene School arriving 8.55 am

SIDLEY-BURWASH   360
via Westfield-Sedlescombe-Hurst Green

Schooldays only

Service no.	360	360	360
Operator	RC	RC	RC
	am	pm	pm
SIDLEY Bexhill Sixth Form Coll	8.50	3.55	.
Sidley Sussex Hotel	8.52	3.58	.
Bexhill St.Mary Magdalene Sch	8.55	4.01	.
Harley Shute Rd Bexhill Rd	.	4.10	.
Hollington Blackman Ave Shops	.	4.15	.
The Harrow Junction	.	4.20	.
Westfield Church	.	4.25	.
The Harrow Junction	.	.	4.20
Kent Street Nortons Farm	.	.	4.24
Sedlescombe Coach & Horses	.	.	4.28
Whatlington Royal Oak	.	.	4.34
Mountfield School	.	.	4.38
Robertsbridge George	.	.	4.42
Hurst Green Royal George	.	.	4.48
Etchingham Post Office	.	.	4.52
BURWASH High Street	.	.	4.57

Operated by Rambler Coaches

RAMBLER COACHES   <u>TIMETABLE</u>

HOOE-BEXHILL SERVICE NO. 31

TUESDAYS AND THURSDAYS ONLY

	<u>OUTWARD</u>	<u>RETURN</u>
HOOE, RED LION	09.05	11.55
WHYDOWN	09.09	11.51
SOUTHLANDS ROAD	09.14	11.46
SIDLEY (PAYLESS)	**09.16**	11.44
BEXHILL TOWN HALL	09.25	11.35
BEXHILL STATION	09.27	11.33
BEXHILL MARINA	09.30	11.30

Rambler Coaches

Local Bus services 1985 - 2018

Until 12/98: Mrs MM & C Rowland & J Goodwin - PK290

From: 12/98: C Rowland & J Goodwin - PK290

O licence increased to 18V by 27/5/88, 22 vehicles by 20/7/90 & granted to expire 30/9/95, then 26 vehs by 27/3/92; 30 vehs by 14/7/95; renewed for 34 to 30/9/2000;

All licences then became continuous so renewal not required from 1/1/96 unless curtailed by Traffic Commissioner.

Rambler Coaches Ltd - PK0003587

Applied for by 3/01, for 35 vehicles, granted by 4/01. Service registrations then in effect were cancelled under the PK290 licence from 6/7/2001, but refreshed local bus service registrations under the new licence PK0003587 were not formally confirmed until various dates in 2002 including 12/2/2002 and 2/9/2002.

Services	Start	Cancelled	Route	Registration reference
2	27/07/1987		Hollington (Tesco) - St Helens (Cemetery) via Wishing Tree, Filsham Road, St Leonards, Milward Road, Elphinstone Road (loop via Ochiltree Road, Pilot Road) *Mondays to Saturdays*	PK0000290/3480
	29/10/1990	26/10/1991	Revised to run only between Stonehouse Drive and Hastings Rail Station and reduced to *Sundays only* with Monday to Saturday service transferred to Stagecoach	
S11	28/09/1998		Pett (Chick Hill) - Rye (Rail Station) via Guestling, Icklesham, Winchelsea, Rye Harbour. *Schooldays*	PK0000290/8348
	07/10/1998	06/07/2001	Diversion via Rye Harbour withdrawn.	
S11 & 311	(09/07/2001)	13/11/2017	Pett (Chick Hill) - Rye (Rail Station) via Guestling, Icklesham, Winchelsea *Schooldays* - Renumbered 311 at the beginning of the autumn term 2002	PK0003587/3
15	29/10/1990	30/10/1994	Sidley - Bexhill (St Mary Magdalene School) *Schooldays*	PK0000290/1916

Previously forming part of service 360 (see below), a morning journey on schooldays only was renumbered 15 at the same time as another 360 journey was renumbered to 361, as part of a new contract award from 29/10/1990. No separate registration has been traced so it is thought likely that this service continued to be registered alongside 360 and 361 (q.v.)

28	See 314 & 328 below			
31	28/05/1985	25/05/1986	Hooe (Red Lion) - Bexhill (Marina) via Whydown, Sidley *Tuesdays and Thursdays only*.	

Although surviving records of this service are fragmented, there is some evidence that in addition to the above return trip (timed for shoppers), school journeys were in operation by February 1984 on all schooldays. All were replaced and incorporated into new service 319 as part of the Battle area County Rider network operated by M J Harmer (Bexhill Bus Company), Bexhill from 27 May 1986. Rambler operation then transferred to service 814 (later 314 - see below) from the same date.

32	30/10/1994		Wishing Tree - Ore (King's Head) via Blackman Avenue, Silverhill, Hastings, Langham Hotel, St Helen's Hospital, *hourly - Winter Sundays* (operated commercially by Stagecoach (South Coast Buses on weekdays and during summer period)	PK0000290/7186
			Exact dates of Rambler operation each season recorded as 30/10/94 to 21/5/95, 17/9/95 to 19/5/96, 22/9/96 to 18/5/97.	
	12/10/1996	06/07/2001	Re-routed in Hastings town centre due to new traffic scheme. Seasonal dates of operation continued as 28/9/97 to 17/5/98, but it appears that Stagecoach continued to operate the 32 on Sundays all-year from 28/9/98, so that Rambler would not have resumed the winter operation after that date.	
44 45 344 345	16/09/1991		Rye (Rail Station) - Hastings (Rail Station) via Winchelsea Beach, Fairlight, Ore *Mondays to Saturdays*	PK0000290/5994
44 344 345	by 10/95		Service 45 school journey renumbered 44	
	05/11/1996		Re-routed in Hastings town centre due to new traffic scheme	
	09/05/2000	06/07/2001	Revised timetable (reduced service)	
	(09/07/2001)	27/10/2002	Registration confirmed for new O-licence during 2002 but cancelled 27/10/2002	PK0003587/8

The rather complex numbering arrangements for the above services arose because some journeys (44/45) were operated commercially in the summer season from 1992 and others (subsequently numbered 344/345) were provided on behalf of East Sussex County Council under the "Local Rider" network brand. Journeys numbered 45/345 additionally served Rye Harbour, and formed only a small proportion of a broader service between Rye and Rye Harbour, with most journeys there provided by other operators (principally Autopoint and Stagecoach). Over the 11 years of Rambler operation, there were several rounds of re-tendering resulting in individual journeys transferring to or from the other operators. See also below for subsequent operation of a service 345 between Fairlight and Rye between 2012 and 2015.

47	10/04/1994	06/04/1997	Rye - New Romney via Brookland, Brenzett, Ivychurch, Old Romney (replacing withdrawn Stagecoach service) *Thursdays only*. (Kent County Council contract).	PK0000290/7000

BUS SERVICES

Service	Start	End	Description	Registration
66	24/11/1993	15/04/1994	Hastings (Town Centre) - Conquest Hospital (The Ridge) via Warrior Square, The Green, Silverhill, Briers, Sainsburys. *Monday to Friday, hourly*	PK0000290/6881
			Service 66 introduced following the opening of the Sainsbury superstore in Sedlescombe Road North, St Leonards	
88	29/10/1990		Hollington (Tesco) - Ore (King's Head) via Church Wood Drive, Tile Barn Road, Lancaster Road, Hollington Post Office, Silverhill, Hastings, Langham Hotel, Halton Flats, Ore (Christ Church), *Mondays to Saturdays.*	PK0000290/5383
	25/11/1991		Diverted between Church Wood Drive and Silverhill via Crowhurst Road, Blackman Avenue, Battle Road.	
	09/08/1983	27/06/1996	Saturday service withdrawn - now *Mondays to Fridays*	
230	03/11/1997	05/01/1998	Tunbridge Wells - Tonbridge (Kings Road) via Penshurst - *Schooldays* (Kent County Council contract).	PK0000290/8159
233	03/11/1997	05/01/1998	Leigh Green - Tunbridge Wells (Bennett Memorial School), *Schooldays* (Kent County Council contract).	PK0000290/8160
			Services 230 & 233 above were operated by vehicles of Autocar, Five Oak Green (Leyland Leopard PSU5C/Wadham Stringer B72F and Leyland Tiger TRCTL11/3R/ECW C53F WPH 133Y), technically on hire to Rambler, until the KCC contract was formally transferred to Autocar from 5 January 1998.	
301	28/09/1987	13/11/1987	Silverhill - Rye (Rail Station) via Westfield, Brede, Broad Oak, Udimore (temporary service) *Mondays to Fridays*	PK0000290/3614
			Single early morning journey operated on a temporary basis, subsequently taken over by Rodemark (Autopoint), Herstmonceux, who at the time was the main operator of service 301 (Hastings - Rye)	
304	30/10/2006	24/09/2018	Hastings - Battle (Claverham College) via St Leonards, Hollington, Telham *Schooldays*	PK0003587/11
305	30/10/1994	06/10/1996	Hastings (Town Centre) - Battle (Abbey) via St Leonards and Silverhill, one journey in each direction, afternoon & early evening peak. *Mondays to Saturdays*	PK0000290/7187
311	See S11 above			
312	09/04/1994	30/10/1994	Rye - Tenterden via Wittersham, Smallhythe *Mondays to Fridays*	PK0000290/7040
			Temporary cover for summer period on Mondays to Fridays only following withdrawal from the service by White-Hide (Rye Coaches), Rye. On Saturdays, Fuggles, Benenden operated the service before and after 9 April 1994. Subsequently the whole service on Mondays to Saturdays passed to Rodemark (Autopoint), Herstmonceux under ESCC contract, replacing both Rambler and Fuggles.	
313	26/04/2015	24/09/2018	Northiam (Coppards Lane) - Rye(Rail Station) via Beckley, Peasmarsh *Schooldays*	PK0003587/21
814	27/05/1986		Crowhurst (Green Street Corner) - Bexhill (Marina) via Telham, Battle, Catsfield, Ninfield, Sidley *Schooldays*	K4954/12
314	26/10/1986		Renumbered from 814 to 314	
28	29/10/1990	30/10/1994	Renumbered from 314 to 28 with revised timetable, *Monday to Friday mornings with additional journeys on schooldays* between Battle and Ninfield.	PK0000290/1915
328	31/10/1994	06/07/2001	Rambler journey renumbered to 328. Battle (Marley Gardens) - Claverham College (single journey) *Schooldays mornings*	PK0000290/7286
	27/09/1998	06/07/2001	Crowhurst journeys re-gained (all now as 328, operating to and from Crowhurst, Green Street) including early morning journey *Mondays to Fridays* to Bexhill Marina (via Claverham College on schooldays) and other journeys *Schooldays* to Ninfield and Bexhill Sixth Form College.	PK0000290/8350
			The reason for separating service 328 into two concurrent registrations from 2002 is unclear. Bexhill 6th Form College moved from Turkey Road, Sidley to Penland Road, Bexhill in September 2004, and it appears that a new journey on service 360 (see below) was introduced under this registration.	
	02/09/2002	29/10/2006	Crowhurst - Bexhill Marina *Schooldays*	PK0003587/7
	04/11/2002	29/07/2011	Battle (Marley Gardens) - Claverham School *Schooldays*	PK0003587/9
	13/11/2006	29/07/2011	Battle - Bexhill via Catsfield, Ninfield, Sidley *Schooldays*	PK0003587/12
342	26/04/2015	24/09/2018	Westfield School - Rye via Brede, Broad Oak and Udimore *Schooldays*	PK0003587/20
344 345	See also 44 & 45 above			
345	05/09/2012	25/04/2015	Fairlight - Rye via Winchelsea Beach	PK0003587/17
347	28/10/2002	29/10/2006	Pett (Chick Hill) - Conquest Hospital via Guestling, Ore, West Hill, Hastings, Silverhill *Mondays to Fridays*	PK0003587/2
355	25/04/2015	24/09/2018	Netherfield (Darvel Down) - Battle (Claverham College) *Schooldays*	PK0003587/18
356	12/04/2015	24/09/2018	Little Common - Battle (Claverham College) via Hooe, Catsfield *Schooldays*	PK0003587/19

357	05/09/2002	29/07/2011	Ore - Bexhill (St Richard's School) via Hastings, St Leonards, Silverhill, Blackman Avenue, Wishing Tree, Glyne Gap *Schooldays*	PK0003587/1
860	27/05/1986	25/10/1986	Burwash (High Street) - Bexhill Sixth Form College via Etchingham, Hurst Green, Roberstbridge, Sedlescombe, Westfield, Harrow Junction, Hollington, Wishing Tree, Harley Shute, St Mary Magdalene School, Sidley *Schooldays*	K4954/13
360	26/10/1986	30/10/1994	Renumbered 360. Participation in 360 suspended after 30/10/1994 but registration continued for 361 only	PK0000290/1916
	26/09/1996	06/07/2001	Operation of certain journeys numbered 360 resumed (route as shown below)	PK0000290/7834
	Bexhill 6th Form College moved from Turkey Road, Sidley to Penland Road, Bexhill in September 2004.			
	(09/07/2001)		Burwash (High Street) - Bexhill Sixth Form College via Etchingham, Hurst Green, Robertsbridge, Sedlescombe, Harrow Junction, Wishing Tree, Harley Shute, St Mary Magdalene School, Sidley *Schooldays*	PK0003587/10
	09/09/2004		Revised timetable with additional journey to provide relief capacity for Stagecoach services 358/359.	
	16/04/2012	24/09/2018	Etchingham (Rail Station) - Bexhill Sixth Form College via Hurst Green, Robertsbridge, Sedlescombe, Harrow Junction, Silverhill, St Leonards *Schooldays*	
361	29/10/1990		Relief short working between Westfield and Bexhill Sixth Form College extended to start at Sedlescombe (Pestalozzi Village) and renumbered 361.	PK0000290/1916
	08/04/1991		Pestalozzi Village to Westfield section of 361 withdrawn	
	05/09/1994	30/10/1994	361 extended from Westfield via Brede to start at Broad Oak	
	30/10/1994	27/09/1998	by 5/98, 361 extended from Broad Oak via Northiam to start at Beckley (Rose & Crown), but contract then transferred to Campbell (J&H Coaches), Rye from 27/9/98	PK0000290/7185
361	03/09/2008		Operation of 361 resumed, but now from Playden to Bexhill Sixth Form College via Peasmarsh, Beckley, Northiam, Broad Oak, Brede, Westfield, St Leonards *Schooldays*	PK0003587/14
	16/04/2012	24/09/2018	Curtailed to start from Peasmarsh and via Beckley, Northiam, Broad Oak, Brede, Westfield, The Ridge West, Blackman Avenue, Harley Shute Road *Schooldays*	
362	03/09/2008	14/04/2012	Rye Harbour - Bexhill Sixth Form College via Udimore, Broad Oak, Sedlescombe, Hollington, St Leonards *Schooldays*	PK0003587/13
375	30/09/1991	30/10/1994	Bexhill 6th Form College - Battle (Abbey) via Harley Shute, Crowhurst, Telham (afternoon journey only) *Schooldays*	PK0000290/6033
380	09/01/1995		Beckley (Rose & Crown) - Robertsbridge College via Northiam, Broad Oak, Sedlescombe *Schooldays*	PK0000290/7303
	02/09/1996		Revised timetable autumn and winter and retain existing timetable for summer term only; diverted between Northiam and Robertsbridge direct via Horns Cross, Staplehurst, Cripps Corner and Johns Cross.	
	24/10/1996		Extended from Broad Oak to Brede (Red Lion)	
	05/09/1997		Revised timetable to match 382 timings in Northiam; second vehicle renumbered 381 and no longer to serve Mountfield	
	03/11/1997		Extended to Westfield Church	
	14/11/1997	06/07/2001	380 terminus reverted to Beckley (381 extended to Westfield in its place)	
	(09/07/2001)	29/07/2011	Beckley - Robertsbridge College via Northiam (no longer operated by Rambler after July 2011)	PK0003587/6
381	05/09/1997		Revised timetable to match 382 timings in Northiam; second vehicle renumbered 381 and no longer to serve Mountfield	PK0000290/7303
	14/11/1997	06/07/2001	Extended to Westfield Church to replace 380	
	(09/07/2001)	29/07/2011	Westfield - Robertsbridge College via Brede, Broad Oak, Cripp's Corner, Sedlescombe, Whatlington (no longer operated by Rambler after July 2011)	PK0003587/6
381	19/09/2017	24/09/2018	Westfield School - Robertsbridge College	PK0003587/22
382	12/09/1997	06/07/2001	Northiam - Robertsbridge College	PK0000290/8113
	(09/07/2001)	29/07/2011	Brede - Robertsbridge College via Broad Oak, Mountfield	PK0003587/4
	05/09/2011	24/09/2018	Northiam (Coppards Lane) - Robertsbridge College via Broad Oak, Brede, Westfield	PK0003587/15
383	03/09/1998	06/07/2001	Peasmarsh - Robertsbridge College via Northiam	PK0000290/8349
	(09/07/2001)	29/07/2011		PK0003587/5
	05/09/2011	24/09/2018		PK0003587/16
384	02/11/1998	06/01/1999	Hastings (Beauport Park) - Robertsbridge College via Battle, John's Cross *Schooldays only*	PK0000290/8416

Appendix 7

Service Vans and Breakdown Trucks

Dick Rowland's only form of personal transport was a car purchased in 1937, a Standard Nine (CLW 404), in use up until the Second World War and then carefully stored away until peacetime resumed. After further use the car was eventually broken up in his Battle Road garage around 1954. After this he never had another car, just the use of a bicycle or public transport, the need of a car or van was not deemed necessary.

By the early 1970's with the fleet of coaches gradually expanding, the need for a service van would now be justified in order to perform a verity of duties from collecting spare parts to transporting the advertising boards from the coach stand and in later years for driver transfers. A number of vans have been owned over the years including Mini-vans and various models of Vauxhall including Viva, Chevette, Astra and more recently a Combo.

The village of Crowhurst has seen a number of incidents over the years due to the narrow and winding country lanes that access it. Seen here is the 1976 Bedford YMT Plaxton Supreme (TAP 461R, originally OTX 41R) that was involved in an unfortunate incident with a motorist who did not see its oncoming presence until it was too late to safely stop. The coach was soon repaired and back in service again. (Colin Rowland)

With John Goodwin's involvement in not only the Rambler Coaches business, he also traded separately as 'The Van Specialist'. One particularly memorable deal would see John acquire fifty mini pick-up vans in varying conditions for resale with one example finding its way into Rambler livery. The notion of owning a break down truck came about around 1981 as the fleet by now was achieving higher annual mileages than in earlier years, so should an unforeseen breakdown occur, in many cases it would be easier to recover the stricken coach for repairs to take place at the premises, with all equipment required available rather than

Mrs Muriel Rowland smartly dressed in attractive green attire, stands with the company Mini pick-up van which was one of fifty examples purchased by John Goodwin. The registration was thought to be in the 'CNY. . .C' series. C1970's. (Colin Rowland)

Minivan (CPM 164K) looks resplendent in Rambler Coaches livery. (Colin Rowland)

Seen at Breeds Place is a Vauxhall Viva (PDY 510K) assisting in advertising duties with a colourful selection of destinations on offer. (Colin Rowland)

attempting repairs on the side of a road, in sometimes less than ideal conditions. The first vehicle owned was a Bedford TK (OBP 310J) that had come from local company VG and was purchased through one of their employees at the time Brian Gain. (Brian would later go on to purchase the business of Cooks Coaches in Westfield). To make the truck suitable for its new role as a breakdown vehicle it was dispatched to local engineer Dennis Wilson (after Colin and John had removed its body to become a store at the depot) to have its chassis shortened for its new role. Around this time trade number plates were obtained (309 DY). These were normally allocated to motor dealers and vehicle testers, used for recovery and general company use, although as they could not be issued to a coach operator, an application under the name Rambler Recovery was granted, being retained up until 2017.

The Bedford TK would be replaced in time by Coombs Motors 1980 Bedford TM (4400) breakdown truck (JUM 787V) rated at some 44

Mrs Rowland is photographed in the driving seat of the company
Vauxhall Chevette van (RJK 211S) (Colin Rowland)

tonnes. With Coombs having at the time run into financial difficulties the TM was purchased for a respectable £2,000. Colin had hankered after this truck for some time as he liked the crane it was fitted with and the A-frame for the ease of lifting and towing vehicles. Powered by a Cummins big cam 14 litre straight six-cylinder engine it was in Colins words 'an ideal vehicle'. It had a Storno radio fitted for direct communication when on the road.

A Volvo F88 six-wheeler was later acquired (Q49 ANJ), although not painted into fleet colours, it was eventually sold on local commercial mechanic Mark Creasy in Rye Harbour. Changes to the licensing system dictated that recovery vehicles could no longer be used displaying trade plates, so the costs of upkeep for what in essence was a lightly used vehicle became less attractive.

With modifications including the fitment of a towing crane and re-paint into fleet livery, we find Bedford TK (OBP 310J) at West Ridge Manor. (Derek Jones)

Captured outside the side entrance of Coombs Motors in Terrace Road in St Leonards on Sea is Bedford TM (JUM 787V) having arrived with Cummins powered Bedford YMT Plaxton Supreme (NCF 715) in tow. (Stephen Dine)

Mechanic Mick Robinson is seen with traffic office manager
Mark Birch and driver John Reid at Claverham Community
College in Battle on 23rd June 2015. (Stephen Dine)

Amongst the long serving members of the Rambler Coaches team are Ivan
Lusted (centre) with his sons Phil and Antony, who between them have
given over eighty years of service to the company. (Colin Rowland)

Appendix 8

Interesting Bedfords

You will have read about the affinity between Rambler Coaches and the commercial vehicle manufacturer Bedford, that in April 1931 had started production of vehicles at the Luton based factory of its owner, Vauxhall cars. In the company's heyday much of its advertising material stated 'You see them everywhere' which was a particularly accurate statement in the world of coaches, buses, trucks and vans around the UK and indeed the most parts of the world, in both home and export markets and with extensive use by the armed forces.

In Rambler's world of coaches, some ninety nine Bedfords have been operated over fifty four years from May 1950, with the last operational coach being sold in July 2004. A number of examples have been retained in preservation since by Colin Rowland personally. The Bedford chassis types owned have ranged from pre-war examples of WLB models dating from 1932 and 1935, OB models from the 1940's and numerous others including SBG, SB3, SB5 (NJM), VAM5, VAM14, VAM70, VAL14, VAL70 (WRQ), VAS5 (PJK), J2, CF, YRT, YRQ, YMT, YLQ, JJL, YNT,

YNV until the close of Bedford production, with the last being two 8m YMP models (known unofficially to many as the YMPS) arriving new in 1987.

The Bedford WLBs owned have been in preservation rather than in earlier commercial use by the company. The first of these was (NG 2414) with Economy 20 seat bus body, new in April 1932 to Jarvis of Swaffham in Norfolk. In August 1941 it was noted with Theobald of Long Melford, giving good service until withdrawn in March 1950 where it was converted into a static caravan, remaining in this guise until being saved for preservation in early 1989. John Goodwin discovered the bus was available for sale in May 1996 and made a purchase based on viewing it from a black and white photograph taken thirty five years before, in what was considered its final role, complete with a makeshift tin roof over it for protection from the elements. The challenge of restoration work to return it back to a bus began when it arrived on the back of a lorry, the vehicle still sporting a sink and gas mantle inside from its last use as a home. Its body was carefully separated from the chassis for shot blasting and painting whilst work on the body commenced with Colin and his cousin Norman French replacing the floor. Norman's son Jason made new upright body supports that he individually shaped and fitted in turn. An effort to conserve as much of the old fabric of the vehicle was maintained when possible. Suitable interior seats were sourced from preservationist Eric Gravelling as the original ones had long since gone. It would eventually receive a livery of cream with green relief and signwriting on the rear in the same style as had been applied to Dick Rowland's BAT Cruiser coach in the 1940's from a surviving photograph as reference. John's vision was to have it running for him to be able to enjoy driving it in the year 2000, something sadly he would not be able to achieve.

Photographed on 2nd September 1961, the Bedford WLB (NG 2414) had by now been in its static role for a number of years. The latter addition of a tin roof over the top of the bus had no doubt assisted to slow down its gradual deterioration. (G R Mills – Colin Rowland collection)

Twelve years later the opportunity arose to buy another Bedford WLB, this time with attractive 20 seat Duple coachwork (CMG 30). Registered in June 1935 it was new to T E Garner of Ealing, London W5. Requisitioned by the Ministry of Supply in World War Two, its registration was changed and in February 1943 it was sold to an E Saunders in Devon, bearing the registration JTA 608. Information after this time is scarce although by 1964 the coach was now with preservationists until 1966 when it was acquired by the coach dealership E J Baker who within months sold it on to an owner in Somerset, now being reunited with its original registration. Latterly thought to have been out of use for around twenty five years. Colin received a call from Julian Brown at

Wealden PSV to discuss a valuation he had been asked to provide for the WLB coach and a lorry. The vehicles were part of a larger collection that were dry stored and after six months of discussion it was purchased. A number of minor jobs were required in order to re-commission it for use with the original engine being exchanged for a later Bedford 214 petrol unit, as the former engine (though itself retained) had a crack in its block. The restored bus has been used and enjoyed by Colin in preservation on numerous occasions since.

1932 Bedford WLB (NG 2414) with Economy bus body is seen at West Ridge Manor on the rare occasion of being seen in the public gaze at the Rambler Coaches 90th anniversary event. (Stephen Dine)

In the capable hands of Ivan Lusted, 1935 Bedford WLB with 20 seat Duple coachwork (CMG 30) is seen in the grounds of the Powdermills Hotel near to Battle in August 2016 on the occasion of the marriage of Miss Hannah Rowland to Mr Tom Foster. (Stephen Dine)

The sole Bedford JJL operated was by far the rarest vehicle to join the Rambler Coaches fleet and the following information has been recorded to provide some background on this interesting concept.

This futuristic small bus design was first exhibited as a mock-up without running units at the 1976 Commercial Motor Show in London, to provide a visual example of the development of the project as a low floor midi-bus. Production started with four examples being built in 1978, showing promise as a new contender for the small bus market, although it did not succeed into volume sales that had been anticipated.

Moving forward to October 1982, John had been reading the Exchange & Mart newspaper and came across an advert with a Bedford for sale noted as 'with the engine in the rear and suitable for making into a motor home'. Pondering the vehicles age Colin immediately thought it must be a Bedford JJL. John called the vendor in Peterborough, who was evidently keen to sell the bus and made the long journey to Hastings the following day for it to be viewed. A deal was struck and in discussion it transpired the vendor was employed by coach builder Marshall, and had acquired the bus for conversion into a caravan, but had had second thoughts so decided to resell it.

It also emerged that Marshall had just rebuilt the front end of the vehicle after serious accident damage whilst on loan to Maidstone Borough Council. Although built with Bedford mechanical components, the concept for what was to become the JJL was originally conceived by Marshall with the intention to use Leyland components. However Leyland declined to participate in the project on the terms proposed, so General Motors, Bedford's owners, were called upon instead. The vehicle was fitted with the trusted and well proven 330ci six-cylinder diesel engine fitted transversely in the rear. The drive was taken up via an Allison automatic gearbox by a Morse chain drive system that ran in an oil bath to ensure constant lubrication, which worked very reliably. This bus had been first used as a demonstrator and was on display at the 1979 Scottish Commercial Motor Show.

Carrying a livery of white and brown relief which was retained, it was duly signwritten with 'Rambler Holiday Tours' advertising and used on local routes with some private hire bookings as it had a tachograph fitted. It normally operated a regular contract, although when this came to an end the bus was advertised for sale. Colin and John were aware that Bournemouth Transport had already tried out the only other three JJL's built with a view to operating one on a particular service it would be well suited for, although the other examples had been rejected having had serious chassis frame fractures on their front ends. This vehicle, having been extensively repaired at Marshall, was now free of such issues. A sale 'circular' was sent to Bournemouth Transport (with the JJL included in it) in April 1983 and the following morning a request came back to take the bus to Bournemouth for an inspection. John made the long journey west at the bus's maximum speed of 45 mph and a successful deal was concluded.

After time in service with Bournemouth Transport, in March 1988 it passed to David Brown's AWD business, the last incarnation of the company that had by now bought the Bedford marque and the JJL was then used as a staff bus. AWD would pass in ownership to Marshall, and by now the JJL with its future hanging in the balance, was sold to John Holloway for intended use as an aid relief vehicle to Kosovo for the

Heading down Junction Road near to the Rambler Coaches premises in April 1994 is the immaculately turned out Bedford JJL Marshall (HKX 553V) working on the route 66 towards Hastings Town Centre. (Terry Blackman)

war effort there. However this plan was abandoned on learning more about the spare parts needed for the long journey across Europe and in view of the vehicle's rarity, it was decided against the idea. It was spotted for sale by Colin at the 'Showbus' event staged at Duxford and would be purchased again, ten years after its previous and somewhat shorter stay in the fleet, now wearing the bright yellow livery of Bournemouth Transport. Soon expertly repainted by John into traditional livery (which suited it very well) it was once more put to work on service 312 between Rye and Tenterden.

A call was received from a representative of Marshall (now under new ownership) who were keen to view the JJL in order to make a study of the vehicle's construction. Marshall was by now also the owners of the Bedford name too. An arrangement was made for the bus to be loaned so their design team could technically understand the vehicle closely and look at

Numerous examples of the Bedford YMT model have been owned over the years, although two less common combinations are found together at West Ridge Manor in December 1991 (on the left) Caetano bodied (AAL 521A) with Silverdale / Van Hool 300 line (NDC 284W). (Stephen Dine)

its entire construction and build, with a new Marshall bodied Dennis Dart loaned in its place. A bus was eventually launched by Marshall to compete with other types now entering this market, with similarities being noted to the JJL although marketed as the Marshall Minibus rather than using the Bedford name. The JJL returned to Rambler and continued operating until the 312 service contract expired. An approach had been made by an operator in Peterborough who wanted to buy the vehicle with the intention to preserve it and operate it on occasions. With Colin and John's blessing, when sold it remained in Rambler livery, with the new owner naming himself 'Rambler of Peterborough'. After the business had ceased trading, it passed to another operator in the same area and was repainted into the livery it had when new as a demonstrator model. In time it would be sold on again, converted into a partial caravan and taken to rally events until changing hands in 2018. It is thought to still be in preservation (2023) as a bus.

Appendix 9

Bedford re-power...
the Cummins project

A number of UK coach businesses were considering an option marketed in the late 1980's by Coombs Motors in St Leonards on Sea, to offer a re-power package on the popular mid-life Bedford YMT chassis with an alternative new Cummins engine. The newer generation Cummins unit offered increased fuel economy and additional power compared to the more traditional standard Bedford 8.2 litre 500 non-turbo diesel unit, should an operator be looking to replace or rebuild their then current engine. Something not so well known was the direct involvement of Rambler Coaches in this project.

One of the then current fleet, a Bedford YMT Plaxton Supreme (VWK 7S) had been treated to a replacement Bedford engine when the manufacturer themselves latterly started providing an in-house service of reconditioning engines. Within days of the fitment this unit proved to be no good, so another replacement engine was fitted. In a short space of time the coach was undertaking a tour of the Lake District when further issues happened, this time the driver took the coach to the local main dealer and yet another engine had to be fitted as a matter of urgency, the warranty to be taken up by Bedford.

Colin had read an article in the trade press about a Bedford TL truck that had had a Cummins B series engine fitted transforming its running and performance and the idea had stuck with him. Discussions between Colin and Alan Marchant at Coombs Motors centred round the proposal of whether an alternative engine could be trialled out for coach application. DAF were contacted but did not seem interested in the idea although Cummins were much more receptive to the possibilities. John Broadway, a Cummins representative, sourced a brand-new Cummins 6 BTA unit with after cooler for the project. Julian Brown from Wealden PSV at nearby Five Oak Green was contacted to source a Bedford chassis for the experimental platform to build a test bed on how both engine and chassis compatibility would be made. Julian did have a suitable Bedford YRT chassis available so the project could now start to take shape. However, when it arrived at Rambler's premises by tow truck there was one initial problem. . .. the Duple Dominant coachwork was still sitting on it! Two weeks later and two skips full of scrap Colin and Alan had cut the body to pieces for removal and they finally had a bare rolling chassis in order to assess how they could now move forward with this project.

Measurements quickly showed that the 5.9 litre Cummins engine was shorter in length in comparison to the 8.2 litre Bedford unit. Colin wanted to keep the same gearbox coupled to the original engine, as the remit would be keeping things as straightforward as possible, without the need to make up numbers of bespoke parts or different additions. The original front engine mountings could be used with new adaptor

With dismantling well underway, Alan Marchant (left) and Colin
Rowland, are evidently adhering to Health and Safety guidelines as
the Duple coachwork is gradually dismantled for its Bedford chassis
to be used on the Cummins repower project. (Colin Rowland)

plates made up by a local fabricator who also made a one foot long metal
tunnel that would bridge the larger gap between the front of the engine
and the radiator unit for the fan cooling. With the engine fitted and work
successful some two months later, a representative of Cummins came to
assess it, the only stipulation being that a new radiator should be fitted
to satisfy a two-year warranty but was more than happy with the progress
made with the only minor chassis modifications needed. The next stage
was to find a complete donor coach, to transfer the running components
into an operational vehicle. David Waterman from Yeates in Salisbury
was contacted and a suitable 1976 Bedford YMT Plaxton Supreme
Express was purchased. Registered OTX 41R (and later re-registered by

Rambler as 419 CLB then TAP 461R) it had at some stage been fitted with a non-standard Leyland 401 engine. In the September of 1987 the coach was towed back to St Leonards on Sea by the Coombs Motors tow truck and all components were transferred from the test bed chassis to what would become the actual operational coach.

The Cummins engine was originally developed with its torque at higher engine revs so the use of 1st gear was needed on pulling away so the clutch would not be burnt out. An original Bedford engine could normally be driven by using 2nd gear for pulling away with 1st gear considered more of a crawler gear for use on a slightly uphill incline. When pulling away from stationary, on its first outing Colin was impressed with having such a different driving experience.

On the first road test heading out of town and the long incline and by-pass on the A21 near to Sevenoaks not far away from the M25 motorway, with the engine revs kept up the coach's performance was remarkably different with its extra turbo-charged power of 180 bhp compared to the original unit's 150 bhp normally aspirated range. The coach now weighed 160kg less than before and was measured in reporting around 13.5 mpg on mixed use (even up to 15 mpg on a long run) in comparison to the Bedford unit at around 10 mpg on the same mixed test.

One minor thing that Colin wasn't comfortable with was that the new Cummins engine oil sump seemed to sit rather low to the ground when the engine was fitted in the chassis, although there were no issues with it grounding, it was indeed low in clearance to the road. This was eventually improved when Cummins spoke with their marine application department, who were using the same power unit with a different shaped oil sump cast in aluminium for use in boats, so this fitment was now an improvement for the PSV application. The sumps did not have baffles in so oil pressure could be an issue, as unlike boats that are never still in the sea, coaches tend to run on even roads, so baffles were put in for the oil feed pipe which was then later used for Marine application too. With the project considered a success, Coombs Motors now marketed the repower package to operators. This could be completed in a respectable seven working days, with advertising in the trade press as the 'Bedford YMT repower specialists'. Orders soon came in to take up this option with the new engine conversion costing £5,500 plus VAT, comparing favourably to fitting a standard *reconditioned* GMX unit from Bedford at £3,250 minus ancillaries. A second coach was now repowered, this time a 1980 Bedford YMT Plaxton Supreme (JJF 880V) later registered

Much to the amusement of its passengers the Cummins B series powered Bedford YMT Plaxton Supreme (SDY 788) is photographed at Pease Pottage Services on 1st June 1988, its driver was Frank Young. (Derek Jones)

SDY 788. Fitted with its new Cummins unit in March 1988 it was on display at that years Brighton Coach Rally, demonstrating the virtues of this alternative re-power package available through Coombs Motors. A full road test was featured in the trade magazine Coachmart, where operators were gaining interest in the repower package that had never previously been thought about. Within a short space of time forty five conversions had been undertaken with another company, United Counties Engineering, having seen the success of the Rambler/Coombs project, now offering the same service and reported at one stage to have already undertaken twenty two conversions themselves.

The conversion work at Coombs Motors was in itself a challenge due to space at their premises. The Western Road site was normally full of customers vehicles, as well as their Bedford Commercial vehicle activities, the building also housed a Vauxhall showroom, parts department and used cars sales. It was not unknown that two coaches could be squeezed in their sub-terranean lower workshops with coaches put onto jacks at the rear in order to turn them in position to work on once the engine transplants were underway. Mechanics such as Derek Wapples, Gordon Green, Steve Wallis and Neil Banks were amongst those mechanics tasked with the jobs.

Alan Marchant soon discussed with Colin the idea of now trying out the more powerful Cummins C series engine as a potential conversion option. No engines could be found in the UK but one was tracked down by John Broadway in Germany, in use with a training school but was brought back to the UK starting the project off. It had no fuel injection pump, although one was sourced with assistance of Dennis Specialist Vehicles in Guildford, as the then new Dennis Javelin chassis used in their range for bodying as coaches used the same Cummins 6CTA engine which was standard in the Javelin chassis. A suitable donor coach was found in May 1988 from Julian Brown at Wealden PSV, another Bedford YMT Plaxton Supreme IV (YEB 105T) later registered as NCF 715. This time without an engine or gearbox, a new ZF 6 speed overdrive gearbox was purchased to marry up with the C series engine. Cummins took this engine to their facility at Darlington to fit it on their Dyno testing machine to check its performance and set up. With adjustments and tweaks this 8.2 litre engine returned an impressive 225 bhp for this straight turbo-charged non-aftercooler engine. Once the work was completed in April 1989, the coach surpassed itself with outstanding performance, returning fuel consumption figures estimated at over 16 mpg.

With the rolling Bedford chassis inside the depot at West Ridge Manor, the brand-new Cummins C Series engine is in place for evaluation on how it will be mounted in the chassis. (Colin Rowland)

Coombs Motors could also offer the option of having a C series engine as a repower package at some £13,800 including a new ZF gearbox for a YMT chassis, £11,500 on a YNT. There was debate from Cummins on the suitability of the air suspended YNV chassis being suitable as the compressor was felt to not be suitable for keeping up with supplying air to the suspension air bags. The B series was still available at a cost of £6,500.

In a Coachmart Trade magazine feature on 4th January 1990, a favourable road test report on the performance of the C series engine in the Bedford YMT followed. A comment from Alan Marchant, that he didn't feel the C series was a viable proposition at this stage, as the idea could easily be picked up by another company and there were concerns about availability of the American built C series engine for this type of work. A representative from Cummins Diesel, Eddie Humphries, stated

Photographed when on a road test report for trade magazine Coachmart, just after receiving its Cummins C series engine, is Bedford YMT Plaxton Supreme IV (YEB 105T). (Coachmart – Colin Rowland collection)

Driver Barry Cannelle stands with the immaculately presented Bedford YMT
Plaxton Supreme IV with Cummins C Series engine, now re-registered as
NCF 715 at Claverham Community College, Battle in 1991. (Stephen Dine)

that Cummins was prepared to proceed if there was sufficient interest,
and UK production was scheduled to start at the Darlington plant on
January 2nd'. The B series was acknowledged in the road test report as
the much cheaper alternative for operators and there was a prospect that
the engine could be uprated to 210 bhp.

As a footnote, mention was made at the time that it was hoped
Cummins might be successful in its bid to supply London Transport
with its C series engine to repower its ageing but hugely successful
Routemaster buses still in operation. Alan Marchant was approached to
undertake the first conversion although he declined in part due to the
practicalities of the Coombs Motors site not suitable to accommodate
double deck buses. Another company did proceed with the engineering
project and the repower proved to be a success, extending the operating

lives of this great British icon of public transport for a number of further years in service.

Colin recalled with a smile the occasion when driving the C series coach on the M25 motorway with a full complement of passengers on board. Up ahead of him a bevy of contemporary heavyweight coaches noted as a DAF, Leyland Tiger and Volvo were all making good progress on their respective journeys. Just a few miles ahead on a long uphill section, Colin overtook all three of the coaches at maximum permitted speed, the only indication for the other coach drivers to see what had just passed them being a long mud flap on the rear with the words 'Bedford' on it. This coach later went on to join the fleet of 'On A Mission' and some years later at the end of its commercial service life was thought to have finally become a caravan in Scotland.

One must remember that the Cummins option was, at the time, considered by coach operators an improvement for the normally aspirated Bedford engine. Many of the vehicles that had the conversion were still being used on long distance work, not suggesting that the Bedford unit was inferior in its design or reliability. In many ways the Cummins re-power idea for the later Bedford YNT model was not seen as such an attractive option, as Bedford's own 500 turbo engines were more than adequate in power and performance in their own right. Bedford's position in the coach and bus market had become greatly diminished due to much competition from other manufacturers mainly from overseas. For example, in 1980 some 905 chassis had been delivered for UK operators, in 1984 (on a high year) it was 356, but by 1988, which proved to be the company's final year of production the number had sadly been a final 45. It was a sad decision by a manufacturer whose products had built so many transport business's. As their advertising once quite correctly stated 'Bedford – you see them everywhere'.

Appendix 10

Coaches for Export

It is not uncommon for coaches and buses to move around large parts of the country after sale by their original operator. Some vehicles are exported overseas to continue in use as a PSV, sometimes thousands of miles away from where they were first in use. A small number of the Rambler Coaches fleet have been exported, the first in March 1995, when a 1950 Bedford OB Duple Vista (LYC 731) joined the Connemara Bus fleet in Moycullen, County Galway in Ireland. Reregistered as ZV 1460 it would enjoy further service before eventually returning to Express Motors of Penygroes in Wales by early 2004, regaining its original registration.

In February 2017 a further member of the fleet to leave for Ireland was Mercedes Benz 1020 Optare Solera (V222 JDY) new to the company in November 1999, joining the Ferry Link operation at Galway.

A number of the fleet have been exported to the Island of Malta through Julian Brown of Wealden PSV Sales. The first coach being the 1985 Volvo B10M-56 Plaxton Paramount 3500 (B191 XJD, NDY 820,

Seen on the day Bedford OB Duple Vista (LYC 731) was soon to depart with its new owners to Ireland, John and Colin stand for a group photograph with the destination display already bearing its new owners name. (Colin Rowland)

B367 RHC) with rare 11 metre long coachwork in May 1991, to join local operator, Emmanuel Cardona of Mosta, then moving to the fleet of Arthur & John's on the Island as LCY 910. In March 2005 a 1995 Volvo B10M-62 Van Hool T8 (N222 EDY) that had been purchased new was exported to join the fleet of Cancu Garage (Supreme Travel) of Zejtun and in December 2002 the same company, owned by Reno Abela, would purchase a Bedford YMT Wadham Stringer bus (C302 RRX). It was never actually licensed for general passenger use in Malta, being imported for use on a contract within the Freeport "dockside". If it needed to return to Zejtun it did so on the Maltese equivalent of trade plates (Trial Run Plates). Buses used within the Freeport were noted to get pretty battered and most ended their days in some accident or other.

Further vehicles would leave UK shores for Malta, with both Volvo B10M-62 Berkhof Axial 50 coachwork (R222 VDY – becoming ZPY 100) and Scania K124 Van Hool Alizee T9 (W222 KDY becoming BPY 012) both arriving in the November of 2006 into the fleets of Zarb and Cancu Garage (Supreme Travel) respectively. A final purchase by Cancu Garage of a Rambler vehicle would be slightly more unusual in being a 1950 Austin CXB with Plaxton 29 seat coachwork (FCO 314) that had been purchased by Colin personally in April 2004. After export to Malta in March 2007 it would now gain the Maltese registration LCY 003 (and later LXY 003) being used for local tours on the Island. It was still in use in 2023, having gained a replacement diesel engine for improved fuel economy and ease of having continuous regular operation.

Both Julian Brown of Wealden PSV Sales (on the left) and Colin Rowland are photographed when delivering a former Rambler Volvo B10M-62 Van Hool (N222 EDY) on the long overland trip to Malta. (Colin Rowland)

Seen in Malta in March 2005 having just arrived from the UK and now in the ownership of local operator Cancu Supreme of Zejtun, is Volvo B10M-62 Van Hool T8. Formerly N222 EDY. It briefly received the UK registration N625 PYJ before allocation of Maltese registration number BCY 902. Remaining in Rambler livery with Supreme fleet names until taken out of service in 2017, it received a full body and frame rebuild, re-entering service by 2020 in the operators white based livery, still in use in 2023. (Colin Rowland)

The first Rambler coach to be exported to Malta was the 1985 Volvo B10M-56 Plaxton Paramount 3500 (B191 XJD/ NDY 820/ B367 RHC) with rare 11 metre long coachwork in May 1991, first to Emmanuel Cardona of Mosta, then moving to the fleet of Arthur & John's Garage in 1999 as LCY 910. It has enjoyed a long time in operation on the island until withdrawn in late 2020, still in immaculate condition, as it had finally reached the thirty-five year age limit now in place for coaches operating there. It was still owned by the company in 2023. (Richard Stedall)

The 1950 Austin CXB Plaxton (FCO 314) was acquired by Colin Rowland from Hickmott, Kingsnorth, Kent in April 2004, being sold to Cancu Supreme, Zejtun in March 2007. Initially registered LCY 003, it became LXY 003 in 2015, up until 2021 retaining its cream with green band livery it had carried for many years. Between 2021 and 2022 it underwent a thorough rebuild appearing in a bright light green base livery, still with a dark green stripe. It has retained its original interior, other than a number of Maltese-style sliding side windows that have been fitted. Its petrol engine has now been replaced with a Perkins diesel unit. (Richard Stedall).

Still giving sterling service at twenty five years of age to local operator Zarb when seen at Valetta Docks on 21st April 2023 is the former Rambler Coaches Volvo B10M-62 Berkhof Axial 50 (R222 VDY) which since November 2006 has been registered in Malta as ZPY 100. (Joshua Dine)

Appendix 11

Fleet list

Firstly, I would like to thank Derek Jones for his huge amount of time of the large task in checking, amending and verifying Colin Rowland's own fleet list of vehicles operated, to Paul Green, Bob Cook and the late David Padgham for their years of research into the earlier years of operation. One must remember that details recorded by companies first hand on the vehicles they operate can sometimes differ from information shared amongst enthusiast circles.

Every effort has been made to ensure accuracy within this fleet list although with a large number of coaches operated in later years, many treated to different personalised registrations within their time of ownership, some information may differ from what is recorded in other publications.

Especially for Dick Rowland's early years of operation, tracing details of vehicles has been challenging for David, Derek and Bob over their years of research. For example, between the ownership of a Lancia (TT 6226) purchased in August 1932 and the next recorded coach, a

Passing along Marina, St Leonards on Sea on 8th March 1986 is Bedford
OB Duple Vista (LYC 731) on the occasion of the Rambler Coaches
hosted S.E.C.O.A Coaching Weekend staged locally. This nicely
captured image shows off its sleek lines to its best. (Derek Jones)

Star Flyer, a further coach or charabanc, possibly a Bean, may have been
purchased, although records with enough information to confirm this
have as yet eluded us.

The fleet numbering system has not continued in sequence, nor has it
allocated a unique number for each coach operated over the decades. As
vehicles have been sold and newer stock would arrive, the previous fleet
number could be reused in its place. Dick generally reused the numbers
from 1 to 3 as coaches were sold and replaced with newer stock, as up
until 1954 the maximum of three vehicles had been the largest number
operated. With the arrival of the then new Bedford SB (GDY 888) at this
time it became number 4, and the numbers 5 to 7 would first be used
between 1960 and 1966. When Bedford VAM (DDY 250D) arrived in

1966 just after Dick's death, he had already specified number 8 on its build sheet for the Plaxton signwriter, so the coach duly arrived as per his instructions.

The fleet numbering system has seen numbers reused or a higher number issued as the fleet increased in size at any one time. The highest official fleet number used by 2018 had been 41 in 2010. The only exception to this was Ford R1114 Plaxton Paramount (ETA 101Y) which came into stock for just two months in 1998 and was given the fleet number 50 because of its expected temporary stay in the fleet. The number 13 has never been used for reasons of traditional superstition, being considered unlucky, although with typical tongue in cheek humour it would be allocated to the company breakdown trucks as their dedicated lucky number.

RAMBLER COACHES

Recorded ownership

Albert George White (1926-1928)

Richard George Rowland from April 1928

Richard George Rowland & Bertram Bernard Greenslade by February 1935 (E&T licence referenced K199)
   (Greenslade remained a partner in 1939 but left the business at an unknown subsequent date)

R G Rowland as sole trader again by April 1948 (K199)

Richard George Rowland & William Samuel Pocklington by October 1950 (E&T licence referenced K3484)

R G Rowland as sole trader again by November 1962 (E&T licence referenced K4698)

to Mrs MM Rowland in 1967

to Mrs MM & C Rowland and J Goodwin in May 1979

Original operator licence PK290 - Mrs MM & C Rowland & J Goodwin

to C Rowland & J Goodwin in 12/98 following the death of Mrs M Rowland (23.12.1998)

to Rambler Coaches Ltd (incorporated 23 March 1999) and new Operator licence PK0003587 issued April 2001

Business sold to Rambler Group Holdings Ltd, Barrowford, Lancashire, with effect from 25 September 2018.

Vehicles still in stock in 9/18 when the business was sold are shown as R in the "sold" column

Fleet History - known vehicles 1924 - 2018

Registration when acq'd	Chassis	Fleet No.	Body make and type	Seats	New	Acq'd	Sold
TB 1227	Lancia Z	---	?	Ch17?	-/20	7/26	c-/31
CP 3468	Lancia Z	---	?	-14-	6/24	?	9/29
KK 9777	Unic	---	?	Ch13	-/24	7/26	-/30
KE 8836	?	---	?	C13?	4/22	4/28	?/??
BP 8879	Unic	---	?	C14?	-/22	5/28	-/30
RO 9427	Lancia	---	?	C20?	3/28	7/30	?/??
TT 6226	Lancia	2	?	C14?	-/25	8/32	8/39
ON 9387	Lancia	---	?	C???	-/26	?	?
KD 2343	Studebaker	3	?	C23?	6/28	7/35	10/40
WM 3151	Star Flyer VB4	---	Spicer ?	C26?	3/29	7/38	-/40
GE 7766	B.A.T.Cruiser	1	Eaton	C20F	-/29	-/46	-/49
RD 9779	Dodge	2	Real	C26F	5/37	1/48	7/51
-?-	Gilford		?	?	?	8/39	-/40
CKE 23	Commer Greyhound B3	3	Waveney	C25F	4/35	1/48	6/52
JUF 637	Bedford OB	1	Duple Vista	C29F	5/49	5/50	6/60
JCD 176	Bedford OB	2	Duple Vista	C29F	1/48	3/51	8/54
DCK 565	Bedford OB	3	Duple Vista	C29F	5/50	5/53	5/57
GDY 888	Bedford SBG	4	Duple Vega	C36F	8/54	NEW	11/63
LFJ 737	Bedford SBG	3	Duple Vega	C33F	-/51	5/57	4/62
ODY 544	Bedford SB3	5	Duple Super Vega	C41F	6/60	NEW	11/66
UOT 585	Bedford SB3	6	Duple Super Vega	C41F	-/59	4/62	10/65
VDY 207	Bedford SB5	7	Duple Bella Vega	C41F	4/64	NEW	10/69
DDY 250D	Bedford VAM5	8	Plaxton Vam	C45F	2/66	NEW	12/70
EDY 565E	Bedford VAM14	1	Duple Viceroy	C45F	4/67	NEW	11/73
KDY 300H	Bedford SB5	2	Duple Vega 31	C41F	4/70	NEW	9/83
ATU 53F	Bedford VAL70	3	Plaxton Panorama	C52F	2/68	12/70	1/75
GPC 58C	Bedford VAL14	---	Plaxton Val	C52F	5/65	4/73	6/73
TDY 494L	Bedford YRT	---	Duple Dominant	C53F	6/73	NEW	11/78

VDY 626M	Bedford YRQ	---	Duple Dominant	C45F	2/74	NEW	12/80
AEX 45B	Bedford J2SZ10	---	Plaxton Embassy	C18F	8/64	8/74	12/74
NKJ 769F	Bedford J2SZ10	---	Plaxton Embassy	C20F	-/68	12/74	10/78
YXD 470M	Ford R1114	---	Duple Dominant	C53F	6/74	1/75	6/76
FOU 216K	Ford Transit	---	Deansgate	C12F	-/72	8/75	11/78
LJK 335P	Bedford YMT	04	Duple Dominant	C53F	6/76	NEW	2/94
CUF 490C	Bedford SB5	---	Duple Bella Vega	C41F	-/65	6/76	9/77
HJM 772H	Bedford VAL70	---	Plaxton Panorama Elite	C53F	1/69	3/77	6/85
YOR 111J	Bedford YRQ	---	Plaxton Panorama Elite	C45F	-/71	9/77	11/80
DME 998A	Bedford SB5	---	Duple Bella Vega	C41F	-/63	10/78	2/82
JFX 657N	Bedford J2	---	Caetano	C20F	-/75	10/78	5/80
MPK 71L	Commer PB	---	Rootes	C12F	8/72	11/78	10/81
VWK 7S	Bedford YMT	07	Plaxton Supreme III	C53F	8/77	11/78	11/89
VWK 8S	Bedford YMT	---	Plaxton Supreme III	C53F	8/77	11/78	1/83
HRD 12N	Bedford YRQ	12	Plaxton Panorama Elite II	C45F	4/75	5/79	10/84
JAA 507E	Bedford VAM14	---	Plaxton Panorama	C45F	4/67	11/79	3/82
KUW 540P	Bedford YMT	6	Willowbrook 008	C53F	5/76	11/79	1/85
LVS 447P	Bedford PJK	---	Plaxton Supreme III	C25F	3/76	3/80	12/82
HVD 588N	Bedford YRT	---	Plaxton Panorama Elite III	C53F	4/75	5/80	2/82
EDY 565E	Bedford VAM14	10	Duple Viceroy	C45F	4/67	9/80	12/99
VNU 75K	Bedford YRQ	---	Willowbrook 002	C45F	5/72	9/80	6/84
UFT 911T	Bedford YLQ	11	Plaxton Supreme III	C45F	8/78	11/80	10/83
HVC 10V	Bedford YMT	10	Plaxton Supreme IV	C53F	9/79	12/80	10/84
YWA 444G	Bedford VAM70	---	Plaxton Panorama Elite	C45F	2/69	1/81	11/82
PPO 122M	Ford Transit	16	Strachan	C16F	11/73	11/81	2/86
CNY 338V	Bedford PJK	25	Plaxton Supreme III	C29F	1/80	2/82	6/86
GDY 500X	Bedford YNT	05*	Plaxton Supreme V	C53F	4/82	NEW	2/88
HKX 553V	Bedford JJL	---	Marshall	B24F	9/79	10/82	4/83
JDY 888Y	Bedford VAS5 (PJK)	29	Plaxton Supreme IV	C29F	1/83	NEW	4/87
ATU 51F	Bedford VAL70	---	Plaxton Panorama I	C52F	4/68	1/83	4/83
RPB 222L	Bedford VAL70	19	Plaxton Panorama Elite III	C53F	5/73	3/83	4/92
KDY 888Y	DAF MB200DKFL600	08	Plaxton.Paramount 3500	C53F	3/83	NEW	2/91
LYC 731	Bedford OB	01	Duple Vista	C29F	1/50	4/83	3/95
5421 CR	Bedford J4LZ1	---	Plaxton Consort III	C29F	6/60	9/83	3/84
A888 MDY	DAF MB200DKFL600	24	Plaxton Paramount 3500	C53F	1/84	NEW	1/92
6881 R	Bedford SB5	---	Yeates Pegasus	DP45F	-/63	4/84	4/84
JJF 881V	Bedford YMT	17	Unicar	C53F	5/80	4/84	10/86
NBW 704L	Bedford YRT	11	Duple Dominant	C53F	3/73	6/84	10/90
LUX 503P	Bedford YLQ	03	Duple Dominant	C45F	4/76	6/84	12/84
YUJ 926T	Bedford CFL	26	Reeve Burgess	C17F	5/80	11/84	9/86
ECB 791W	Bedford YMQ	03	Duple Dominant II	C45F	9/80	12/84	1/96
A273 KEL	Bedford YNT	02	Plaxton Paramount 3200	C53F	2/84	1/85	11/86
RHX 190L	Volvo B58-56	09	Duple Dominant	C53F	4/73	2/85	11/87
B888 PDY	Bedford YNV	38	Plaxton Paramount 3200	C53F	2/85	NEW	12/89
C588 SJK	Volvo B10M-61	28	Plaxton Paramount 3500	C49FT	1/86	NEW	12/93
PGR 620N	Bedford YRT	20	Willowbrook	B60F	10/74	4/86	9/90
MAX 331X	Bedford VAS5 (PJK)	31	Plaxton Supreme IV	C29F	1/82	6/86	1/87
D941 UDY	Freight Rover	16	Dixon Lomas	C16F	8/86	NEW	8/92
PAM 516M	Bedford YRT	06	Duple Dominant	C53F	1/74	11/86	5/89
D133 VJK	Bedford YMP 8m	33	Plaxton Paramount 3200	C33F	4/87	NEW	9/18
D137 VJK	Volvo B10M-61	37	Plaxton Paramount 3500	C53F	4/87	NEW	5/10
D134 VJK	Bedford YMP 8m	34	Plaxton Paramount 3200	C33F	5/87	NEW	12/01

TDT 624L	Seddon Pennine IV/236	25	Seddon	DP25F	5/73	7/87	5/89
OTX 41R	Bedford YMT	21	Plaxton Supreme Exp	C53F	11/76	9/87	2/93
WNH 52W	Bedford YMQ 8m	14	Lex Maxeta	B33F	5/81	10/87	10/98
JJF 880V	Bedford YMT	23	Plaxton Supreme IV	C53F	5/80	12/87	3/93
E184 XJK	Volvo B10M-61	18	Van Hool Alizee	C51FT	3/88	NEW	11/05
GUR 487L	Bedford YRT	---	Plaxton Panorama Elite III	C53F	11/72	3/88	--/88
YEB 105T	Bedford YMT	22	Plaxton Supreme IV	C53F	6/79	5/88	2/98
B191 XJD	Volvo B10M-56	09	Plaxton Paramount 3500	C38F	3/85	12/88	5/91
710 VCV	Volvo B10M-61	17	Plaxton Paramount 3500	C53F	4/83	11/89	12/92
G135 UWV	Volvo B10M-60	35	Plaxton Paramount 3500	C51FT	4/90	NEW	12/95
AAL 521A	Bedford YMT	05	Caetano Estoril 2	C53F	3/78	4/90	10/92
FRP 855T	Bedford YMT	06	Duple Dominant II	C53F	1/79	6/90	10/91
DMT 904V	Bedford YMT	07	Duple Dominant II	C53F	3/80	6/90	2/94
NDC 284W	Bedford YMT	11	Silverdale (on Van Hool McArdle frames)	C53F	5/81	9/90	3/94
910 OCV	Bedford YMT	20	Duple Dominant II	C53F	8/77	9/90	2/98
TCD 481J	Bristol RESL6L	15	Marshall	B45F	10/70	11/90	12/92
G168 ODH	Dennis Javelin	32	Plaxton Paramount 3200	C53F	8/89	11/90	12/93
F27 HGG	Volvo B10M-60	27	Plaxton Paramount 3500	C51FT	2/89	4/91	11/94
F28 HGG	Volvo B10M-60	28	Plaxton Paramount 3500	C51FT	2/89	4/91	11/94
EYL 319V	Bedford YMT	08	Plaxton Supreme IV	C53F	7/80	8/91	2/94
KUR 585Y	Bedford YNT	31	Plaxton Paramount 3200	C53F	5/83	8/91	7/04
MGS 437V	Bedford YLQ	12	Alexander Y (1973)	DP45F	-/76	8/91	10/92
D558 MVR	Volvo B10M-61	19	VanHool Alizee	C53F	2/87	3/92	12/09
PKO 260W	Bedford YMT	06	Duple Dominant II	C53F	3/81	3/92	3/01
CKN 142Y	Bedford YMT	10	Wright TT	B53F	10/82	6/92	2/96
CKN 143Y	Bedford YMT	11	Wright TT	B53F	10/82	6/92	1/97
K16 ADY	DAF 400	16	Crystals	C16F	8/92	NEW	8/00
MUY 41X	Bedford YMQ	12	Wright TT	B45F	1/82	11/92	5/00
F507 MAA	Volvo B10M-61	17	Van Hool Alizee T8	C49FT	2/88	12/92	8/97
A244 KFJ	Bedford YNT	29	Plaxton Paramount 3200	C53F	8/83	1/93	1/99
A383 BNP	Bedford YNT	30	Plaxton Paramount 3200	C53F	3/84	1/93	1/97
A627 YWF	Bedford YNT	21	Plaxton Paramount 3200	C53F	2/84	4/93	1/97
F609 EHE	Mercedes-Benz 609D	15	Whittaker	C24F	3/89	7/93	1/99
A67 NPP	Bedford YNT	25	Plaxton Paramount 3200	C51F	3/84	8/93	5/01
A68 NPP	Bedford YNT	26	Plaxton Paramount 3200	C51F	3/84	8/93	4/00
HKX 553V	Bedford JJL	05	Marshall	C24F	9/79	10/93	3/99
A440 HJF	Bedford YNT	32	Plaxton Paramount 3200	C53F	3/84	11/93	4/99
H631 UWR	Volvo B10M-60	36	Plaxton Paramount 3500	C50F	3/91	1/94	11/10
H612 UWR	Volvo B10M-60	38	Plaxton Paramount 3500	C49FT	3/91	1/94	1/96
B929 AAX	Bedford YNT	23	Plaxton Paramount 3200	C53F	4/85	1/94	3/95
B930 AAX	Bedford YNT	24	Plaxton Paramount 3200	C53F	4/85	1/94	9/01
KWB 695W	Bedford YMT	07	Duple Dominant (Bus)	B55F	1/81	3/94	3/95
C345 RSG	Bedford YNT	04	Plaxton Paramount 3200	C55F	8/85	8/94	1/99
M222 CDY	Scania K113CRB	27	Van Hool Alizee T8	C51FT	1/95	NEW	3/98
M222 DDY	Scania K113CRB	28	Van Hool Alizee T8	C51FT	1/95	NEW	3/00
E232 GPH	Bedford YNV	23	Plaxton Paramount 3200	C55F	1/88	2/95	9/01
C203 GKR	Bedford YMT	07	Wright TT	B51F	5/86	3/95	4/02
G48 VVM	Mercedes-Benz 609D	01	Made to Measure	DP24F	5/90	4/95	2/03
L571 FVU	Volvo B10M-62	35	Jonckheere Deauville P599	C51FT	3/94	11/95	7/99
HSK 834	Volvo B10M-61	02	Jonckheere Jubilee P599	C49FT	5/88	12/95	12/96
HSK 835	Volvo B10M-61	03	Jonckheere Jubilee P599	C49FT	5/88	12/95	12/96

N222 EDY	Volvo B10M-62	38	Van Hool Alizee T8	C51FT	1/96	NEW	3/05
H170 EJF	Toyota HDB30R	10	Caetano Optimo	C21F	1/91	5/96	3/98
SJI 2586	Bedford YNV	08	Plaxton Paramount 3200	C53F	1/88	9/96	5/01
NG 2414	Bedford WLB	1	Economy	B20F	4/32	11/96	9/18
M127 UWY	Volvo B10M-62	02	Plaxton Premiere 350	C49FT	5/95	12/96	8/00
M128 UWY	Volvo B10M-62	03	Plaxton Premiere 350	C49FT	6/95	12/96	2/02
C302 RRX	Bedford YMT	11	Wadham Stringer Vanguard	B49F	7/86	1/97	12/02
E953 KDP	Volvo B10M-61	21	Plaxton Paramount 3200	C57F	3/88	1/97	9/00
E968 KDP	Volvo B10M-61	30	Plaxton Paramount 3200	C57F	2/88	1/97	3/09
C538 OTY	Bedford YMT	09	Duple 320 Express	C53F	7/86	5/97	9/04
R222 WDY	Volvo B10M-62	17	Berkhof Axial 50	C49FT	8/97	NEW	10/03
R222 XDY	Dennis Javelin GX	05	Berkhof Axial 50	C53F	9/97	NEW	2/02
M211 UYD	Toyota HZB50R	10	Caetano Optimo 3	C21F	1/95	3/98	11/99
R222 VDY	Volvo B10M-62	27	Berkhof Axial 50	C49FT	3/98	NEW	11/06
ETA 101Y	Ford R1114	50	Plaxton Paramount 3200	C53F	3/83	6/98	8/98
BPL 459T	Leyland-National 10351B/1R	14	Leyland-National	B41F	4/79	8/98	4/03
H532 WGH	Volvo B10M-60	20	VanHool Alizee T8	C53F	4/91	8/98	9/08
H533 WGH	Volvo B10M-60	22	VanHool Alizee T8	C53F	4/91	9/98	4/10
GDY 500X	Bedford YNT	32	Plaxton Supreme V	C57F	4/82	11/98	8/09
P884 FMO	Dennis Javelin GX	04	Berkhof Axial 50	C53F	4/97	1/99	8/03
T222 ADY	Mercedes-Benz 614D	15	Autobus Classique	C24F	5/99	NEW	8/13
T222 GDY	Volvo B10M-62	35	VanHool Alizee T9	C49FT	5/99	NEW	4/14
YUT 628Y	Volvo B10M-61	29	Plaxton Supreme V	C57F	1/83	9/99	2/22
V222 JDY	Mercedes-Benz O1120L	10	Ferqui Solera	C35F	11/99	NEW	2/17
SJI 3929	Dennis Dorchester	26	Caetano Algarve	C51FT	9/88	2/00	11/01
W222 KDY	Scania K124IB4	28	VanHool Alizee T9	C49FT	3/00	NEW	11/06
JDY 888Y	Bedford VAS5 (PJK)	29	Plaxton Supreme IV	C29F	1/83	6/00	9/18
T110 SOA	Mercedes-Benz 0404	-	Hispano Carrocera	C49FT	6/99	6/00	9/00
G75 PKR	Mercedes-Benz 609D	16	Reeve Burgess	B20F	11/89	7/00	2/03
NPJ 476R	Leyland-National 11351A/1R	12	Leyland-National	B49F	10/76	7/00	2/02
R777 GSM	Dennis Javelin	21	Plaxton Premiere 3200	C57F	4/98	8/00	2/04
X500 GDY	Mercedes-Benz 0404	02	Hispano Carrocera Vita	C49FT	9/00	NEW	2/15
all subsequent vehicles entered the fleet under the Rambler Coaches Ltd operator's licence (PK0003587)							
Y222 PDY	Volvo B10M-62	06	Berkhof Axial 50	C49FT	4/01	NEW	R
P427 LJH	Volvo B10M-62	08	Plaxton Premiere 350	C53F	8/96	5/01	5/17
P428 LJH	Volvo B10M-62	25	Plaxton Premiere 350	C53F	8/96	5/01	R
SIB 8243	Volvo B10M-60	26	Plaxton Paramount 3500	C49FT	3/91	11/01	7/04
D122 EFH	Bedford YMT	12	Plaxton Derwent	B55F	4/87	2/02	5/04
D123 EFH	Bedford YMT	11	Plaxton Derwent	B55F	4/87	2/02	9/04
GX02 AED	Volvo B10M-62	05	Plaxton Panther	C49FT	3/02	NEW	R
GX02 AEE	Volvo B10M-62	03	Plaxton Panther	C49FT	3/02	NEW	R
M513 VJO	Dennis Dart	07	Marshall	B40F	3/95	9/02	11/06
G200 PAO	Mercedes-Benz 709D	24	Alexander Sprint	DP25F	5/91	10/02	4/10
M649 KVU	Volvo B10M-62	23	VanHool Alizee T8	C49FT	1/95	12/02	4/09
E22 XHL	Bedford YNT	14	Plaxton Paramount 3200	C53F	4/88	4/03	10/03
NCF 715	Bedford YNT	---	Plaxton Paramount 3200	C53F	3/84	8/03	7/04
M605 ORJ	Volvo B10M-62	16	Jonckheere Deauville	C53F	4/95	11/03	4/13
M613 ORJ	Volvo B10M-62	17	Jonckheere Deauville	C53F	4/95	11/03	R
CR04 RAM	Volvo B7R	04	Plaxton (Transbus) Profile	C53F	2/04	NEW	9/15
JG04 RAM	Volvo B7R	14	Plaxton (Transbus) Profile	C53F	2/04	NEW	5/15

FCO 314	Austin CXB	1	Plaxton	C29F	5/50	4/04	3/07
JIL 5279	Volvo B10M-61	12	Northern Counties	B51F	5/88	5/04	12/11
J505 GCD	Dennis Dart	21	Alexander Dash	B41F	3/92	6/04	7/15
J507 GCD	Dennis Dart	26	Alexander Dash	B41F	3/92	6/04	8/04
J534 GCD	Dennis Dart	11	Alexander Dash	B41F	4/92	7/04	4/11
TIL 1185	Volvo B10M-61	26	Plaxton Derwent	B55F	1/93	8/04	7/09
JG54 RAM	Mercedes-Benz 814D	34	Plaxton Cheetah	C33F	9/04	NEW	4/13
CA52 LAO	Volvo B12M	31	Berkhof Axial 50	C49FT	2/03	4/05	1/08
W87 RRU	Volvo B10M-62	18	Plaxton Panther	C53F	5/00	9/05	R
JUF 244E	Bedford VAM14	02	Duple Viceroy	C45F	4/67	3/06	9/18
CR06 EDY	Volvo B12B	09	Berkhof Axial 50	C53FT	5/06	NEW	R
H649 PVW	Leyland Olympian	28	Alexander Belfast RH	H47/31F	3/91	9/06	12/09
J706 CEV	Leyland Olympian	29	Alexander Belfast RH	H47/31F	12/91	9/06	3/13
N301 XRP	Mercedes-Benz 709D	27	Alexander Sprint	B23F	5/96	9/06	5/13
N191 LPN	Mercedes-Benz 709D	07	Alexander Belfast Sprint	DP25F	8/95	10/06	8/14
N962 NAP	Mercedes-Benz 709D	---	Alexander Sprint	B23F	2/96	10/06	2/07
UUD 12	Bedford J2SZ7	---	Plaxton Consort	C20F	12/61	10/06	2/14
F709 WCS	Volvo B10M-56	20	Duple 300	B53F	1/89	11/06	7/09
JG07 RAM	Volvo B12B	01	Volvo 9700 Prestige	C49FT	6/07	NEW	R
M606 UTV	Volvo B10B-58	31	Plaxton Verde	B51F	6/95	11/07	11/15
M607 UTV	Volvo B10B-58	33	Plaxton Verde	B51F	6/95	11/07	1/16
JG08 RAM	Volvo B12B	22	Plaxton Panther	C49FT	2/08	NEW	11/15
CR08 RAM	Volvo B12B	38	Volvo 9700 Prestige	C49FT	3/08	NEW	R
CMG 30	Bedford WLB	2	Duple	C20R	6/35	11/08	9/18
YR52 MEU	Volvo B10M-62	30	Plaxton Paragon	C53F	9/02	1/09	R
SK07 FUW	Volvo B12B	23	VanHool Alizee	C49FT	4/07	2/09	R
FY02 WHA	Mercedes-Benz 413CDI	39	Ferqui Soroco	C16F	6/02	5/09	2/13
P330 RVG	Volvo B10M-62	26	Plaxton Interurban	C57F	6/97	6/09	11/14
N617 APU	Volvo B10M-62	20	Plaxton Interurban	C57F	1/96	7/09	4/15
S136 RLE	Volvo Olympian OLY-50	28	Alexander RV	H43/29F	9/98	12/09	2/16
YN51 WGY	Volvo B10M-62	40	Plaxton Paragon	C53F	9/01	1/10	R
YN51 WGZ	Volvo B10M-62	41	Plaxton Paragon	C53F	9/01	1/10	R
YN55 WSW	Volvo B12B	19	Plaxton Panther	C53F	11/05	8/10	R
R710 YWC	Dennis Dart	11	Plaxton Pointer	B43F	10/97	1/11	2/16
M525 WHF	Volvo B10B	12	Wright Endurance	B53F	11/94	8/11	3/16
PE56 XMJ	Mercedes 1022L	24	Unvi Cimo	C33F	2/07	8/11	R
CR12 RAM	Mercedes Tourismo	36	Mercedes Benz	C49FT	3/12	NEW	R
JG12 RAM	Volvo B9R	37	Plaxton Panther 2	C53FT	3/12	NEW	R
MX07 NTA	Mercedes 0815D	39	Ferqui Toro	C28F	8/07	2/13	R
X661 LLX	Volvo B7TL	29	Plaxton President	H47/33F	1/01	3/13	R
BK09 LVD	Mercedes Tourismo	32	Mercedes Benz	C53F	5/09	1/14	R
CR14 RAM	Mercedes Tourismo	34	Mercedes Benz	C49FT	3/14	NEW	R
S775 BLG	Mercedes 0814D	07	Plaxton Beaver	B31F	9/98	7/14	8/17
BG14 OOE	Volvo B11R	35	Jonckheere SHV	C53FT	4/14	8/14	R
UK15 RAM	Mercedes Tourismo	15	Mercedes Benz	C51FT	3/15	NEW	R
MV54 BLU	DennisDart SLF	26	Alexander Pointer 2	B38F	9/04	4/15	R
MW54 BLU	DennisDart SLF	27	Alexander Pointer 2	B38F	9/04	4/15	R
J 7247	Bedford OB	---	Duple Vista	C29F	5/50	5/15	9/18
SK52 OJD	Dennis Dart SLF	31	Plaxton Pointer	B42F	12/02	5/15	R
SN53 AUW	Transbus Dart SLF	20	Transbus Pointer	B42F	10/03	6/15	3/16
EK51 XXC	Dennis Dart SLF	14	Alexander	B29F	11/01	9/15	R
YN13 EHD	Irizar i6	22	Irizar	C57FT	6/13	11/15	R

CR65 RAM	Yutong ZK6938HQ	02	Yutong TC9	C35F	1/16	NEW		R
R853 PRG	Volvo B10BLE	33	Wright Renown	B44F	4/98	1/16		R
YK53 GXO	Volvo B7RLE	20	Wright Eclipse Urban	B43F	12/03	3/16		R
YK53 GXP	Volvo B7RLE	28	Wright Eclipse Urban	B43F	12/03	3/16		R
CR17 RAM	Mercedes Tourismo M	10	Mercedes-Benz	C53FT	3/17	NEW		R

Colin Rowland's own O-licence for Fairlight Private Hire granted 1/03 (with 4 discs) and licence renewed in 2023 until 12/27.

Registration when acq'd	Previous Operator	Subsequent Operator
TB 1227	-?-, Lancashire	Used as lorry, last licensed 7/31
CP 3468	-?-, unknown location	Untraced
KK 9777	-?-, Margate	Untraced
KE 8836	Myers, Margate	Untraced
BP 8879	Overton, Goring-by-Sea	Untraced
RO 9427	Dell, Ware, Herts	Untraced
TT 6226	Smith, Buntingford	Untraced
ON 9387	Pritchard, London E14	Untraced
KD 2343	E J Jones (Imperial), Liverpool, via Pearson, Liverpool (not used)	Tunbridge Wells Fire Brigade (as fire tender)
WM 3151	Marriner, Southport, possibly via another operator	Hastings Fire Service (requisitioned)
GE 7766	Sydenham Coaches, SE26	Bailey (shopkeeper), St Leonards-on-Sea (non-PSV)
RD 9779	Newman & Sons, Hythe	Waterhouse, Burwash
{Gilford}	Untraced (believed South London area)	Hastings Fire Service (requisitioned)
CKE 23	Newman & Sons, Hythe	Unknown Mobile Shop, Tonbridge, Kent
JUF 637	Unique, Brighton	Gaytime, Alresford, Hampshire
JCD 176	Unique, Brighton	Reedman, Thirsk, Yorkshire
DCK 565	Barnes (Premier), Preston	Martin, Hillingdon, Middlesex
GDY 888	NEW	Croad (contractor), Portsmouth, Hampshire
LFJ 737	Kingdom, Tiverton	Richmond (Epsom Coaches), Epsom, Surrey
ODY 544	NEW	Furlong, Wantage, Oxfordshire
UOT 585	Coliseum, Southampton	Perkins, Woodley, Berkshire
VDY 207	NEW	Davey (Blue Iris), Nailsea, Somerset
DDY 250D	NEW	Lucas, Hollington, Staffordshire
EDY 565E	NEW	Plumridge, Horley, Surrey
KDY 300H	NEW	Bexhill Swimming Club (non-PSV)
ATU 53F	Shearing, Altrincham	Eagle Line, Faringdon, Oxfordshire
GPC 58C	Bodman, Worton	Patten (Empress), Hastings
TDY 494L	NEW	Freeman, Uffington, Oxfordshire, 3/79
VDY 626M	NEW	Marchwood, Totton, Hampshire
AEX 45B	Bluebird, Weymouth	Clark, Havant, Hampshire
NKJ 769F	Cox (Streamline), Maidstone	Williams, Cwmdu, Powys, 1/79
FOU 216K	Epsom Coaches, Surrey	Martin, West End, Woking, Surrey 9/79
YXD 470M	Courtline, Luton, Bedfordshire	Farnham Coaches, Surrey
LJK 335P	NEW	Cordery & Matthews (Whites Coaches), Heathfield, East Sussex (as NUF 828P)
CUF 490C	Oakley Coaches, Hampshire	Plumridge, Horley, Surrey
YOR 111J	Banstead Coaches, Surrey	Wise, Upper Dicker, East Sussex
HJM 772H	Browne, Brabourne, Kent	Gain (Cooks), Westfield, East Sussex
DME 998A	Martin, West End, Woking, Surrey	Broad Oak & Punnetts Town Scouts, Heathfield, East Sussex
JFX 657N	House (Mercury), Boscombe, Dorset	Calloway, Rowley Regis, West Midlands
MPK 71L	Nelmes Travel, Hornchurch, Essex	Unknown
VWK 7S	Shaw, Coventry	Gain (Cooks), Westfield, East Sussex

FLEET LIST

VWK 8S	Shaw, Coventry	Freeman, Uffington, Oxfordshire
HRD 12N	Tappin, Wallingford, Oxfordshire	J2T Video, Newhaven (non-PSV)
JAA 507E	Smith & Ball, Waterhouses, Staffordshire	Caravan, Bournemouth
KUW 540P	National Travel (South East)	J2T Video, Newhaven (non-PSV) (as 6751 KP)
LVS 447P	Armchair, Brentford, Greater London	Fuggle, Benenden, Kent
HVD 588N	Premier, Watford, Hertfordshire	Freeman, Uffington, Oxfordshire, by 10/82
EDY 565E	Plumridge, Horley, Surrey	Peter Simpson, Whittlesey, Cambridgeshire (preservation)
UFT 911T	Curtis, Dudley, Tyne & Wear	Fuggle, Benenden, Kent
HVC 10V	Shaw, Coventry	Fuggle, Benenden, Kent
VNU 75K	Worthington, Collingham, Notts	Spencer, Buckland Filleigh, Devon
YWA 444G	Wilde, Heage, Derbyshire	Accident damage, 6/82; Day & Butland (Vernon's), Hailsham, E Sussex for spares
PPO 122M	Barnes, Runcton, W Sussex	Hills, Hersham, Surrey (as 6881 R)
CNY 338V	Thomas, Clydach Vale, Glamorgan	Haynes, Christchurch, Dorset
GDY 500X	NEW	Southlands, Bromley, Greater London
HKX 553V	Marshall, Cambridge (via private owner, Peterborough)	Bournemouth Transport (Yellow Buses), Bournemouth
JDY 888Y	NEW	Stamp, Honiton, Devon
ATU 51F	Freeman, Uffington, Oxfordshire	Smith (Farleigh Coaches), East Farleigh, Kent
RPB 222L	Chivers, Wallington, Surrey	Withdrawn 4/92; Bibby, Ingleton, North Yorkshire (as EUF 738L) 7/92; Chivers, Wallington, Surrey, 11/92
LYC 731	Jones, Orpington (preservation); licensed as PCV from 1986 until c1991	Ryan (Connemara Bus), Moycullen, Galway, Eire (re-registered as ZV 1460)
KDY 888Y	NEW	Grindle, Ruardean Hill, Cinderford, Gloucestershire (as NIJ 8067)
5421 CR	Bexhill Swimming Club (NPSV)	Dawson (mobile caravan), Rye (as XUF 34A)
A888 MDY	NEW	Bourne, Birmingham (as A673 NJK)
6881 R	Thorn, Newhaven (NPSV)	Caravan (as XUF 52A)
JJF 881V	Wainfleet, Nuneaton, Warwickshire	Maybury, Cranborne, Dorset
NBW 704L	Arlott, Aldermaston, Berkshire	Gain (Cooks), Westfield (as EUF 683L)
LUX 503P	Arlott, Aldermaston, Berkshire	Caravan
YUJ 926T	Whittle, Highley, Shropshire (26)	Amanda Coaches, Bedfont, Greater London
ECB 791W	Turner, Chulmleigh, Devon	Evans, Tregaron, Ceredigion (as OUF 669W), 5/96
A273 KEL	Tedd (Amport & District), Thruxton, Hants	Turner, Chulmleigh, Devon (as A72 NHC) by 7/87
RHX 190L	Brooks, ?London?	Southern Land Tours, Eastbourne
B888 PDY	NEW	Alexcars, Cirencester, Gloucestershire
C588 SJK	NEW	Burton, Haverhill, Suffolk (as C164 CCD) by 12/94
PGR 620N	Yeoman, Hereford (34)	Wealden, Five Oak Green, Kent, for scrap
MAX 331X	Thomas, Clydach Vale, Glamorgan	Empress, Hastings
D941 UDY	NEW	Brown, Robertsbridge (non-PSV), 8/92; Cook, Sampford Moor, Somerset by 2/93
PAM 516M	Barnes, Aldbourne, Wiltshire	Gain (Cooks), Westfield
D133 VJK	NEW	Withdrawn & to preserved status 5/07; C Rowland (preservation) 9/18
D137 VJK	NEW	Hill, Hersham, Surrey (re-reg to HIL 9322)

D134 VJK	NEW	Way (Reading & Wokingham Coaches), Wokingham, Berkshire
TDT 624L	Maun, Mansfield, Nottinghamshire (24)	D & N Travel, Tycroes, Carmarthenshire
OTX 41R	Morgan, Nantyglo, Gwent	Taylor, Sutton Scotney, Hants (as TAP 461R)
WNH 52W	Milton Keynes City Bus (2052)	Wealden, Five Oak Green, Kent, for scrap
JJF 880V	Watson, Annfield Plain, Durham	Turner, Maidstone, Kent (re-registered as TCT 51)
E184 XJK	NEW	Whincop, Peasenhall, Suffolk
GUR 487L	Rimmer, Ramsgate, Kent	Autopoint, Herstmonceux, East Sussex
YEB 105T	Portrest, Southam, Warwickshire	Exodus, Ravensden, Bedfordshire
B191 XJD	Glenton, London SE15	E Cardona, Mosta, Malta; A & J Galea (Arthur & John's), Qormi, Malta, 1999 as LCY 910; withdrawn 2020
710 VCV	Coliseum, West End, Hampshire	Prout, Port Isaac, Cornwall
G135 UWV	NEW	Farmer (Kent Coach Tours), Ashford, Kent (as G791 VYJ)
AAL 521A	Davies, Bridport, Dorset	Thorn, Rayleigh, Essex
FRP 855T	Ashby, London E17	Gain (Cooks), Westfield, East Sussex (and re-registered to HFG 281T)
DMT 904V	WHM (Brentwood) Ltd, Little Waltham, Essex	Cordery & Matthews (Whites Coaches), Heathfield, East Sussex (as JNJ 365V)
NDC 284W	Shalder, Scalloway, Shetland	Perkins, New Haw, Surrey
910 OCV	Coliseum, West End, Hampshire	Exodus, Ravensden, Bedfordshire
TCD 481J	Kent Coach Tours, Ashford, Kent	Withdrawn 12/92; Mulpeter & Cutbush, Newhaven, East Sussex, 4/93
G168 ODH	Shirley (Elizabethan Travel), Walsall, West Midlands	Phillips (Bow Belle), Crediton, Devon (as G238 VYJ)
F27 HGG	Parks, Hamilton, Strathclyde	Dixon, Wednesfield, West Midlands (as F295 CJK), by 9/95
F28 HGG	Parks, Hamilton, Strathclyde	Meek, Chasetown, Staffordshire (as F294 CJK), 1/95
EYL 319V	Royal Ordnance Factory, Bishopton, Renfrewshire	Cordery & Matthews (Whites Coaches), Heathfield, later sold to Evans, Tregaron, Dyfed and re-registered to JNJ 567V in 9/95
KUR 585Y	Taylor (Reliance), Meppershall, Bedfordshire	Curtis (Driver Training Centre), Hastings (non-PSV)
MGS 437V	The King's Ferry, Gillingham, Kent	Evans, Tregaron, Dyfed, 4/93
D558 MVR	Shearings, Wigan (558)	S Gilkes (West Kent), West Kingsdown, Kent
PKO 260W	Moore & Verge (Aantelope Travel), Cliftonville, possibly via Beulah Court Hotel, Cliftonville (non-PSV), Kent	Cass Packaging, Hoo, Kent (became Amberlee, Southfleet, Kent during 2002)
CKN 142Y	Maidstone Borough Transport (Boro'line Maidstone) (242)	Withdrawn 7/95 due to accident damage; Ripley, Carlton, South Yorkshire for scrap
CKN 143Y	Maidstone Borough Transport (Boro'line Maidstone) (243)	Taylor, Redhill, Surrey (as driver trainer, and re-registered CYJ 790Y) 3/97
K16 ADY	NEW	St Mary's School, Folkestone, Kent (non-PSV)
MUY 41X	Martin Perry, Bromyard, Herefordshire (56)	Paterson, Bearsted, Kent (preservation)
F507 MAA	CSGB Engineering, South Newton, Wilts	Davies & Jones, Letterston, Pembrokeshire
A244 KFJ	Hodson, Navenby, Lincolnshire	Kingswinford Coaches, Pensnett, West Midlands (as A774 ODY)
A383 BNP	Associated, Worcester	North & Williams, Totternhoe, Bedfordshire (as A473 ODY)

A627 YWF	Sheffield United Transport (387)	Annetts & Porter (Mervyn's), Micheldever, Hampshire (as A462 ODY)
F609 EHE	Williams, St Albans, Hertfordshire	Mower (Cheam Coaches), Cheam, Greater London (as F675 DDY)
A67 NPP	Hil-Tech, Hillingdon, Greater London	Gale, Haslemere, Surrey
A68 NPP	Hil-Tech, Hillingdon, Greater London	Kingswinford Coaches, Pensnett, West Midlands (as A918 ODY)
HKX 553V	Holloway, Denham, Suffolk	Withdrawn by 11/95; Ely (First Choice), Peterborough
A440 HJF	Barnes, Aldbourne, Wiltshire	Gain (Cooks), Westfield, East Sussex (as A729 ODY) and re-registered NCF 715 in 7/99
H631 UWR	Wallace Arnold, Leeds, West Yorkshire	Fowler, Holbeach Drove, Lincolnshire (as H392 GBD)
H612 UWR	Wallace Arnold, Leeds, West Yorkshire	Barnes, Aldbourne, Wiltshire (as H131 DFG), 4/96
B929 AAX	JD Cleverly Ltd (Capitol Coaches), Cwmbran, Gwent	Gain (Cooks), Westfield, East Sussex (as 8876 FN)
B930 AAX	JD Cleverly Ltd (Capitol Coaches), Cwmbran, Gwent	Wealden, Five Oak Green (dlr)
KWB 695W	Rider (York) (1177)	Coach Services, Thetford, Norfolk
C345 RSG	Wilson, Dalkeith, Midlothian	Port Erin Hotels, Isle of Man (re-registered to KMN 106), 2/99
M222 CDY	NEW	Bowers, Chapel-en-le-Frith, Derbyshire (as M134 GAP)
M222 DDY	NEW	Ward, Alresford, Essex by 6/01; later to Hulleys, Baslow, Derbyshire
E232 GPH	Banstead Coaches, Surrey	Annetts & Porter (Mervyns Coaches), Micheldever, Hampshire
C203 GKR	Evans, Tregaron, Dyfed	Wealden, Five Oak Green (dlr); Southern Film Services, New Haw, Surrey (non-PSV) 10/03
G48 VVM	Whitehead, Rochdale, Greater Manchester	Wealden, Five Oak Green for scrap
L571 FVU	Shearings, Wigan, Greater Manchester (571)	Holywell, Eastbourne (as L772 THC), 9/99
HSK 834	Abridge, Hadleigh, Essex	Barnett, Feltham, Greater London (as E238 HCD), 3/97
HSK 835	Abridge, Hadleigh, Essex	Harmer (Renown Coaches), Bexhill (as E235 HCD), 2/97
N222 EDY	NEW	Cancu Supreme, Zejtun, Malta (re-registered as BCY 902)
NG 2414	M Betterton, Forncett St Peter, Norfolk (Preservation)	C Rowland (preservation)
H170 EJF	Munro (Curness Travel), Uddingston, Lanarkshire	Premier Albanian, Watford (as H917 DFG)
SJI 2586	Davies, Shipton Oliffe, Gloucestershire	Hodge, Sandhurst, Berkshire
M127 UWY	Wallace Arnold, Leeds, West Yorkshire	Watts (TM Travel), Old Tupton, Derbyshire
M128 UWY	Wallace Arnold, Leeds, West Yorkshire	B&J Travel, Barnoldswick, Lancashire
C302 RRX	Hunting Brae, Aldermaston, Berkshire	Cancu Supreme, Zejtun, Malta, 12/02, (for dockside use at Freeport, Birzebbuga, Malta)
E953 KDP	Owen, Yateley, Hampshire	Jackman (Spearings), Willand, Devon, 1/01
E968 KDP	Owen, Yateley, Hampshire	Big Lemon, Brighton
C538 OTY	OK Motor Services, Bishop Auckland, Durham (9254)	Hoar & Savage (Red Kite), Tilsworth, Leighton Buzzard, Bedfordshire, 10/04
R222 WDY	NEW	Abbey, High Wycombe, Buckinghamshire

R222 XDY	NEW	Baker, Enstone, Oxfordshire, 8/02
M211 UYD	Barnes, Aldbourne, Wiltshire	Premier Albanian Coaches, Watford, Hertfordshire (as M353 FWV)
R222 VDY	NEW	Zarb Coaches, Iklin, Malta as ZPY 100
ETA 101Y	Turner & Gilson, Chulmleigh, Devon	Brylaine Travel, Boston, Lincolnshire
BPL 459T	Arriva Croydon & North Surrey (previously London & Country) SNB459	Eastonways, Ramsgate, Kent, 5/03
H532 WGH	Epsom Coaches, Surrey	Hodge, Sandhurst, Berkshire (as H973 KDY)
H533 WGH	Epsom Coaches, Surrey	Clark (Brentons of Blackheath), London SE6
GDY 500X	Craker, Maidstone, Kent	Mobile caravan (as HWV 260X)
P884 FMO	Q-Drive, Battersea, London	Gain (Cooks), Westfield, East Sussex
T222 ADY	NEW	Brown (Crawley Luxury Coaches), Crawley, West Sussex
T222 GDY	NEW	Rogerson Coach Travel, Tranent, East Lothian
YUT 628Y	Gabriel, Rhoslefain, Gwynedd	Hosking (Rosevidney Travel), Ludgvan, Penzance, 4/03
V222 JDY	NEW	Naughton Coach Tours, Spiddal, Galway, Ireland
SJI 3929	Geoff Amos, Eydon, Northamptonshire	Hills Driving School (non-PSV), Plumpton (as F436 OFG); then to Stone, Edenbridge, Kent
W222 KDY	NEW	Cancu Supreme, Zejtun, Malta 2/07 as BPY 012; still in use 3/23
JDY 888Y	Maye (Mayfield Travel), Astley, Greater Manchester	C Rowland (preservation); Tyrrell, Bournemouth (preservation) by 6/21
T110 SOA	Adams (Victory Tours), Handley, Wiltshire	Clarkson, South Elmsall, West Yorkshire, 11/00
G75 PKR	Arriva Kent & Sussex (1075)	Wealden (dlr), Nettlestead; Caravan, Warehorne, Kent, 10/03
NPJ 476R	Shearer (Fleetwing), Mayford, Surrey	Cass Packaging, Hoo, Kent (became Amberlee, Southfleet, Kent during 2002)
R777 GSM	Mayne, Buckie, Moray	Western Isles Council, Stornoway
X500 GDY	NEW	Sandfields Farms Ltd, Luddington, Warwickshire, 3/15
Y222 PDY	NEW	[DDY 222] - R
P427 LJH	Bus Eireann, Dublin (VP34)	Scrapco, Paddock Wood, Kent (technically as P360 RCR), for scrap
P428 LJH	Bus Eireann, Dublin (VP35)	[GDY 493] - R
SIB 8243	Stone, Edenbridge, Kent	Ronan, Callan, Kilkenny, Eire (as H786 KDY), 8/04
D122 EFH	Stolzenberg (Llynfi Coaches), Maesteg, Glamorgan	McKenna Bus Hire, Armagh, Northern Ireland
D123 EFH	Stolzenberg (Llynfi Coaches), Maesteg, Glamorgan	Hoar & Savage (Red Kite), Tilsworth, Leighton Buzzard, Bedfordshire, 10/04
GX02 AED	NEW	[DDY 557] - R - sold for scrap 3/22
GX02 AEE	NEW	[BDY 389] - R
M513 VJO	Fleetmaster, Horsham, West Sussex	Autocar, Five Oak Green, Kent 3/07
G200 PAO	Renown, Bexhill via Wealden, Five Oak Green (dlr)	Sold for scrap
M649 KVU	Shearings, Wigan (649)	Davies, Llanelli, Carmarthenshire
E22 XHL	Roffey, Flimwell	Hoar & Savage (Red Kite), Tilsworth, Leighton Buzzard, Bedfordshire, 1/04

NCF 715	Gain (Cooks), Westfield	Wealden (dlr), Five Oak Green, Kent
M605 ORJ	Shearings, Wigan, Greater Manchester (605)	Wise, Hailsham, East Sussex
M613 ORJ	Shearings, Wigan, Greater Manchester (613)	[ODY 607] R - Scrapco, Paddock Wood, for scrap 2/19
CR04 RAM	NEW	Fowler, Holbeach Drove, Lincolnshire
JG04 RAM	NEW	Fowler, Holbeach Drove, Lincolnshire
FCO 314	Hickmott, Kingsnorth, Ashford, Kent	Cancu Supreme, Zejtun, Malta as LCY 003, re-registered as LXY 003 in 2015; rebuilt in 2021/2, converted to diesel engine and repainted two-tone green and white
JIL 5279	Birmingham Omnibus Company, Tividale, West Midlands	Withdrawn 6/11; Wealden PSV (dlr), Five Oak Green, Kent (as E364 NEG), 12/11
J505 GCD	Stagecoach (East Kent) (32505)	Wealden PSV (dlr), Five Oak Green, Kent
J507 GCD	Stagecoach South (32507)	Guildford College, Guildford, Surrey (non-PSV)
J534 GCD	Mee (RedRoute), Northfleet, Kent	Bartletts Metal Recycling, Three Oaks, East Sussex, for scrap
TIL 1185	St Buryan Garage, St Buryan, Cornwall	Brown (Crawley Luxury Coaches), Crawley, West Sussex (as K180 PAP), 5/11
JG54 RAM	NEW	Holder, Charlton-on-Otmoor, Oxfordshire
CA52 LAO	Bebb, Llantwit Fardre, Rhondda Cynon Taff	R&D (Formby Travel), Formby, Merseyside
W87 RRU	Amport & District, Thruxton, Hants	[LDY 173] - R
JUF 244E	Peter Simpson, Whittlesey, Cambridgeshire (preservation)	C Rowland (preservation)
CR06 EDY	NEW	[PDY 272] - R
H649 PVW	Dublin Bus (RH79)	Bone (Newnham Coaches), Hook, Hants, 1/10
J706 CEV	Dublin Bus (RH123)	Bone (Newnham Coaches), Hook, Hants, 4/13
N301 XRP	Stagecoach (United Counties) (40301)	Bean, -?- for preservation, 8/13
N191 LPN	Stagecoach (Southdown) (40891)	Wealden PSV (dlr), Five Oak Green, Kent
N962 NAP	Stagecoach (East Kent) (40962)	Hoare, Chepstow, Monmouthshire, 3/07
UUD 12	Robertson, Stockport, Greater Manchester (preservation)	Ecosse Classic Wedding Cars, Glasgow
F709 WCS	Mullany, Watford, Herts (709)	Fowler, Holbeach Drove, Lincolnshire, 9/09
JG07 RAM	NEW	R
M606 UTV	Hoggans European (Gemini Travel), Neath, Glamorgan	Scrapco, Paddock Wood, Kent, for scrap
M607 UTV	Hoggans European (Gemini Travel), Neath, Glamorgan	Scrapco, Paddock Wood, Kent, for scrap
JG08 RAM	NEW	SMS, Towcester, Northamptonshire
CR08 RAM	NEW	R
CMG 30	Taylor, Tintinhull, Somerset	C Rowland (preservation)
YR52 MEU	Princess, West End, Hants	[GDY 500X] - R
SK07 FUW	Brown, Broxburn, West Lothian	[VDY 468] - R
FY02 WHA	Lee (Beewise), High Green, South Yorkshire	Little & Massey (Lathkill Coaches), Monyash, Derbyshire, 4/13
P330 RVG	First Eastern Counties (20120)	Coastal Red, North Runcton, Norfolk
N617 APU	First Eastern Counties (20117)	Norman (W&M Travel), Parson Drove, Cambridgeshire
S136 RLE	Ensign, Purfleet, Essex (136)	Accident damage; Jonathan Lloyd Commercial Salvage, Hixon, Staffordshire, for scrap, 3/16
YN51 WGY	Flight Delay Services, Manchester Airport	[RDY 155] - R

YN51 WGZ	Flight Delay Services, Manchester Airport	*[UDY 512]* - R
YN55 WSW	TGM Group, Manchester Airport	*[SDY 788]* - R
R710 YWC	Bluebird Buses (Stagecoach), Aberdeen (32360)	Scrapco, Paddock Wood, Kent, for scrap
M525 WHF	Beestons, Hadleigh, Suffolk	Dews Coaches, Somersham, Cambridgeshire
PE56 XMJ	McCabe, Dundalk, Eire	*[HDY 405]* - R
CR12 RAM	NEW	R
JG12 RAM	NEW	R
MX07 NTA	Astons, Worcester	*[ODY 395]* - R
X661 LLX	Metroline, Cricklewood, London (VPL161)	R - *Ripley (dealer), Hailsham for scrap by 7/20*
BK09 LVD	Evo Travel, Acton, Greater London	*[1924 RH]* - R
CR14 RAM	NEW	R
S775 BLG	Finney (W&G Coaches), Heron Cross, Stoke-on-Trent, Staffordshire	Empress, St Leonard's-on-Sea (100)
BG14 OOE	Volvo, Coventry (Demonstrator)	R
UK15 RAM	NEW	R
MV54 BLU	Greater Manchester Buses South Ltd (Stagecoach Manchester) 33863	R - *scrapped c2019*
MW54 BLU	Greater Manchester Buses South Ltd (Stagecoach Manchester) 33864	R - *scrapped c2019*
J 7247	Tantivy Blue, St Helier, Jersey	C Rowland (preservation)
SK52 OJD	Lothian Buses, Edinburgh (60)	R - *scrapped 12/19*
SN53 AUW	Lothian Buses, Edinburgh (86)	Accident damage; sold for scrap
EK51 XXC	Regal Busways, Great Wakering, Essex	R - *Big Lemon, Brighton, 6/19*
YN13 EHD	Clarkes of London, Lower Sydenham, London	*[CR13 RAM]* - R
CR65 RAM	NEW	R
R853 PRG	Go Northern (Go North East), Gateshead, Tyne & Wear (4853)	R - *Ripley (dealer), Hailsham for scrap by 7/20*
YK53 GXO	Glenvale (Stagecoach), Gilmoss, Liverpool 21253	R - *Scrapco, Paddock Wood, for scrap 12/19*
YK53 GXP	Glenvale (Stagecoach), Gilmoss, Liverpool 21254	R
CR17 RAM	NEW	R

Appendix 12

The Gallery

Through the chapters of this book many of the fleet feature in some excellent photographs over their working lives with the company. A further selection of images have been included as a final gallery to illustrate the fleet up until Colin's retirement in 2018.

Driver Dave Whiting is pictured with Bedford YMPS Plaxton Paramount (D133 VJK) that was new to the company in April 1987. It survives in preservation with Colin Rowland in 2023. (Colin Rowland)

Seen at Hastings Station is Volvo B10M-62 Van Hool T9, new to the company as T222 GDY in May 1999 and latterly bearing the registration number PDY 272. It was sold in April 2014 to Rogerson in Edinburgh. (Alan Snatt)

In a sole experiment with a slightly different variation of the traditional fleet livery, a 1983 Volvo B10M-61 with Plaxton Supreme V 57 seat coachwork (YUT 628Y) carried white side panels above its green and black livery. Purchased from Gabriel, Rhoslefain in late 1999 it would receive the registration TDY 946 and was sold three years later to Rosevidney in Penzance. (Paul Green)

A moment in time has been captured as the 1976 Bedford YMT Duple Dominant (WUF 44) driven by Mick Cousens makes steady but slow progress up the steep incline of Battery Hill in Fairlight on his way back to Hastings on a glorious afternoon. (Terry Blackman)

Driver Paul Green takes a moment to photograph Mercedes Benz Tourismo (CR14 RAM) on an Irish tour to Kilkenny on 30th April 2015. (Paul Green)

HVC 10V was a 1980 Bedford YMT Plaxton Supreme IV,
new to Harry Shaw in Coventry. (Bob Cook)

Bedford YMPS Plaxton Paramount (D134 VJK) is seen at the Ardingly
South of England Show on 10th June 1989 (Derek Jones)

BDY 389 was a 1991 Volvo B10M-60 Van Hool Alizee T8,
previously with Epsom Coaches. It is seen at the Millennium
Dome in London. (Unknown – Colin Rowland collection)

This 1977 Bedford YMT Duple Dominant II (910 OCV) had previously
operated for Coliseum in Southampton before joining the fleet in
1990, enjoying a stay of eight years. Driver Peter Wilson poses for
the camera at Michelham Priory in East Sussex. (Stephen Dine)

Seen when only a few months old on 22nd July 2015 is Mercedes Benz Tourismo (UK15 RAM) at The Pilot Inn, Dungeness. (Philip Cattermole)

Captured on film travelling along Eastbourne seafront on a pleasant summers afternoon on 2nd June 1968, is Bedford SB5 Duple Bella Vega (VDY 207) its driver was Mr Anderson. (Alan Snatt)

Passing through the village of Sedlescombe on 15th September 2011 is the 1997 Volvo B10M-62 with Plaxton Interurban coachwork (TDY 946). Previously with Eastern Counties as P330 RVG, it was soon joined by a similar example from the same operator, N617 APU. Both were 57 seat examples. (Terry Blackman)

Representing the smaller coaches in the fleet is Mercedes Benz 1022L (HDY 405, formerly PE56 XMJ) with 33 seat Unvi Cimo coachwork (sold in the UK by Esker Bus and Coach) seen near to the historic Battle Abbey in East Sussex on 8th July 2016. (Paul Green)

This 1969 Bedford VAM 70 Plaxton Elite (YWA 444G) arrived via dealer Yeates in January 1981, having previously been with Wild of Heage, Derbyshire. It was captured on film by enthusiast Bob Cook at West Ridge Manor on 7th March 1982 in close company of two other Bedfords in the fleet. (Bob Cook)

Seen in Pestalozzi Children's Village at Sedlescombe when on hire to Cooks Coaches of Westfield in October 1991, is the 1978 Bedford YMT Caetano Estoril (AAL 521A) previously with Davies of Bridport. After just over two years of service it was sold to Thorn (APT Travel) in Rayleigh, Essex. (Stephen Dine)

Mercedes Benz Tourismo (1924 RH) is captured in London after
dropping its passengers off, with driver Geoff Casey at the wheel.
It was new as BK09 LVD to Evo Travel in Acton. (Alan Snatt)

Folkestone Football Club provides the backdrop for Bedford YMT
Willowbrook 008 'Spacecar' (6751 KP) with driver Les Morris. It was new
in 1976 to National Travel South East as KUW 540P. (Colin Rowland)

With its driver taking a rest break between shifts on the local service
88 route we find Bedford YMPS with 33 seat Maxeta body (WNH 52W)
parked in Rye Road, Hastings on 15th August 1991. (Paul Gainsbury)

Awaiting its passengers near to Dover's Western Docks we find Bedford
YNT with 12 metre Plaxton Paramount 3200 body (A72 NHC). New
to Amport & District in February 1984 as A273 KEL, it joined the fleet
just one year later having had substantial accident repairs undertaken
necessitating a DVLA reissued chassis number afterwards. (J T Wilson)

Seen at West Ridge Manor is the Volvo B10M-62 with Berkhof Axial 50 coachwork (TDY 388) new to the company in March 1998 as R222 VDY. In late 2006 it was exported to Malta joining the fleet of Zarb and registered ZPY 100. It was still in service in 2023. (Colin Rowland)

Waiting to collect students for EF language school in St Leonards on Sea on a day trip to Canterbury, we find Bedford YNT Plaxton Paramount 3200 (WUF 44) previously registered as A244 KFJ. (Stephen Dine)

St Dunstans in Ovingdean near Brighton provides the backdrop for 1988 Bedford YNV Plaxton Paramount 3200 (PDY 42). It joined the fleet in February 1995 from Banstead Coaches in Surrey as E232 GPH. (Stephen Dine)

Drivers Brian 'Yorkie' Wood and Bill Palmer stand with their identical 1988 Volvo B10M-61 Plaxton Paramount 3200 coaches on 11th July 1997. Both previously with Owens of Yateley. (Stephen Dine)

After dropping its passengers off at Thorpe Park on 29th
June 2010, Volvo B7R Plaxton Profile (JG04 RAM) shows
off its immaculate livery to its best. (Stephen Dine)

Arriving at the Port of Dover's Eastern Docks on a 'travelsphere' feeder
for an on-going continental tour on 13th June 1998 is the 49 seat Volvo
B10M-62 Berkhof Axial 50 (R222 WDY) driven by Tony Cloutt. It was
sold to Abbey Travel in High Wycombe in April 2004. (Paul Green)

This stunning scenery is the perfect backdrop for Volvo B12B with 9700 Prestige coachwork (JG07 RAM) whilst on a continental tour. (Unknown – Colin Rowland)

Captured near to the Snooty Fox Public House at Three Bridges is a 2005 Volvo B12B Plaxton Panther (SDY 788) previously with Tellings-Golden Miller as YN55 WSW. Purchased in August 2010 it had first worn the 'Just Go' tour company livery, eventually receiving fleet colours. (Alan Snatt)

NPJ 476R was a 1976 Leyland National that was new to Alder Valley and operated until the companies take over by Stagecoach in 1992 where it would receive their own corporate livery. Arriving with Rambler from Fleetwing Travel, Surrey in July 2000 it is seen at Broad Oak on a school service. (Paul Green)

Seen at the Hastings MOT Test Station in Ivy House Lane is 1967 Bedford VAM14 with Plaxton Panorama 45 seat coachwork (JAA 507E). Purchased in November 1979 from dealer Yeates, it had previously operated with Smith & Ball, Waterhouses, Staffordshire. (Colin Rowland)

Seen whilst working rail replacement duties at Lewes Station in East Sussex we find Volvo B12B with Berkhof Axial 50 coachwork PDY 272. It was new to the company in 2006 as CR06 EDY. (Alan Snatt)

A number of coaches have operated in customer's liveries over the years. HRD 12N was a 1975 Bedford YRQ Plaxton Elite that came from Tappins of Wallingford in 1979, receiving EF livery not long afterwards. (Colin Rowland)

Representing smaller coaches in the fleet is a 2007 Mercedes Benz 0815 Ferqui Toro (ODY 395) seating 28, seen emerging onto Hastings Seafront from Harold Place, driven by Darren Stewart. It was new to Britannia Parking in Bournemouth as MX07 NTA. (Alan Snatt)

New in November 1999 as V222 JDY, Mercedes Benz 1020 with Optare Solera 35 seat coachwork is seen on Eastbourne seafront. By now it has gained the cherished registration HDY 565. (Alan Snatt)

Awaiting shipping for export to Malta in March 2007 is the 1950 Austin CXB with Plaxton body (FCO 314) still to be found on the Island (2023) in regular use. Compare the image of this coach in its later livery under the chapter 'Coaches for Export'. (Colin Rowland)

Captured on Eastbourne seafront is Volvo B10M-62 with Berkhof Axial 50 coachwork (DDY 222) new to the company in April 2001 as Y222 PDY. Its driver was Matthew Britton. (Alan Snatt)

JNJ 365V (originally DMT 904V) was a 1980 Bedford YMT Duple Dominant 2 and is seen at West Ridge Manor on 6th March 1993 alongside Bedford YMPS Plaxton Paramount 3200 (UDY 910, originally D133 VJK). (Derek Jones)

Mercedes Benz 814 Vario (JG54 RAM) carried 33 seat Plaxton Cheetah coachwork, new in September 2004. It is seen on Eastbourne seafront, driven by Martin Lee. (Alan Snatt)

Bedford YRT Duple Dominant (405 UPJ) was new to Aldermaston
Coaches in 1973 as NBW 704L, joining the fleet in June 1984.
Sold to Cooks Coaches in nearby Westfield in 1990 as EUF 683L
it would end its days as a static caravan. (John Grubb)

Awaiting collection from the Plaxton works in Scarborough is
a new Volvo B10M-61 Plaxton Paramount 3500 (D137 VJK). It
would later receive the personalised registration HDY 405 and
was sold to Hills of Hersham in May 2010. (Colin Rowland)

NKJ 769F was a 1968 Bedford J2 with Plaxton Embassy body,
acquired in December 1974 from Cox in Maidstone. After nearly
four years of service its subsequent owner became Williams
Coaches of Cwmdu, Wales. (Marriotts Photo Stores)

Bedford YLQ Plaxton Supreme IV (UFT 911T) is captured in slow
moving traffic in Eastbourne. New in August 1978 it was acquired at
just two years old from Curtis in Tyneside and was sold in October 1983
to Fuggles of Benenden. (Unknown – Colin Rowland collection)

In this rare image taken in December 1996 are two Volvo B10M-61 Jonkheere Jubilee coaches (TDY 388 and VDY 468) that have arrived for sale at coach dealer Bob Vale after a stay of just one year in the fleet. Both were new in May 1988 as E697 NNH and E696 NNH consecutively. (Stephen Dine)

Seen at West Ridge Manor is Volvo B10M-60 with 51 seat Jonckheere Deauville coachwork (DDY 222). New to Shearings as L571 FVU in April 1994, it joined the Rambler fleet only eighteen months later, enjoying a stay of just under four years. (Colin Rowland)

In Tenterden coach park the 1984 Bedford YNT Plaxton Paramount 3200 (ODY 607) can be found on hire to Della Holidays on 30th May 1994. It joined the fleet in February 1993 having previously operated for Rover in Bromsgrove as A383 BNP. (Paul Green)

Parked on the Warrior Square coach stand in St Leonards on Sea is the 1976 Bedford YMT Willowbrook Spacecar (KUW 540P) new to National Travel South East. Note that the coachwork features emergency exit doors on both its sides of the rear. (Bob Cook)

Having arrived in Falaise Road, Hastings with an incoming group for EF Language School, is the recently acquired Volvo B10M-60 Plaxton Paramount 3500 (F27 HGG) in April 1991, soon receiving the registration UDY 512. Its driver, Colin Rowland, is seen on the right of the image. (Stephen Dine)

Photographed in Warrior Square with driver Nigel Glover on hire to EF Language School, is Volvo B10M-60 (F28 HGG) the sister coach to F27 HGG, purchased together from Parks of Hamilton. (Stephen Dine)

A popular destination for enthusiasts to photograph coaches is Derby Day, where on the Epsom Downs on 2nd June 1993, Volvo B10M-61 Van Hool Alizee (MDY 397) is arriving. New to Excelsior in Bournemouth in 1988 it initially carried a Belgian registration, then receiving a UK issue as F450 WFX, before becoming XEL 941. It joined the fleet as F507 MAA becoming MDY 397. (Derek Jones)

This 1980 Bedford YMT Plaxton Supreme IV (405 UPJ) was purchased via Julian Brown at Wealden PSV in August 1991, having previously operated for the Ministry of Defence as EYL 319V. Sold in March 1994 to Whites Coaches of Heathfield, it is seen at West Ridge Manor on 28th August 1993. (Derek Jones)

Herstmonceux Science centre in East Sussex is the home of the former
Royal Greenwich Observatory and a Grade II listed building. Seen outside
is Volvo B10M-62 Plaxton Premiere 350 (VDY 468) Formally registered
M128 UNY. It was purchased with sister coach M127 UNY from its
original owner, Wallace Arnold via dealer Bob Vale. (Colin Rowland)

Seen at Warrior Square, St Leonards on Sea on 6th September 1988,
is the DAF MB200 DKFL Plaxton Paramount 3500 (A888 MDY) new in
February 1984. Its driver that day was Fred Pilbeam. (Paul Gainsbury)

Bedford SB5 (NJM) Duple Vega 31 (KDY 300H) received a number
of different coloured lower front panel re-paints to experiment
with its look in its thirteen years of ownership, including sliver,
cream, black and in this photograph, green. (J T Wilson)

This 1991 21 seat Toyota Coaster with Caetano Optimo body (H170 EJF later
re-registered as UDY 512) was the first of two examples owned to cater for
smaller groups. Previously with Munro Travel, it was purchased in 1996. Just
under two years later it moved on to Premier Albanian in Watford. (Stephen Dine)

Entered at the S.E.C.O.A coach operators event staged in Folkestone in April 1984 is the DAF MB200DKFL Plaxton Paramount 3500 (KDY 888Y). Its rear windscreen displays an array of features for passenger comfort. (Derek Jones)

In January 1991 driver Dennis Goodwin stands alongside Bristol RESL6L Marshall (TCD 481J) whilst on service 88, at the Kings Head Public House in Rye Road, Hastings. Purchased from Kent Coach Tours in November 1990 it was new to Southdown Motor Services in October 1970. (Stephen Dine)

Waiting at the Tesco Superstore in Hollington, St Leonards
on Sea in March 1992, Bristol RESL6L (TCD 481J) has now
received full company livery. (Terry Blackman)

1976 Bedford YMT Duple Dominant (WUF 44, originally LJK 335P) was
already into nine years of ownership when seen in Bohemia, Hastings
on 18th April 1985, still in immaculate condition. (Paul Gainsbury)

A very useful vehicle used on mainly contract duties was a
Mercedes Benz 709 Alexander Sprint (TDY 388) seating 23 and
formerly operated by Stagecoach as N301 XRP. (Alan Snatt)

In the picturesque grounds of the Powdermills Hotel near Battle is the 1935
Bedford WLB Duple (CMG 30) seen in August 2016. (Stephen Dine)

The second of two Toyota Coaster's with Caetano Optimo coachwork to grace the fleet was M211 UYD, a 1995 example acquired in March 1998 from Barnes in Swindon replacing the earlier example H170 EJF. It received the cherished registration M222 CDY from a Scania 113 CRB Van Hool that was soon to be sold. It is seen alongside the West Ridge Manor premises on 1st October 1998. (Paul Green)

Seen on 30th June 2010, T222 ADY was a Mercedes Benz 614 with 24 seat Autobus Classique conversion, purchased new in May 1999 via dealer Bob Vale. It enjoyed a long stay of fourteen years in operation, being sold in September 2013 to Crawley Luxury. (Paul Green)

A hard working member of the fleet was the 1976 Bedford YMT Plaxton Supreme Express (TAP 461R) that was purchased via dealer Yeates as OTX 41R from Morgan, Nantyglo. For a time it bore the registration 419 CLB. Used mainly through the narrow lanes in nearby Crowhurst to Claverham Community College in Battle, its powerful roof-mounted air horn was used in certain points to warn motorists of its impending arrival. (Stephen Dine)

Appendix 13

The Skinners AEC

Hastings and St Leonards on Sea's oldest transport operator, Skinners, had acquired a number of new AEC coaches with attractive Harrington coachwork when updating some of their post war fleet in the late 1940's. The last of this batch to be delivered in 1950 (EDY 192) would also have an in-vogue tail fin on the top of the rear dome above its windows. Around the same time, Harrington also supplied a 1/5th scale model of the coach built measuring some six feet in length, for promotional display purposes in the window of Skinners' Cambridge Road premises. An equally impressive revolving backdrop of scenery around it gave the impression of a moving coach for passers-by to see, advertising their coach hire and excursion activities.

Moving on to 1966 and a young Colin was accompanying Skinners employee Peter White between their Western Road site and the Cambridge Road premises (now the site of ESK Warehouses) where Peter was looking for vehicle parts. Up in the loft of the building Colin discovered the by now forgotten Harrington model just sitting amongst

St Leonards on Sea based Skinners Coaches once owned a
1950 AEC Regal with Harrington coachwork (EDY 192) that has
an unlikely connection to the Rambler story. (Rob Crouch)

other discarded items and went to see one of the Skinners Directors,
Michael Hickman, to ask if he could have it. Michael's reply was 'yes, just
for a bottle of whisky'. Colin was later shown more of the jigsaw puzzle
of the coach's story by Peter when they looked through more discarded
things upstairs in the Western Road premises and the eight feet long
revolving scenery complete with the electric motors to drive it was now
found too. Regretfully Colin declined the offer of taking it as it was just
too big to find anywhere to keep it.

Colin kept his prized possession and, in the years ahead, (possibly the
late 1970's, early 1980's) John Goodwin would repaint the large model
into Rambler Coaches livery complete with its own fleet number 1. At the
time two local enthusiasts, Bob Cook and Rob Crouch, had found out

about the former Skinners coach and on a depot visit were pleased to be shown the model by John, proudly wheeled out from inside the depot to be photographed. Rob had also brought along his cine camera and with Bob now filming, Rob took great delight in 'driving' or rather pushing the large model around the yard much to everyone's amusement. It was only afterwards that the discovery was made that Rob had forgotten to put a new film in and it was unfortunately empty.

Many transport enthusiasts traditionally forward reports of new additions or sales from coach and bus fleets to their clubs or societies to share information and Rob would, in due course, report the arrival of this vehicle to the M&D and East Kent Bus Club. Rob's rather keenly abbreviated report though accidently forgot to mention that the coach was in fact a model and not the real coach, so when the club magazine duly put this discovery into print, the new story created much interest. When another enthusiast soon arrived at the Rambler depot to see this prize coach he was taken aback as John Goodwin would now roll the model out again with a smile on his face!

In this rare photograph enthusiast photographer Rob Crouch is himself captured on his own camera by friend Bob Cook kneeling alongside the former Skinners Coaches AEC Harrington (EDY 192) in its 1/5th scale model guise, now wearing its Rambler Coaches livery. (Rob Crouch)

The model was loaned out for an exhibition being staged locally and when the event was over it was temporarily parked up again inside the rear of the depot in one corner until being stored away. Sadly, in the interim a driver reversing a coach inside did not see the model and backed into it causing considerable damage. This unique piece could not be broken up and a local craftsman Mr Pannell very kindly spent many hours in carefully repairing it and conserving it, which after completion would now be re-painted back into its original owner's attractive blue livery by Ivan Lusted, and the model is still retained in the ownership of Colin in 2023.

The Skinners AEC Harrington model shows off its sleek lines when seen in Rambler Coaches workshop just after repainting into its original livery. (Colin Rowland)

Acknowledgements

The Cinemas of Hastings & St. Leonards by Nick Prince (1996)

Buses and Trolleybuses 1919-1945 (David Kaye) (1970)

The Hastings Omnibus 1832 – 1914 (David Padgham)

Hastings & St. Leonards in the front line – Hastings & St Leonards Observer.

Plaxton – A Century of Innovation – Stewart J. Brown (2007)

The Bus Archive, Walsall.

Kent History and Library Centre

Hastings Reference Library